MINING: Filmhaus

nhalt / Content

60 Manifest / Manifesto

59 Interview

Bericht / Report
44 Appendix

38 Demolierung / Demolition
34 Prozess / Process
04 Ausstellung / Exhibition

03 Über das Projekt / Hard Facts

Über das Projekt
Hard Facts

MINING: Filmhaus

Eine räumliche Intervention des MINING Kollektivs (Friedrich Engl & Ursula Gaisbauer)

mit 20 Akteur*innen, realisiert im September 2020

Skulptur, Sound, Performance, Video und Recherche

Space in Transition:
Gebäude der VHS Polycollege / Margareten und des BFI, Stöbergasse 11 – 15, Wien, Österreich

Fläche:
Ca. 1000 m²

Baujahr:
1978

Architektur:
Fred Freyler und Igirien (Werner Appelt, Franz Eberhard Kneissl und Elsa Prochazka)

Bauherrin:
Sozialbau AG

Kooperation:
BauKarussell, Die Kümmerei, Kreative Räume Wien

Intervention:
14 Tage / 11.–25. September 2020

Ausstellung:
3 Tage / 25.–27. September 2020

MINING: Filmhaus ist eine künstlerische urbane Spurensuche im ehemaligen Filmhaus Stöbergasse. Das Programmkino war in ein traditionsreiches Bildungszentrum integriert und von kulturhistorischer Bedeutung. Innerhalb von zwei Wochen wurde das Gebäude vom MINING Kollektiv szenografisch und filmisch erschlossen. Es konnte ein letztes Mal vor seinem Abriss für ein kurzes Zeitfenster von drei Tagen besucht werden.

Parallel zur künstlerischen Bespielung des Ortes fanden die Abbruch-Vorbereitungen statt und wurden von sozialen und ökologischen Maßnahmen begleitet. In experimentellen Arbeitsprozessen, die mit der Kamera dokumentiert wurden, entstanden auf der Baustelle Synergien mit den Abbrucharbeitern und anderen Akteur*innen. Baustoffe, die recycelt oder entsorgt werden mussten, dienten den Künstler*innen als Konstruktionsmaterial. Aus diesen vor Ort gefundenen Objekten und Materialien entstand eine atmosphärische Rauminterpretation an der Schnittstelle zwischen Dokumentation und Inszenierung, Zufälligkeit und Künstlichkeit.

MINING: Filmhaus

A spatial intervention by the MINING Kollektiv (Friedrich Engl & Ursula Gaisbauer)

with 20 acteurs, realised in September 2020

Sculpture, sound, performance, video and research

Space in transition:
VHS and BFI building, Stöbergasse 11–15, Vienna, Austria

Area:
Approx. 1000 m²

Year of construction:
1978

Architecture:
Fred Freyler and Igirien (Werner Appelt, Franz Eberhard Kneissl and Elsa Prochazka)

Builder:
Sozialbau AG

Cooperation:
BauKarussell, Die Kümmerei, Kreative Räume Wien

Intervention:
14 days / 11–25 September 2020

Exhibition:
3 days / 25–27 September 2020

'MINING: Filmhaus' is an artistic urban investigation of the former Filmhaus Stöbergasse. The art house cinema was integrated into a traditional educational centre of cultural and historical significance. Within two weeks, the building was scenographically and cinematically explored by the MINING Kollektiv. It could be visited for only three days before its final demolition.

Parallel to the artistic performance on the site, the demolition preparations took place simultaneously and were accompanied by social and ecological measures. In experimental processes, which were documented with a camera, synergies between the demolition workers and other acteurs emerged on the construction site. Building materials that had to be recycled or disposed of served the artists as construction material. These objects and materials found on site were used to create an atmospheric interpretation of the space at the intersection of documentation and staging, coincidence and artificiality.

AUSSTELLUNG
(Höhepunkt)

EXHIBITION
(Climax)

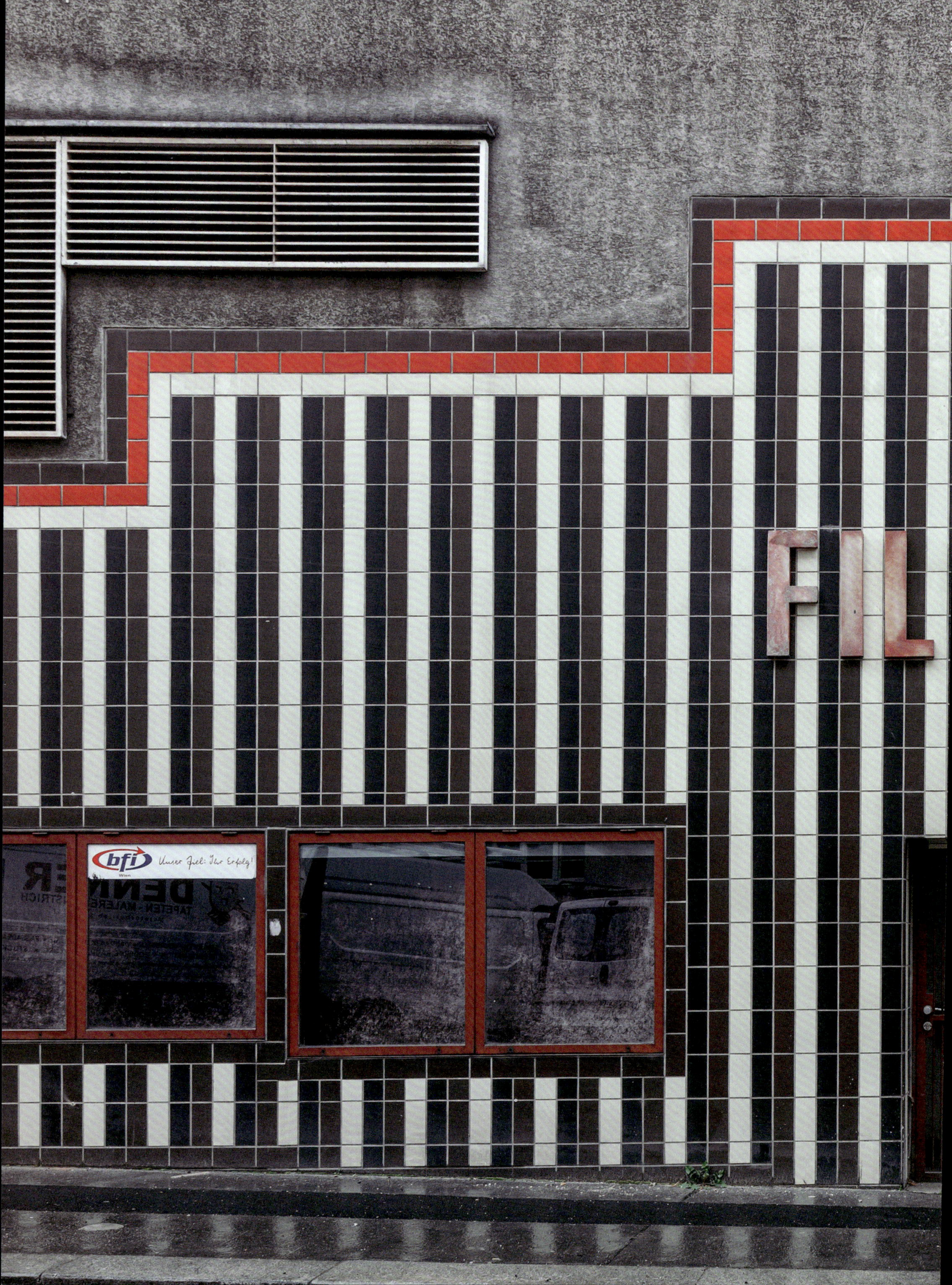
FIL
bfi
Wien
Unser Ziel: Ihr Erfolg!

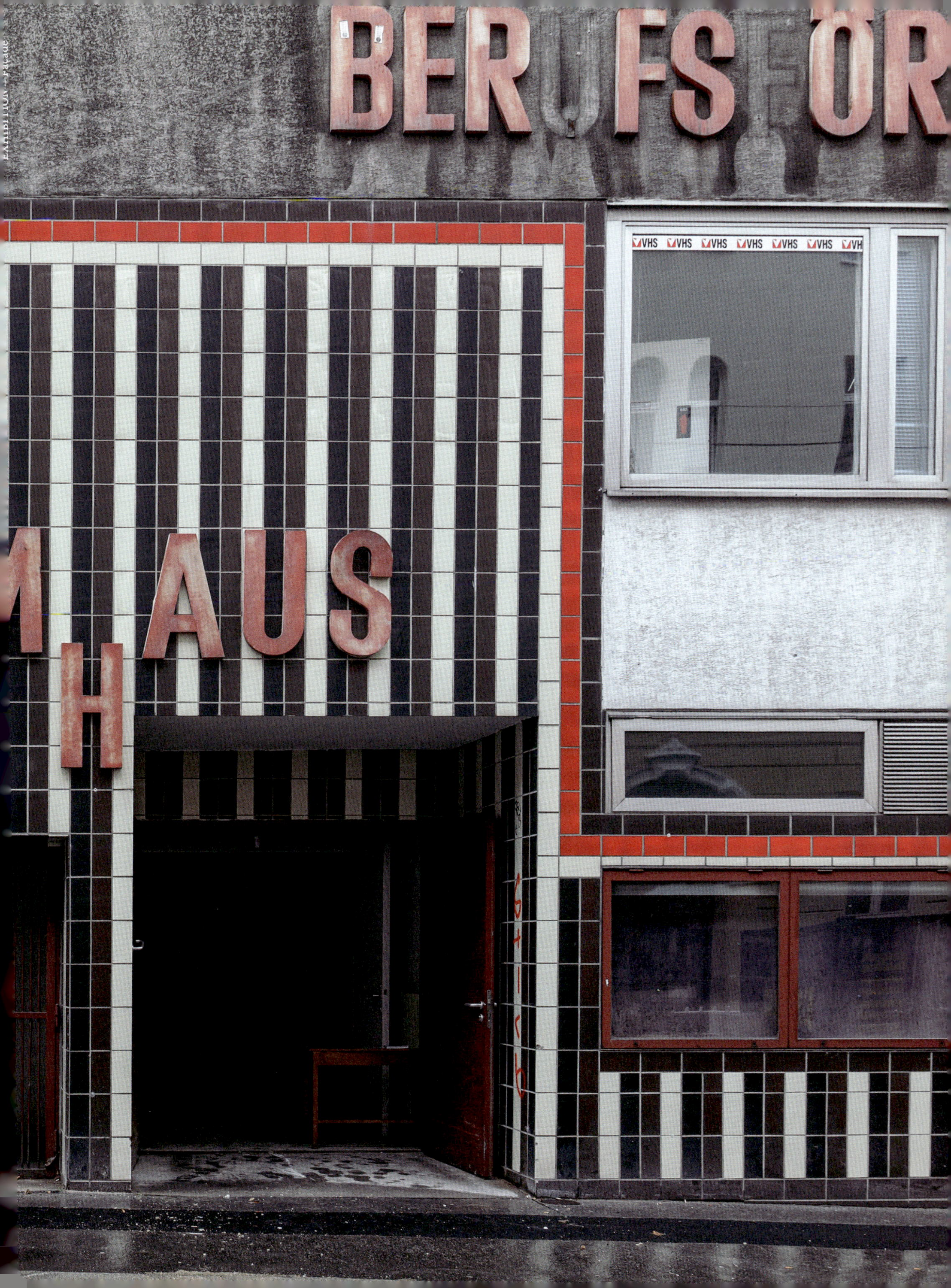
BERUFSFÖR
VHS VHS VHS VHS VHS VHS VH
M HAUS
H

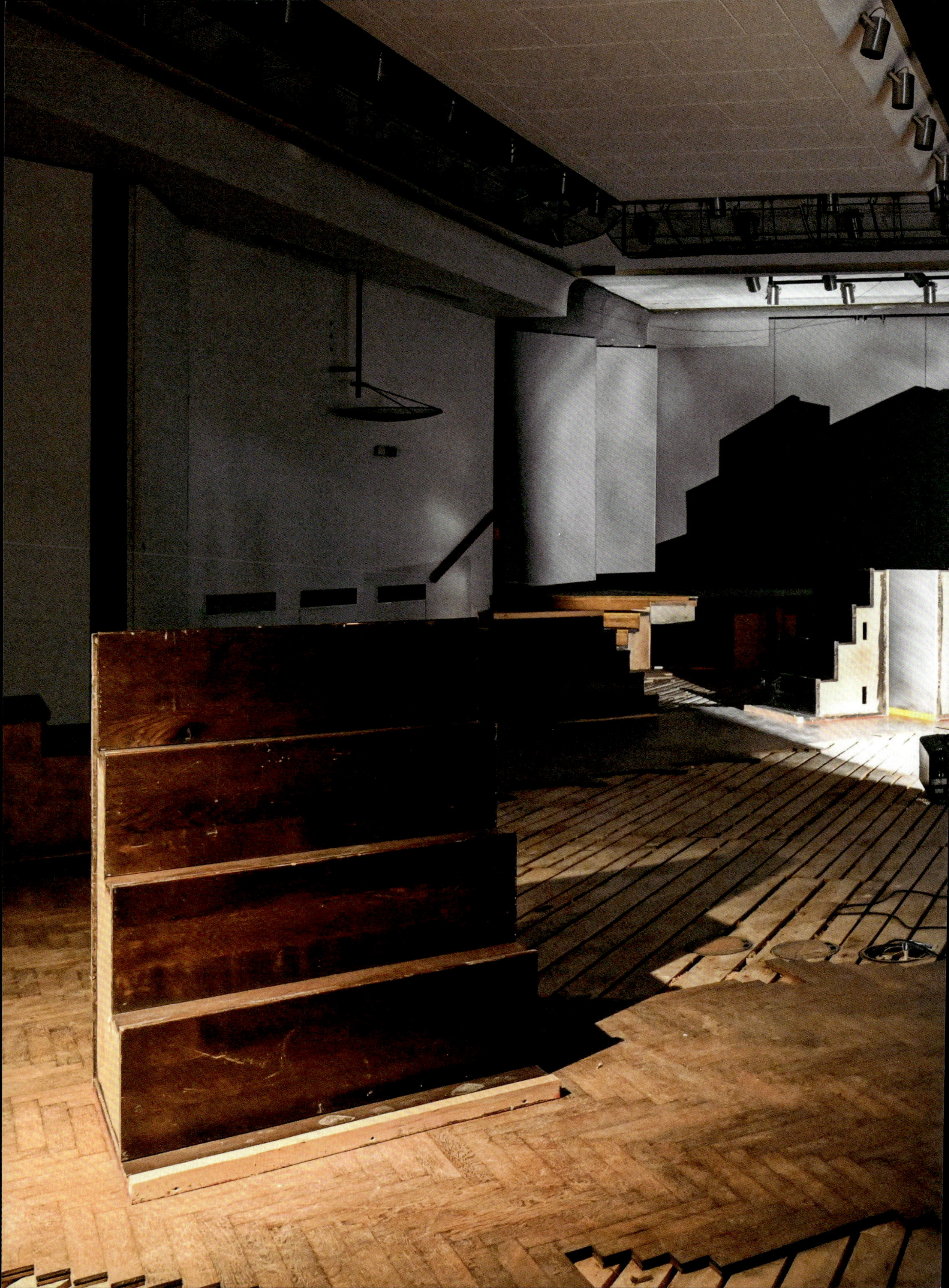

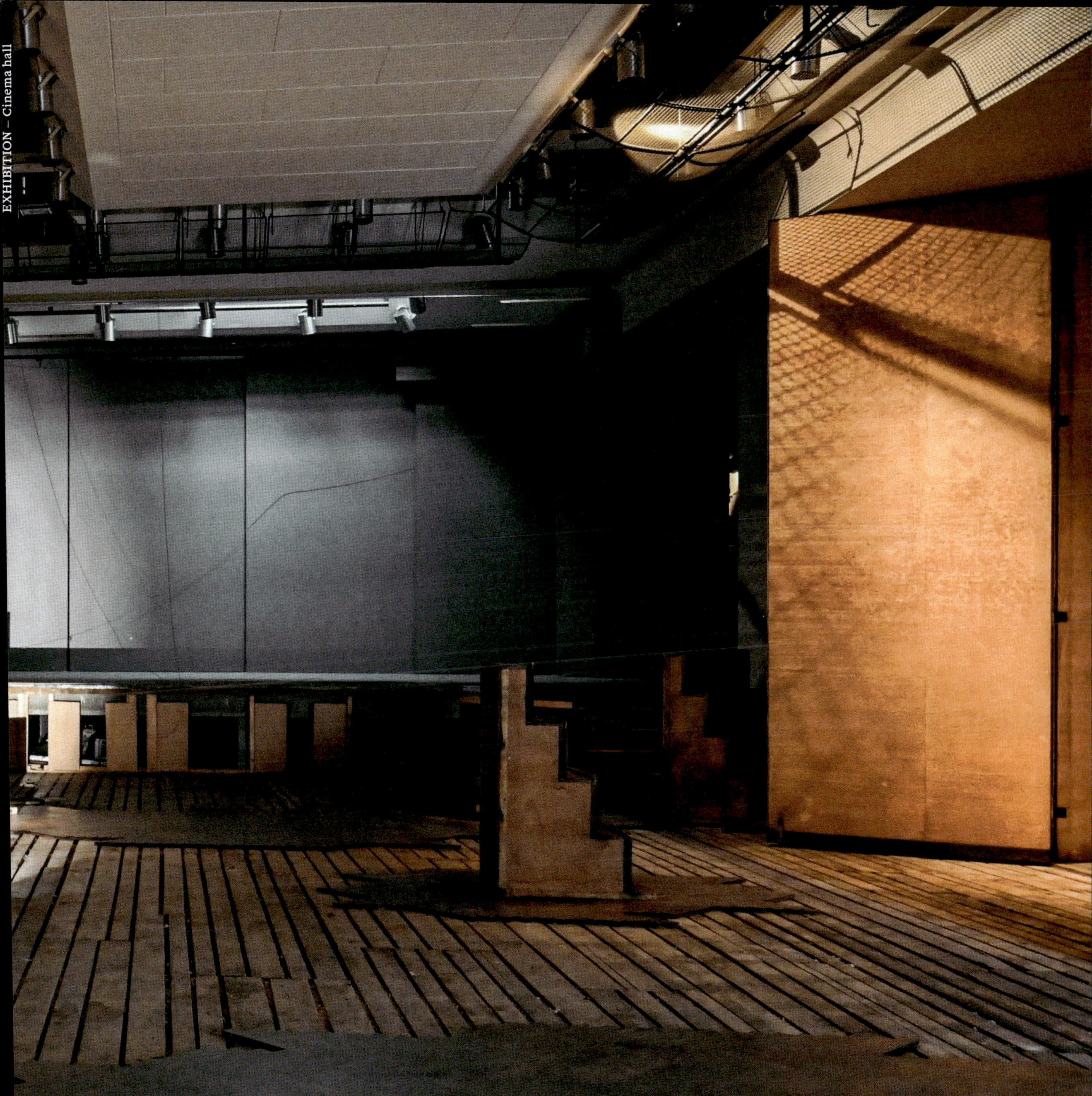

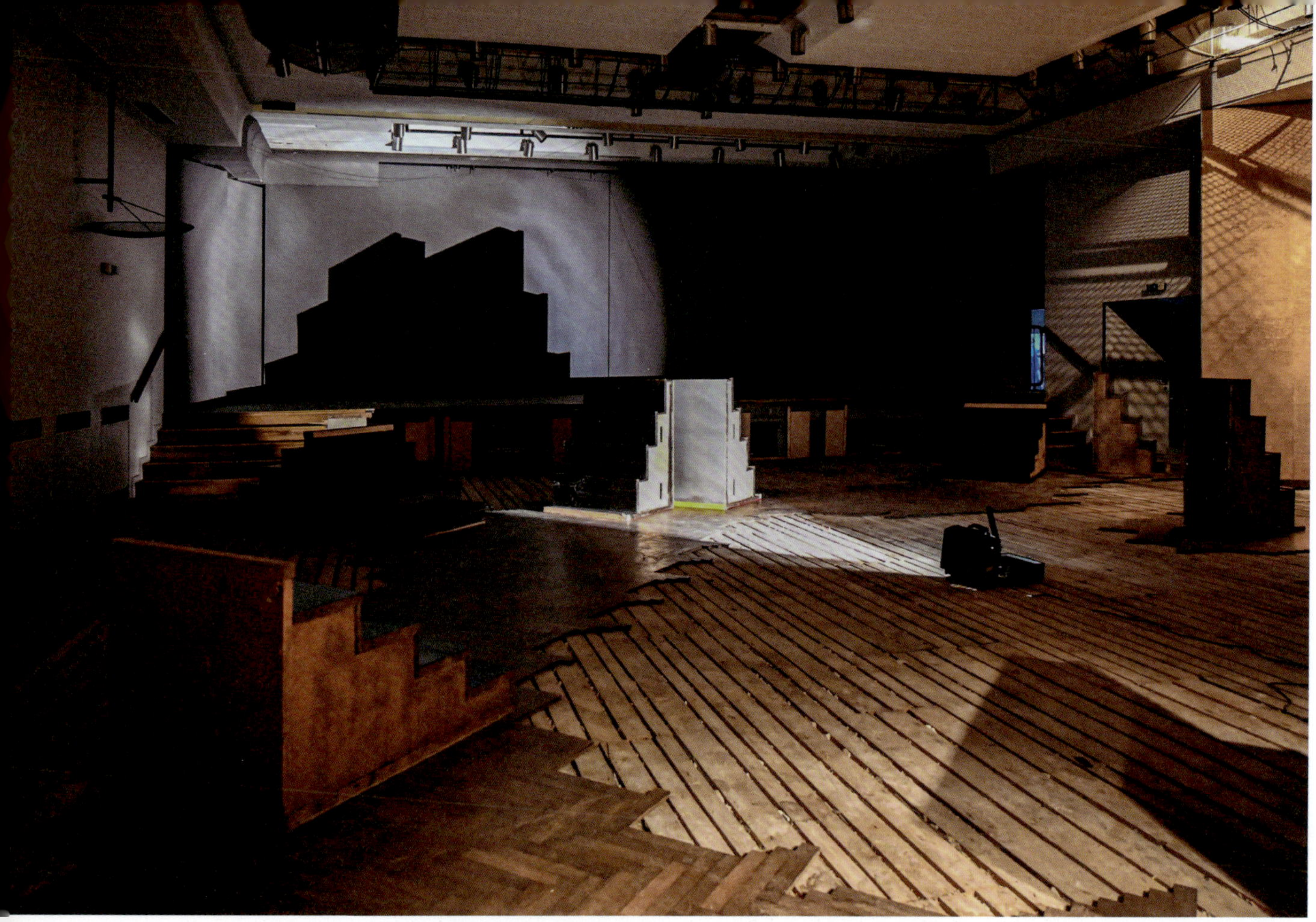

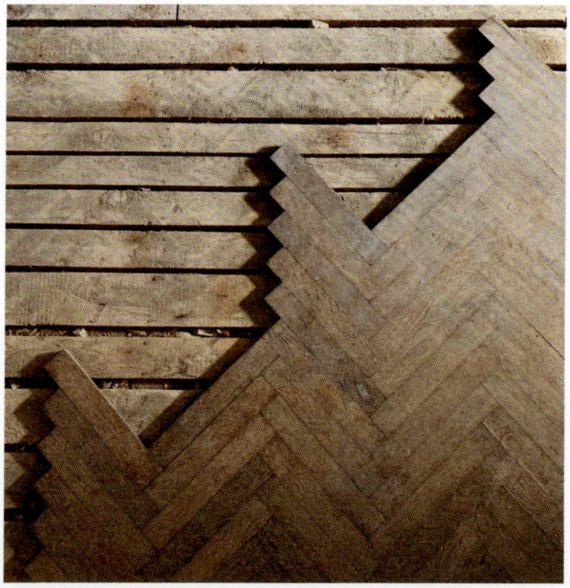

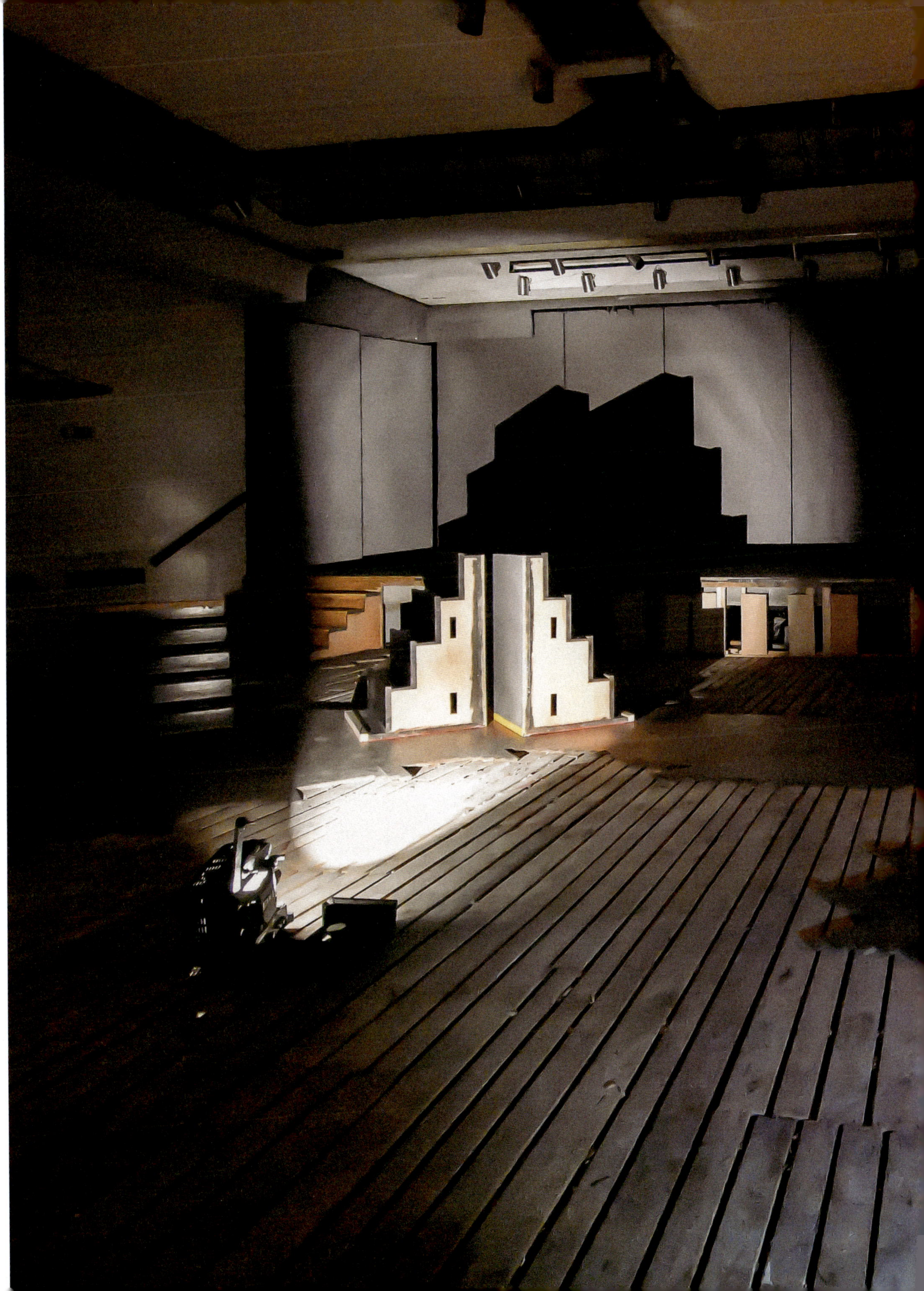

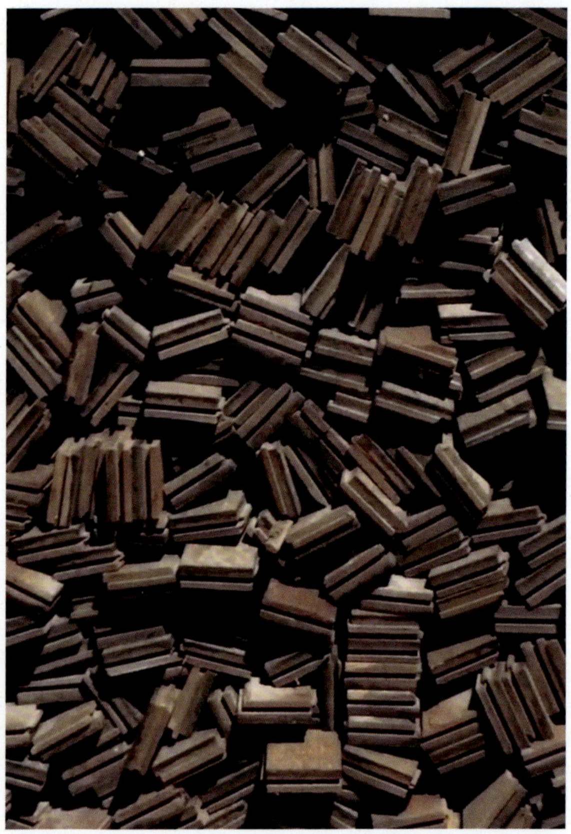

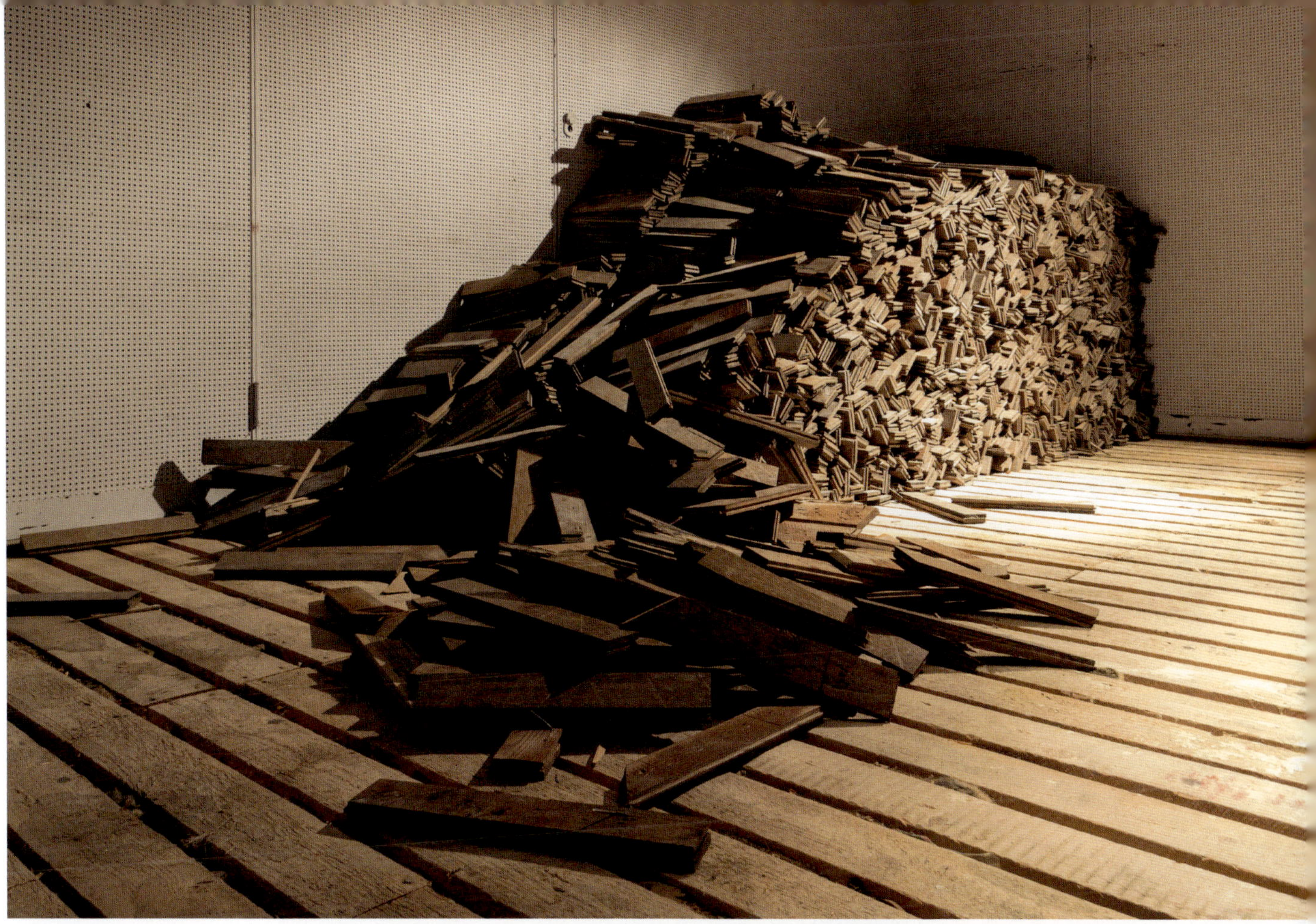

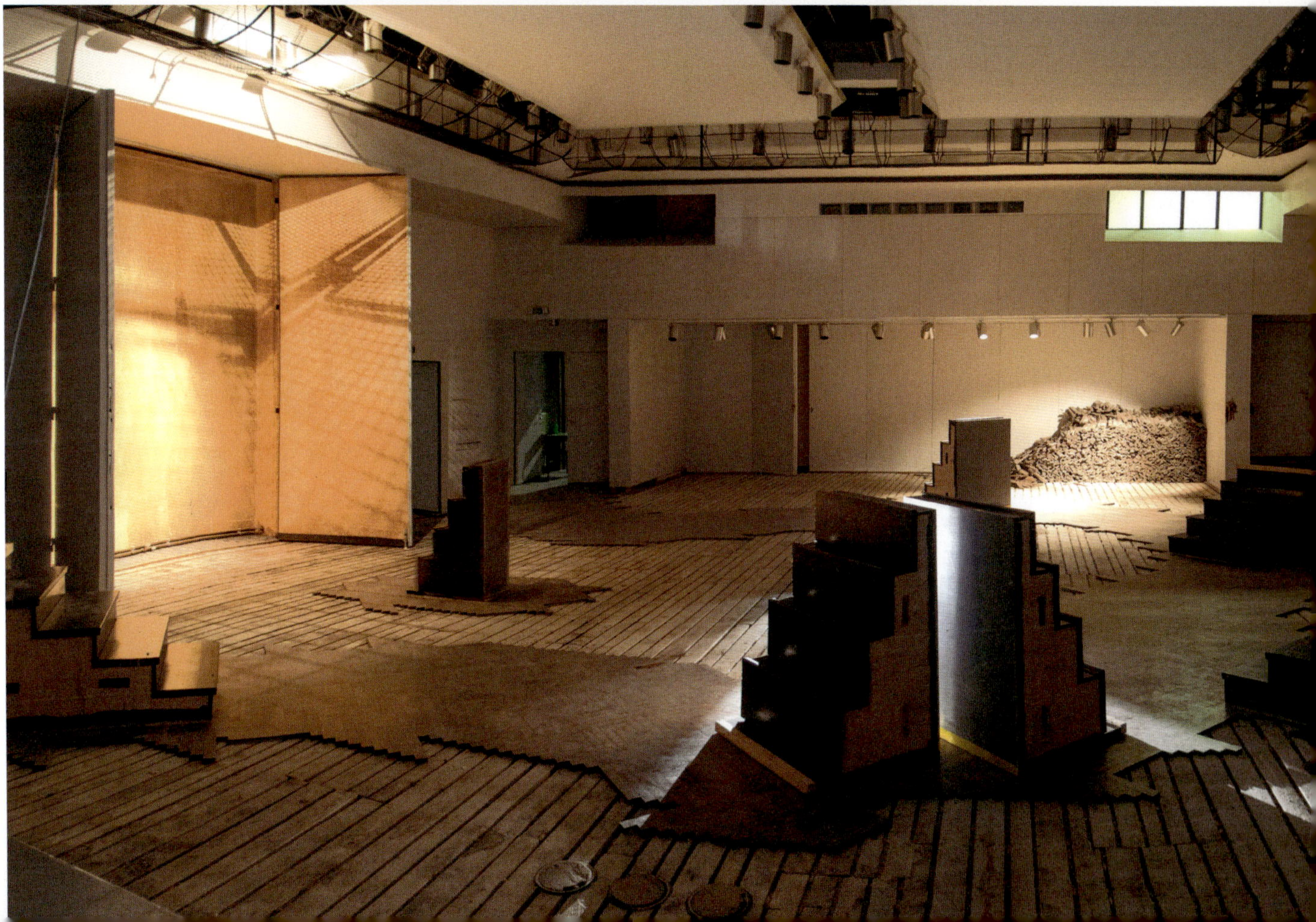

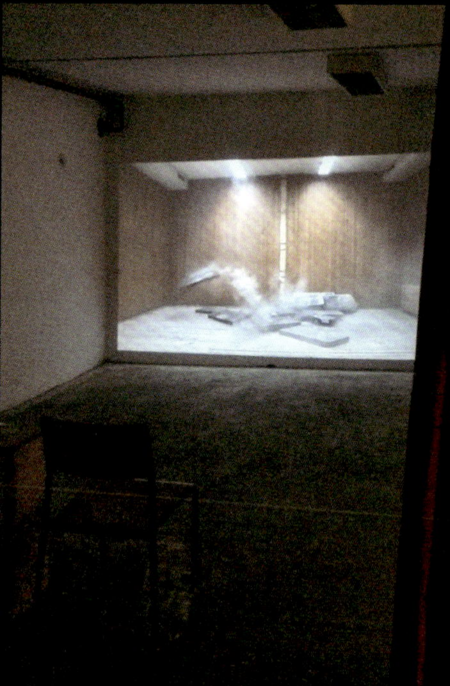

[Lautes Knallen auf den Boden]
[Loud banging on the floor]

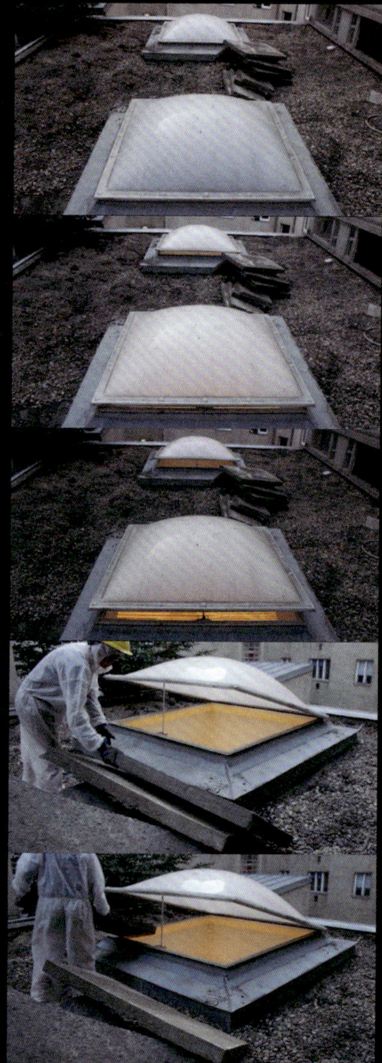

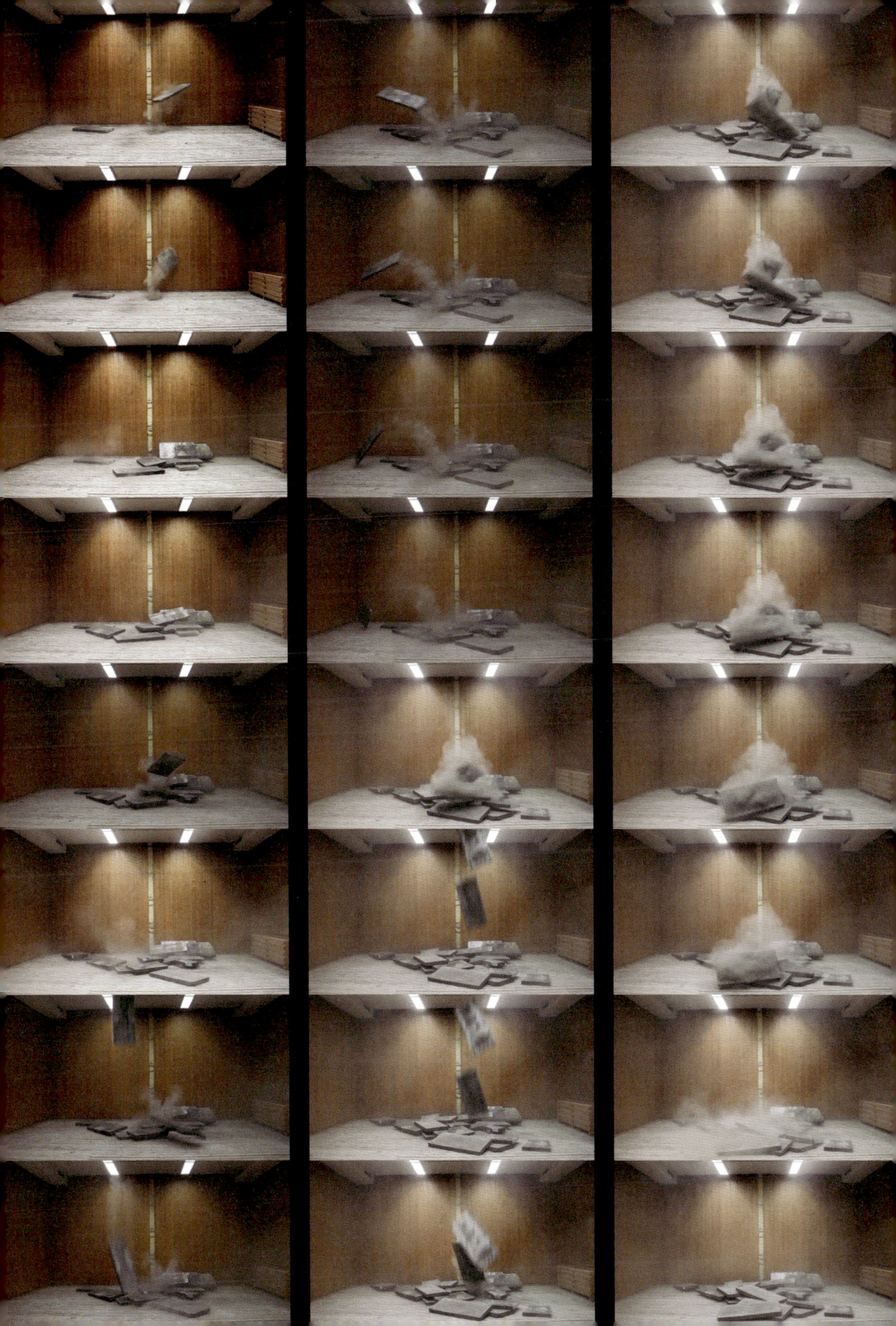

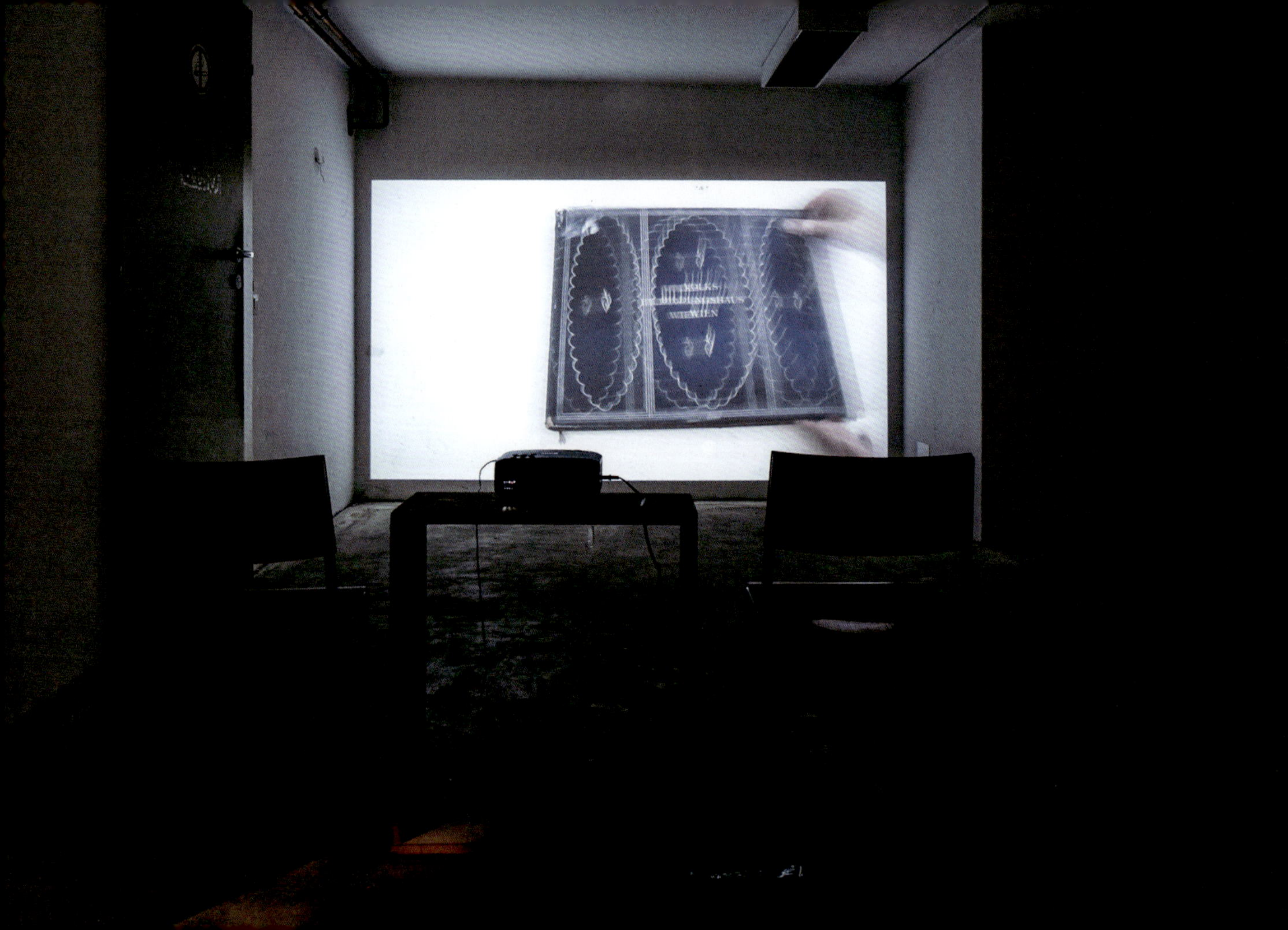

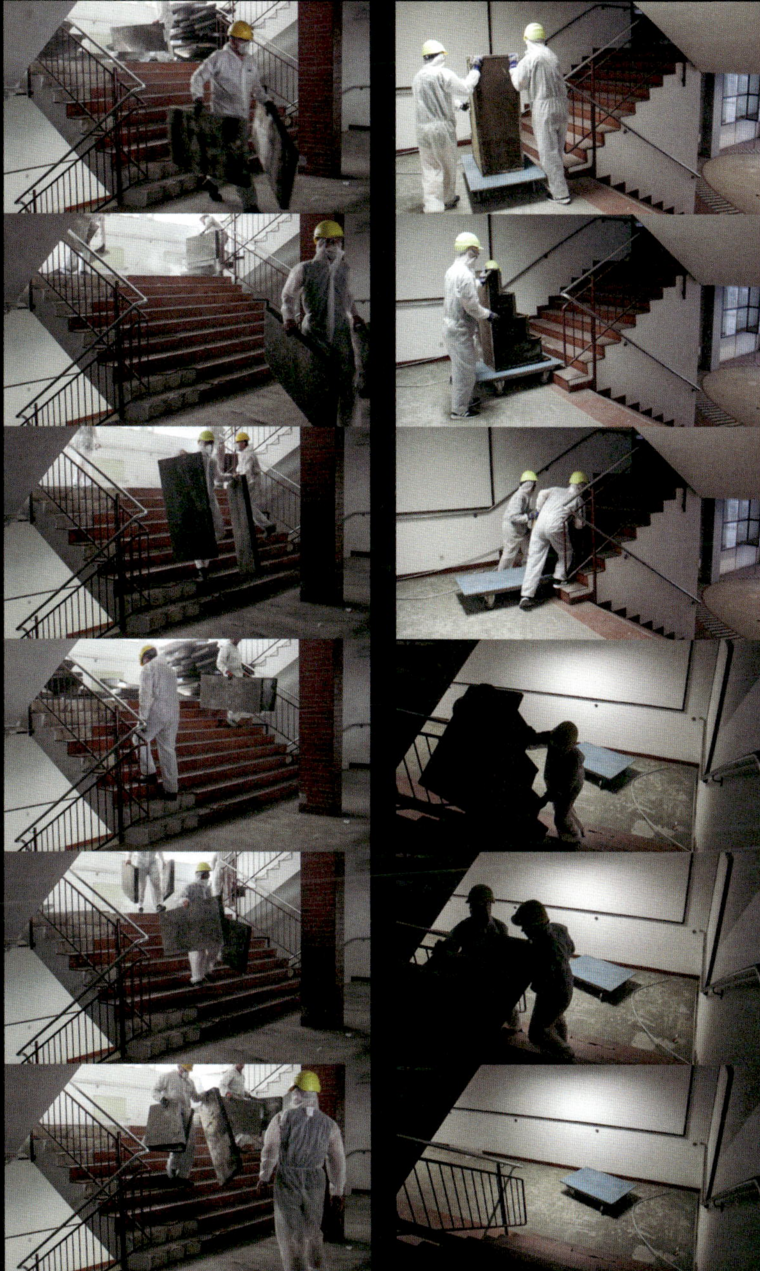

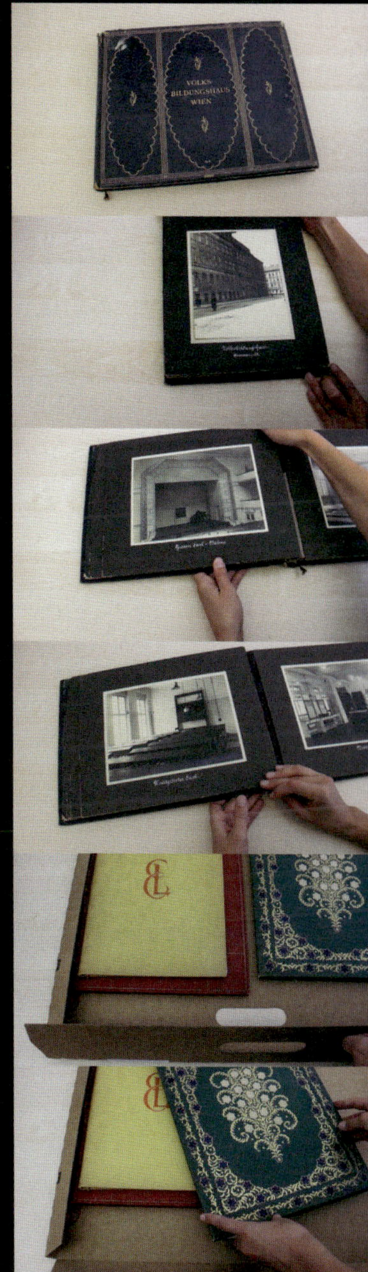

Video: *MINING: Filmhaus – Großer Videosaal*, 2020
14:45 min / Teil 2, Die Arbeiter
Video: 'MINING: Filmhaus – Big video room', 2020
14:45 min / Part 2, The Workers

Video: *MINING: Filmhaus – Großer Videosaal*, 202
14:45 min / Teil 3, Das Archiv
Video: 'MINING: Filmhaus – Big video room', 202

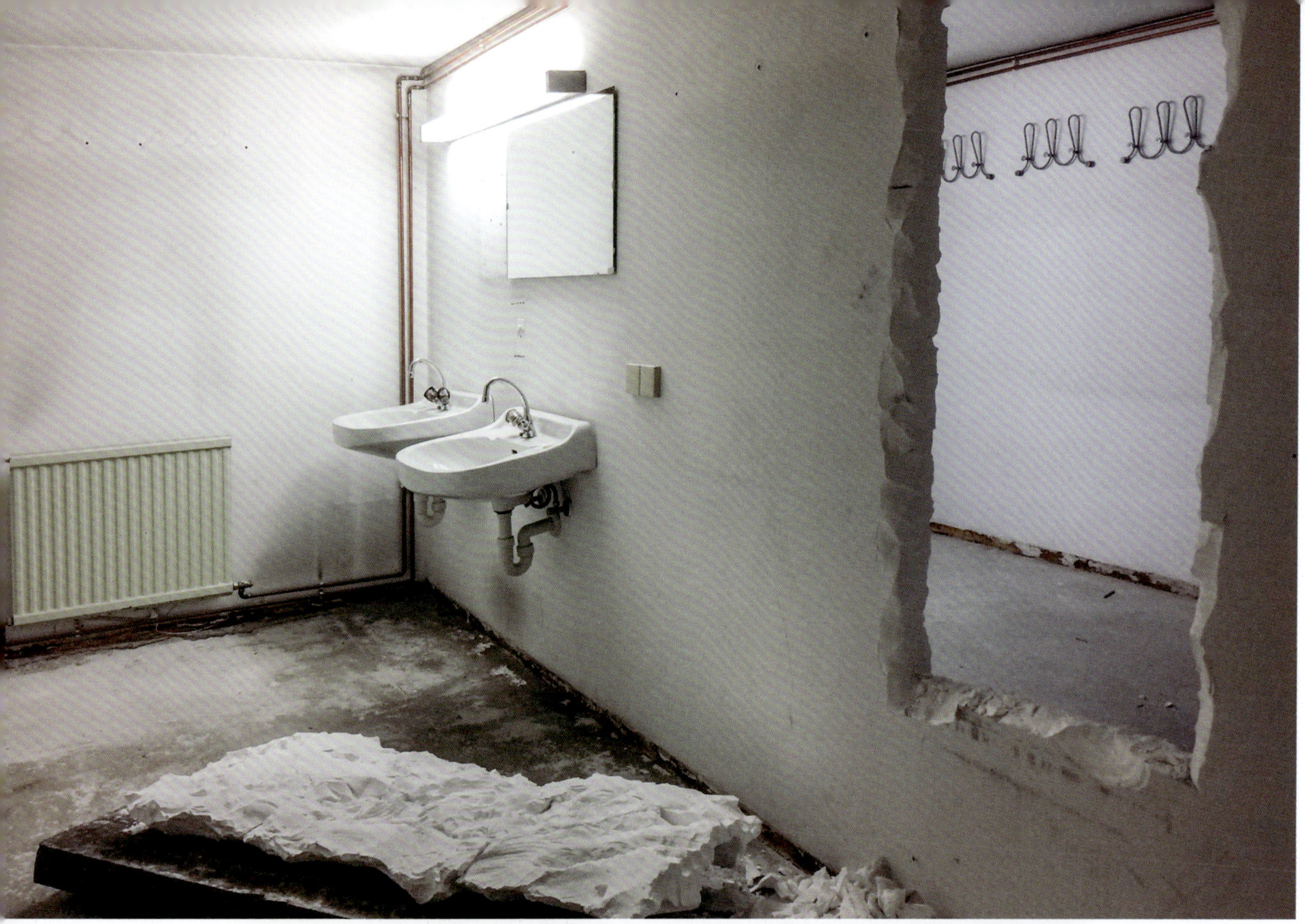

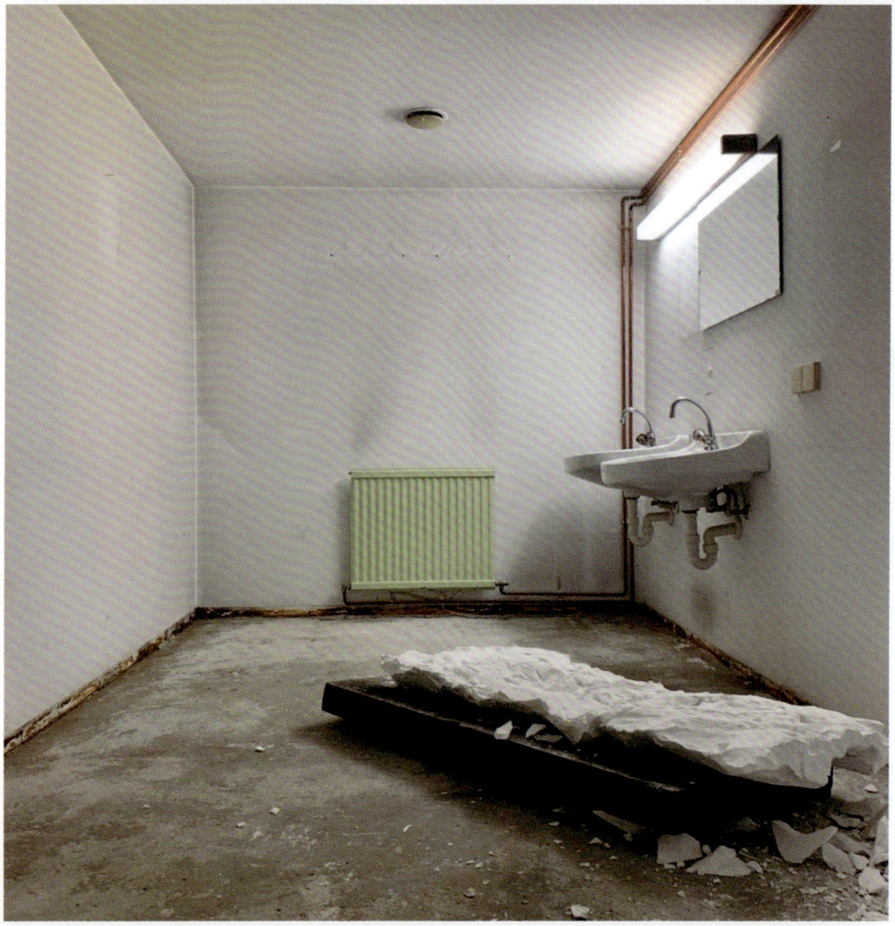

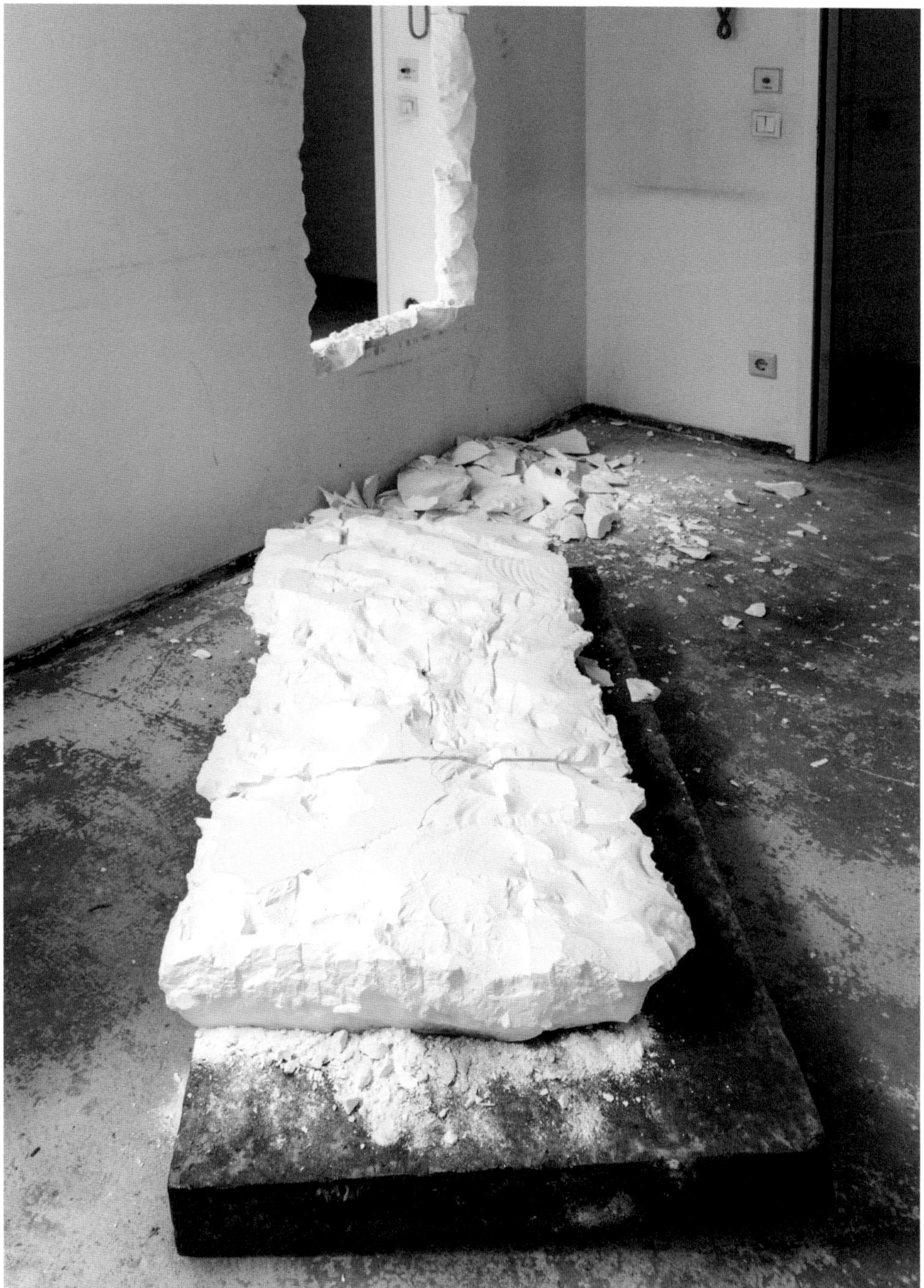

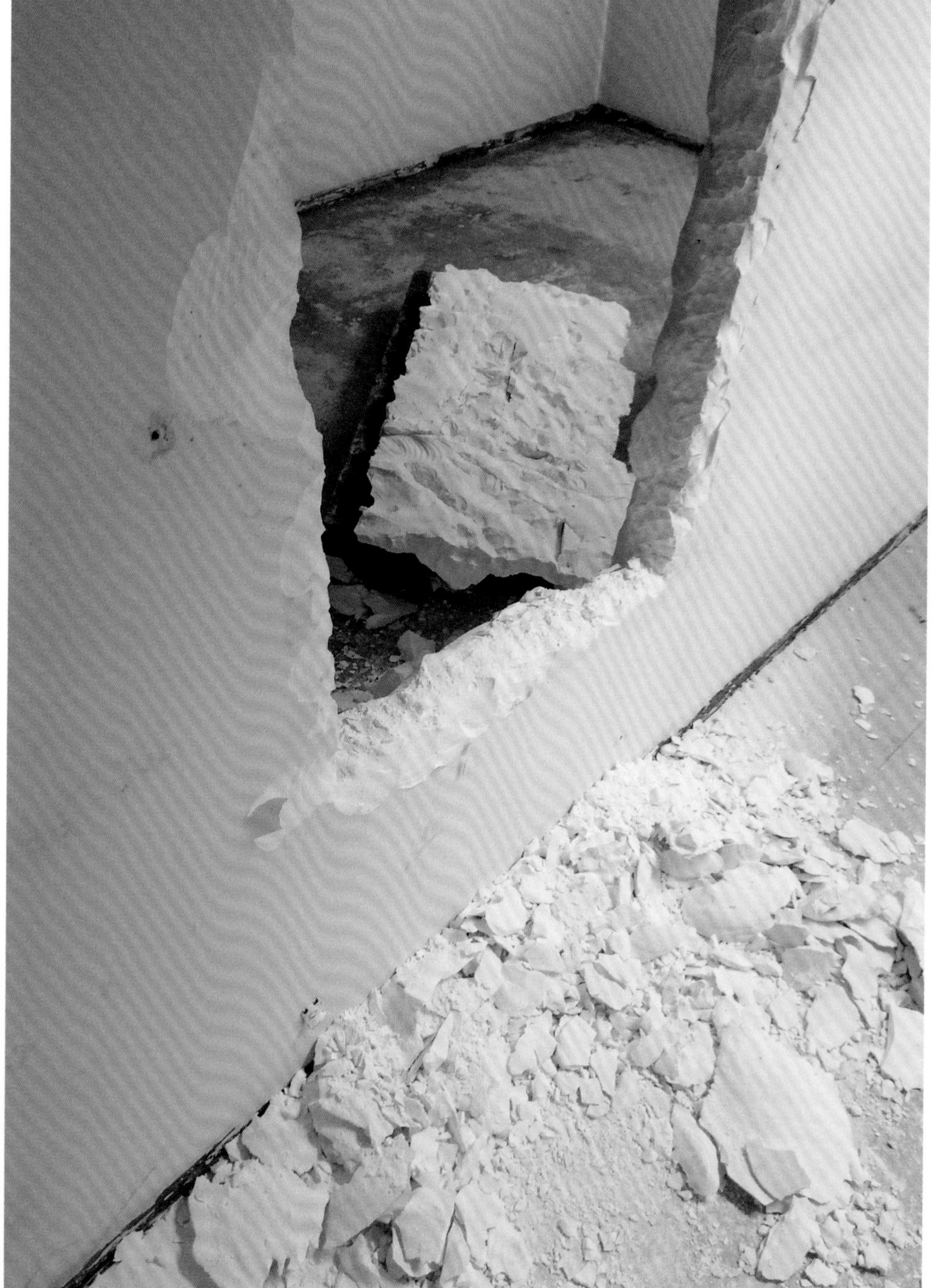

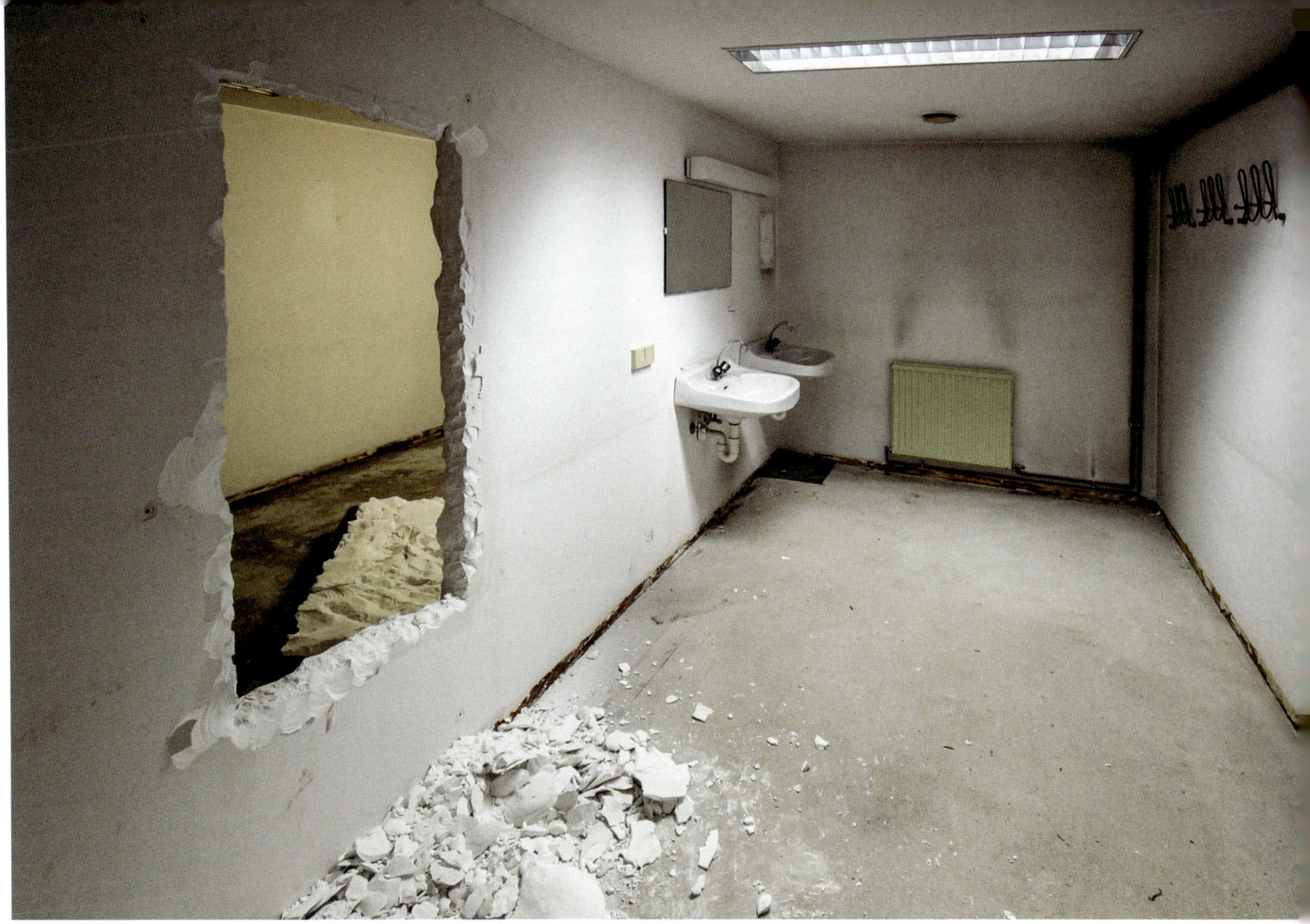

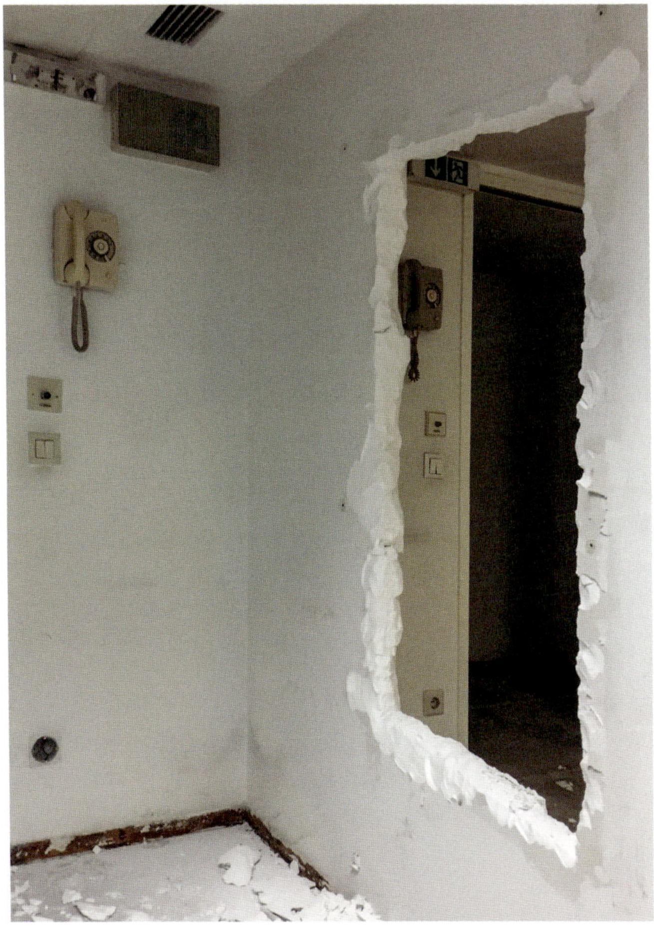

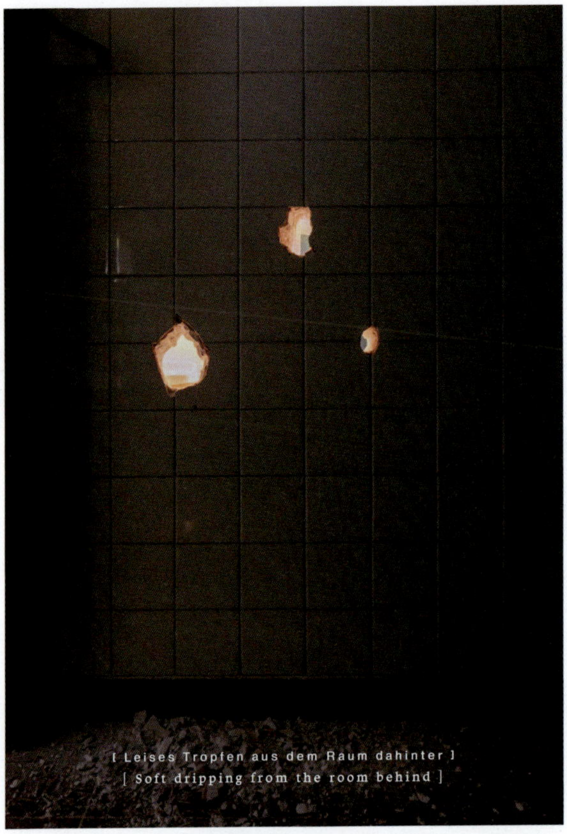
[Leises Tropfen aus dem Raum dahinter]
[Soft dripping from the room behind]

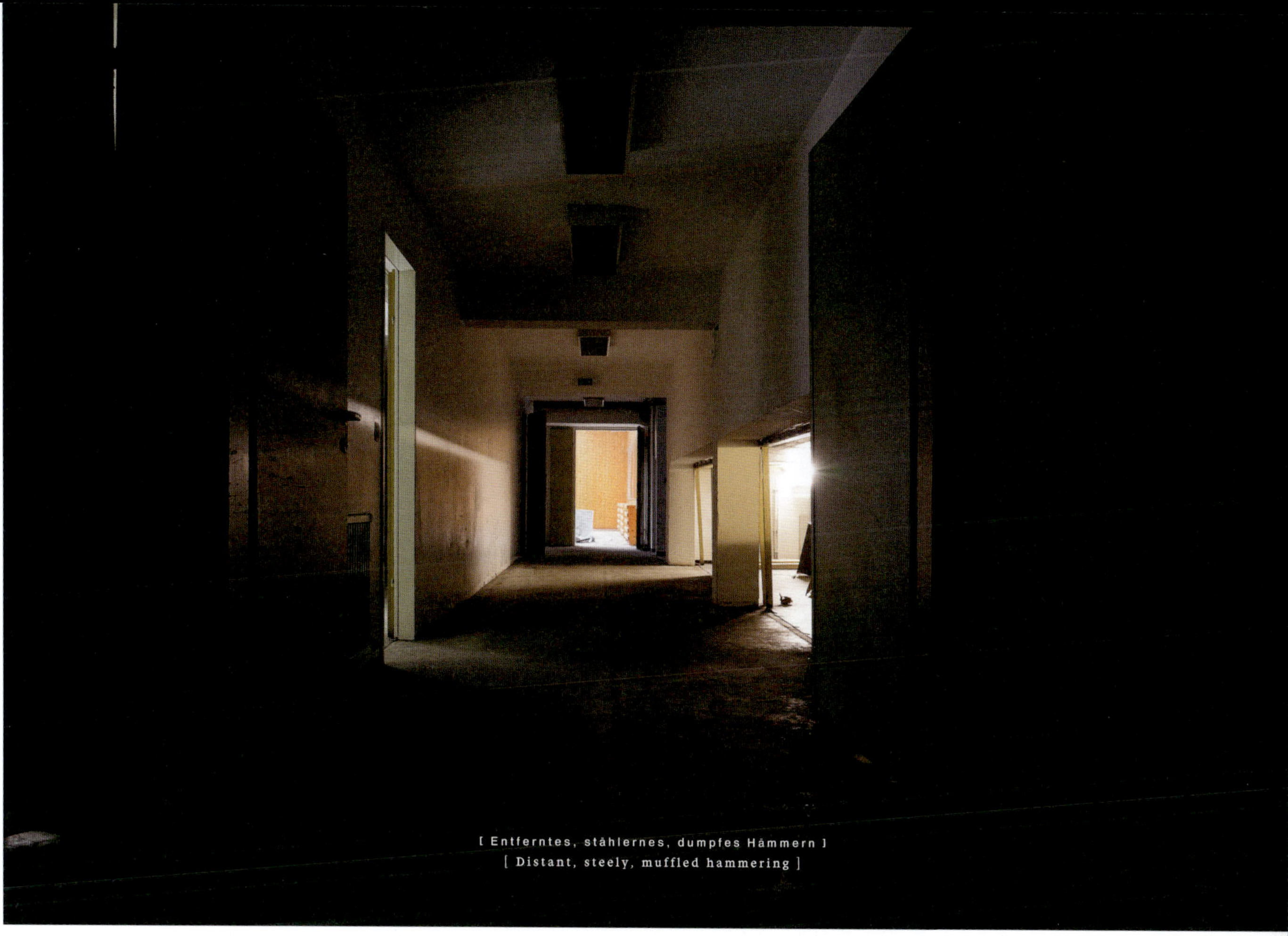
[Entferntes, stählernes, dumpfes Hämmern]
[Distant, steely, muffled hammering]

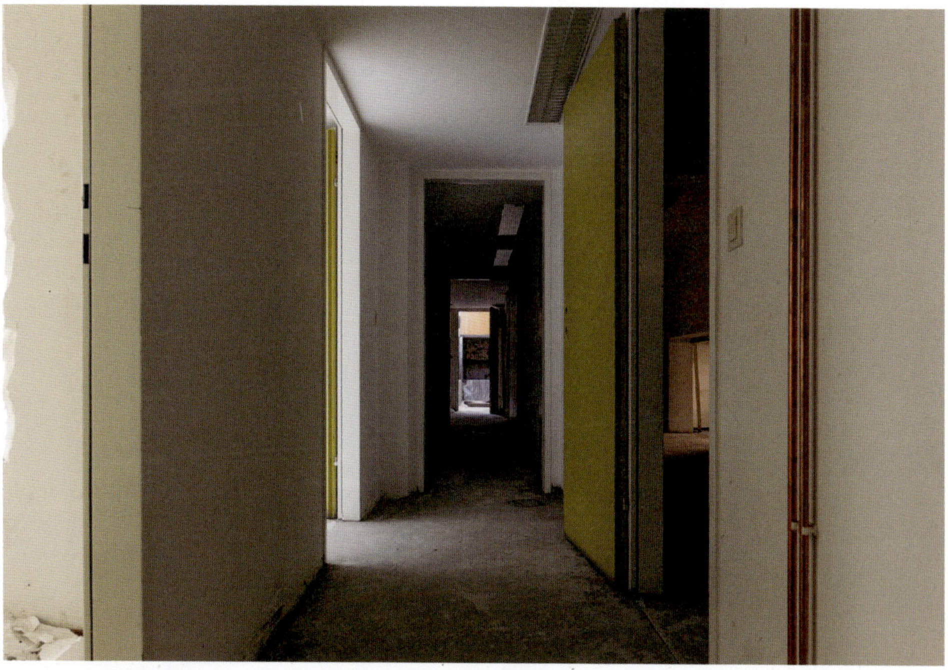

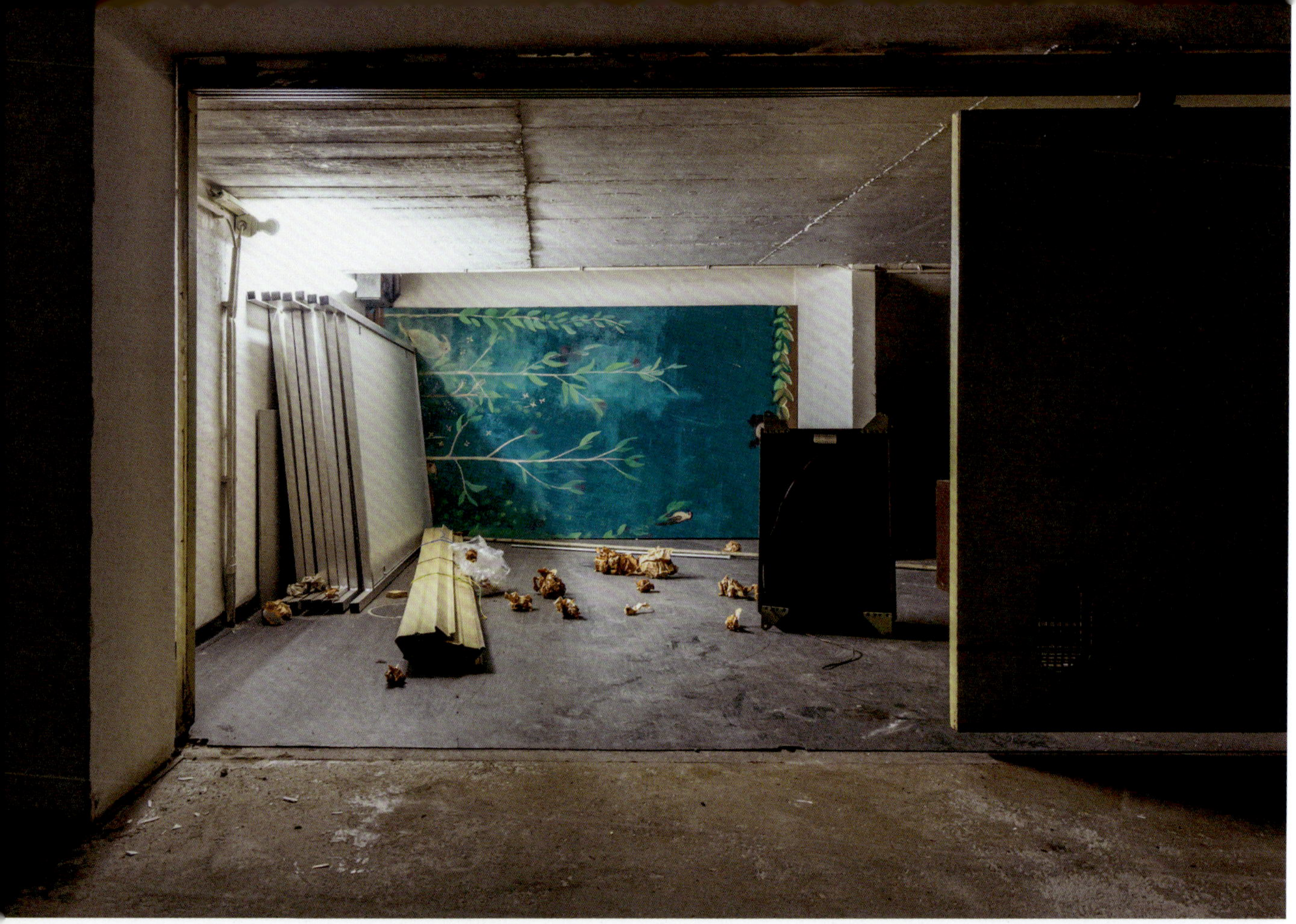

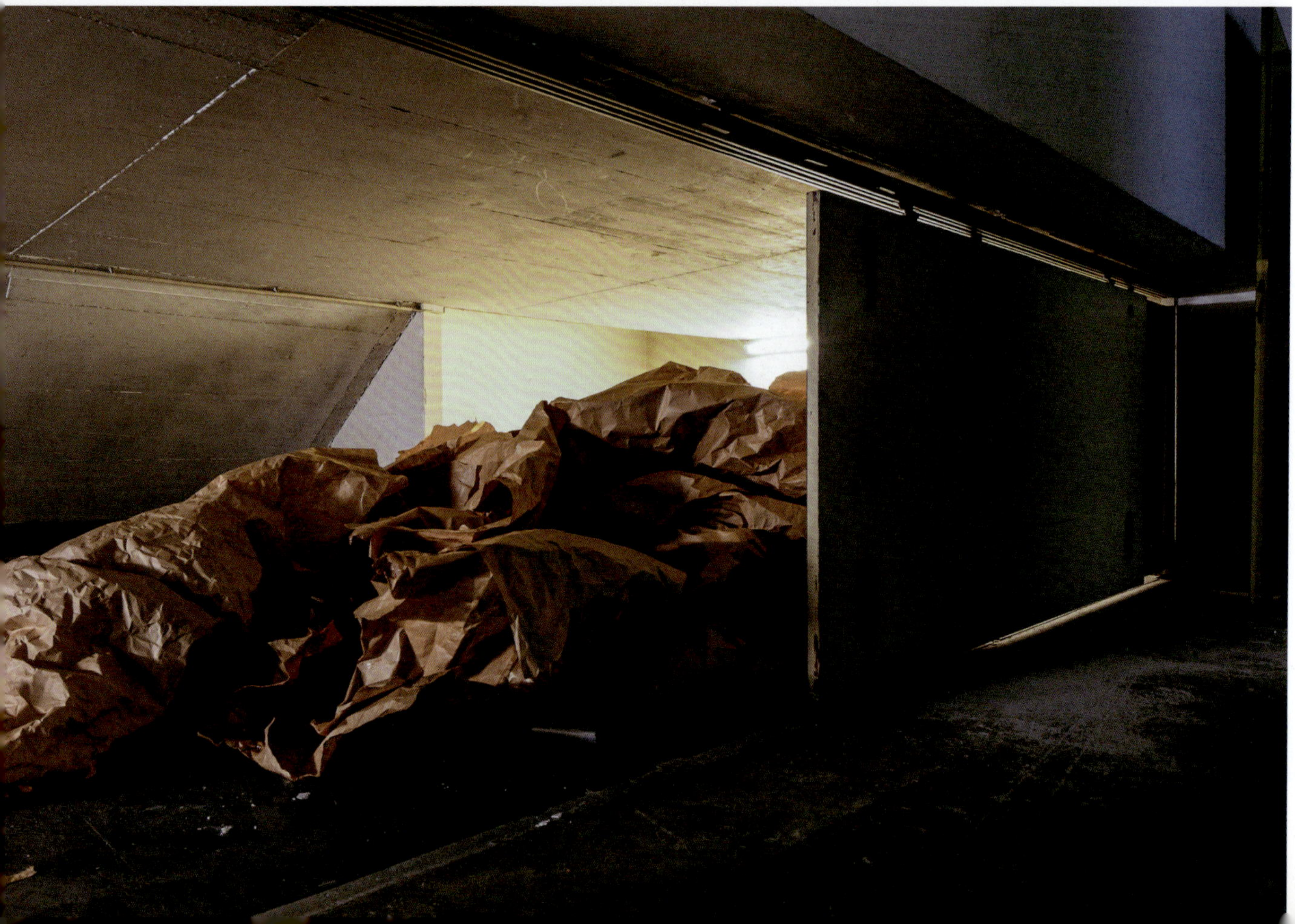

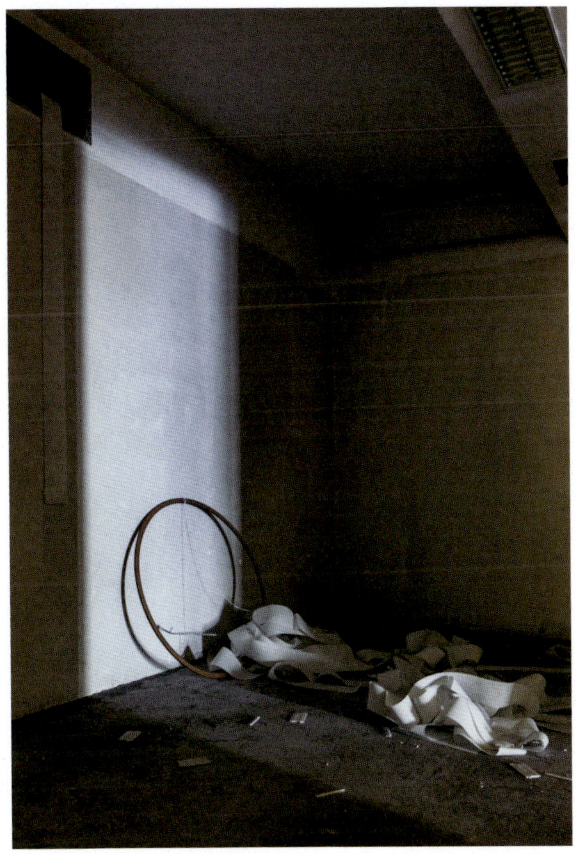

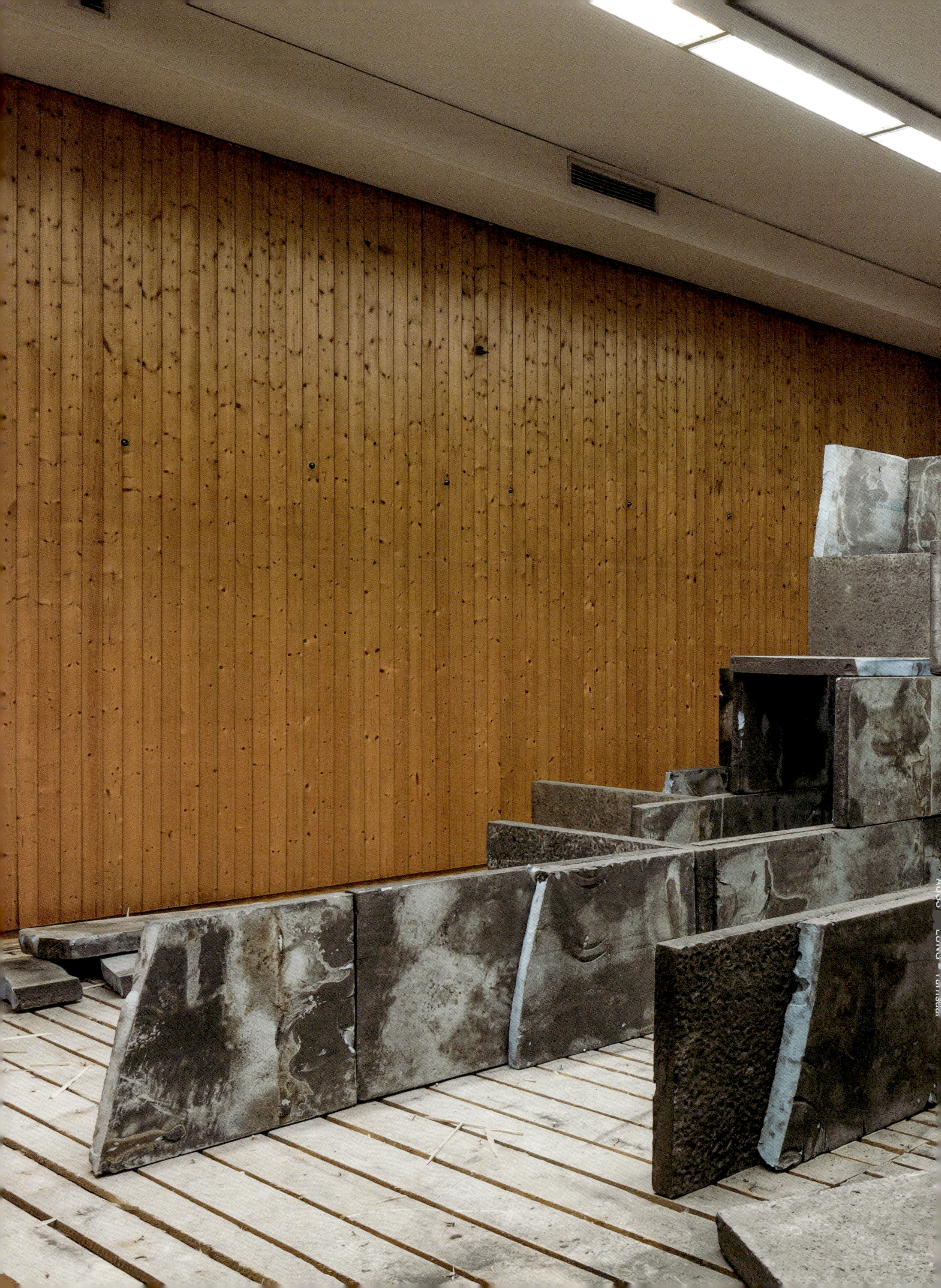

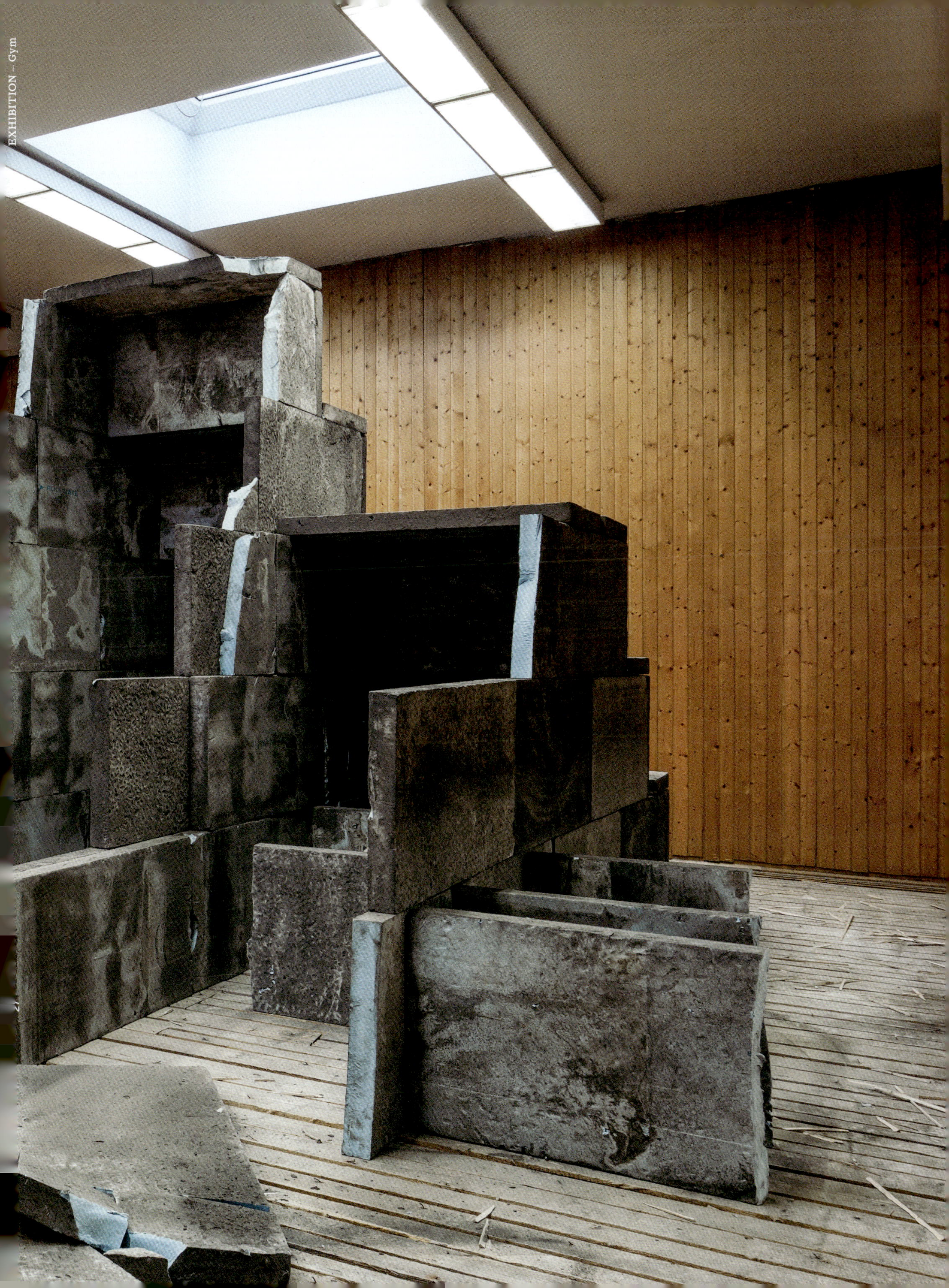

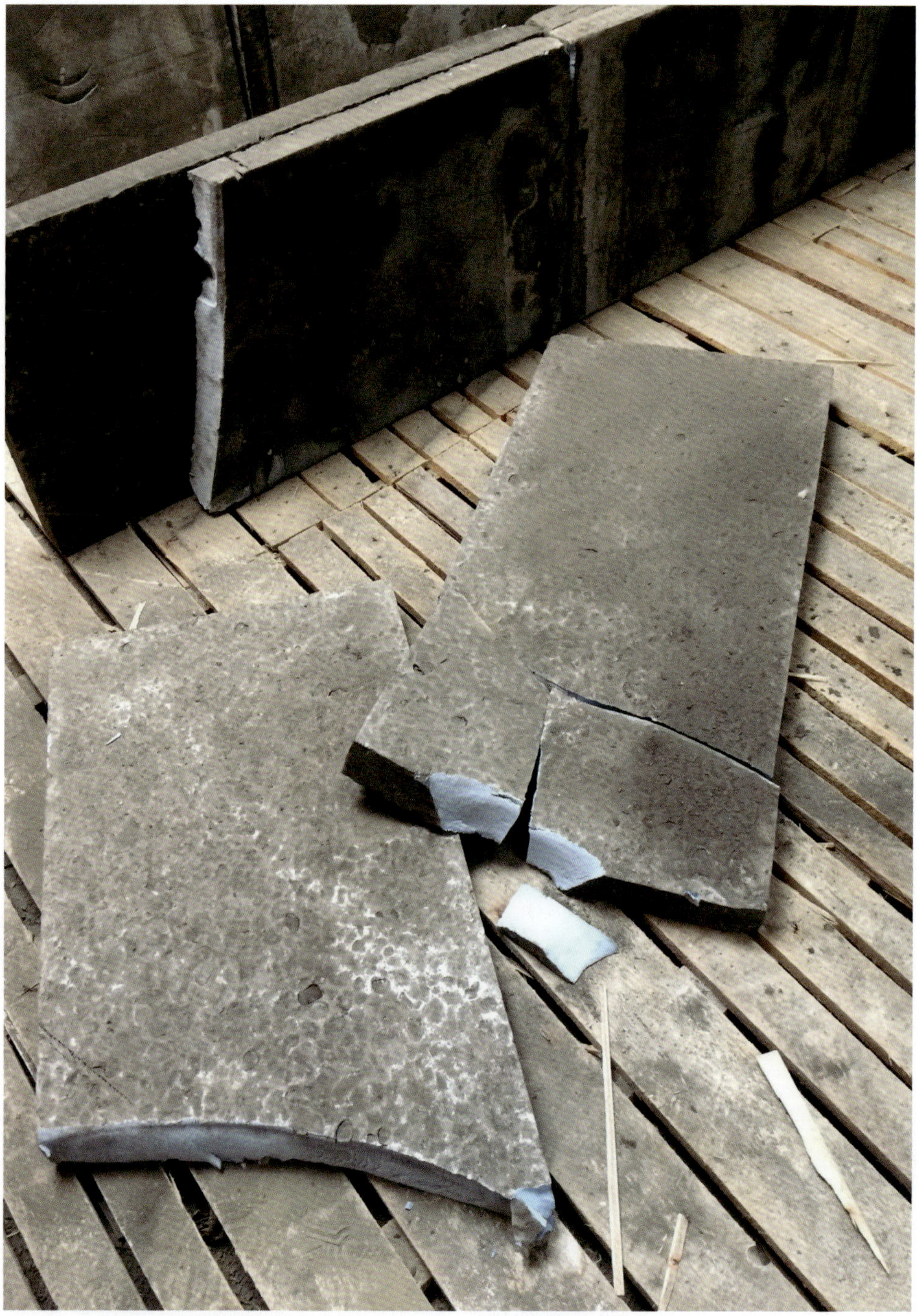

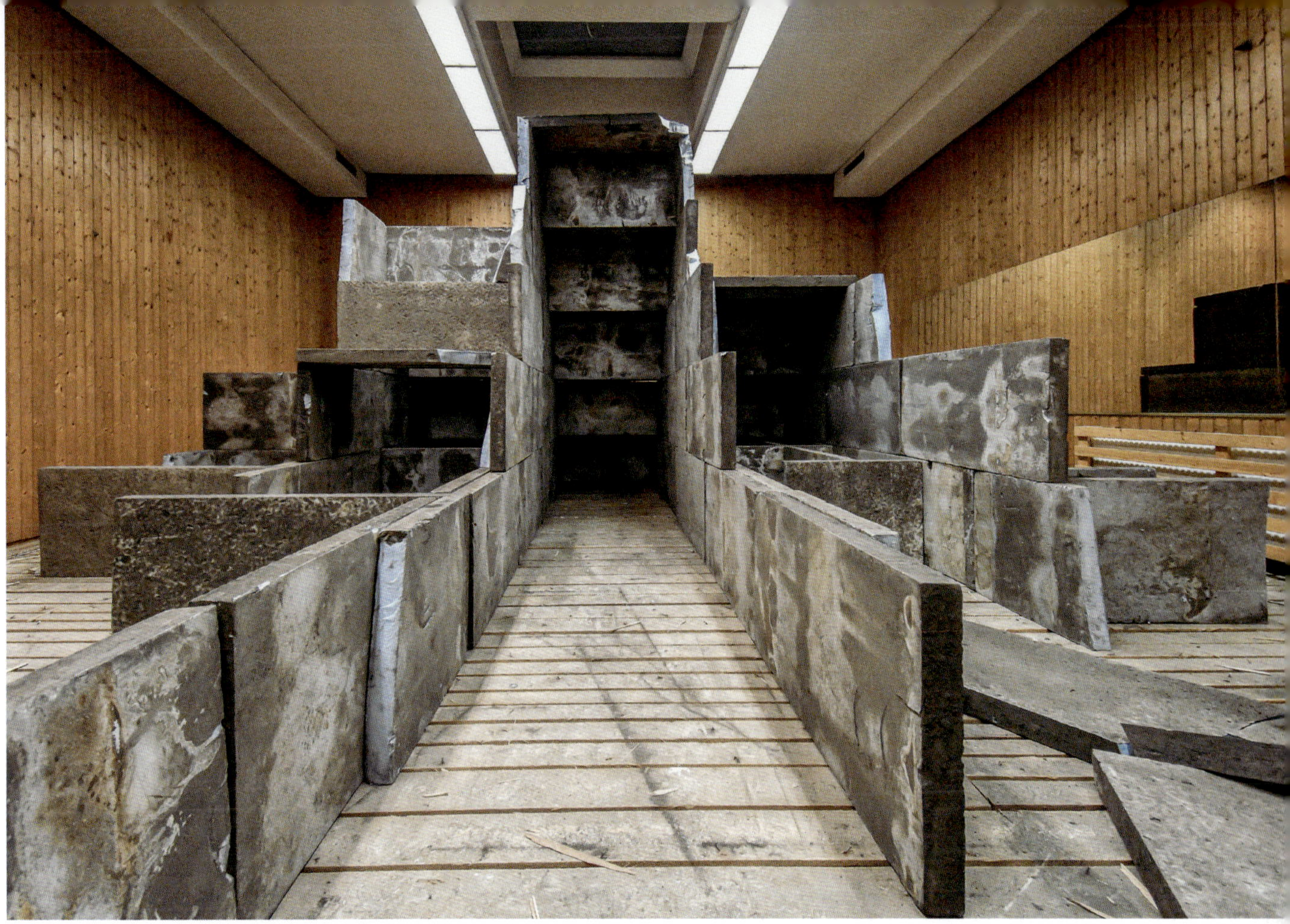

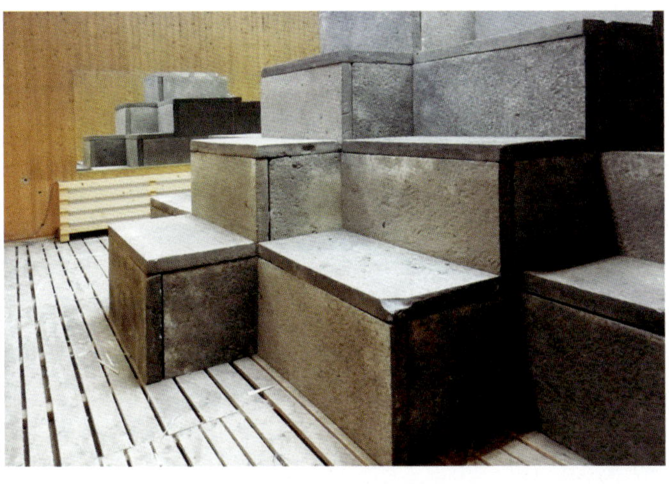

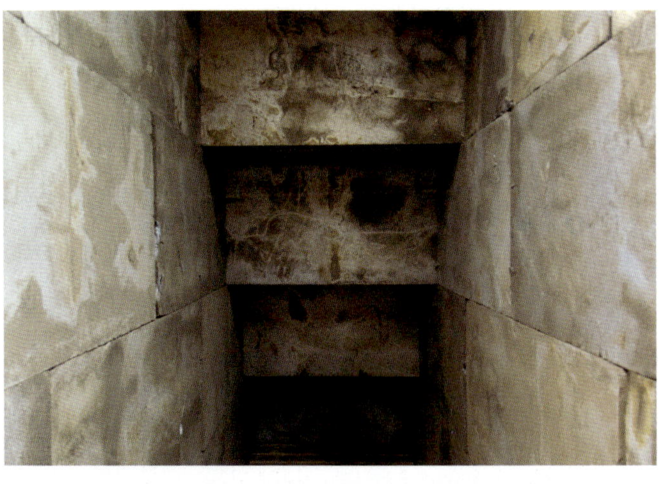

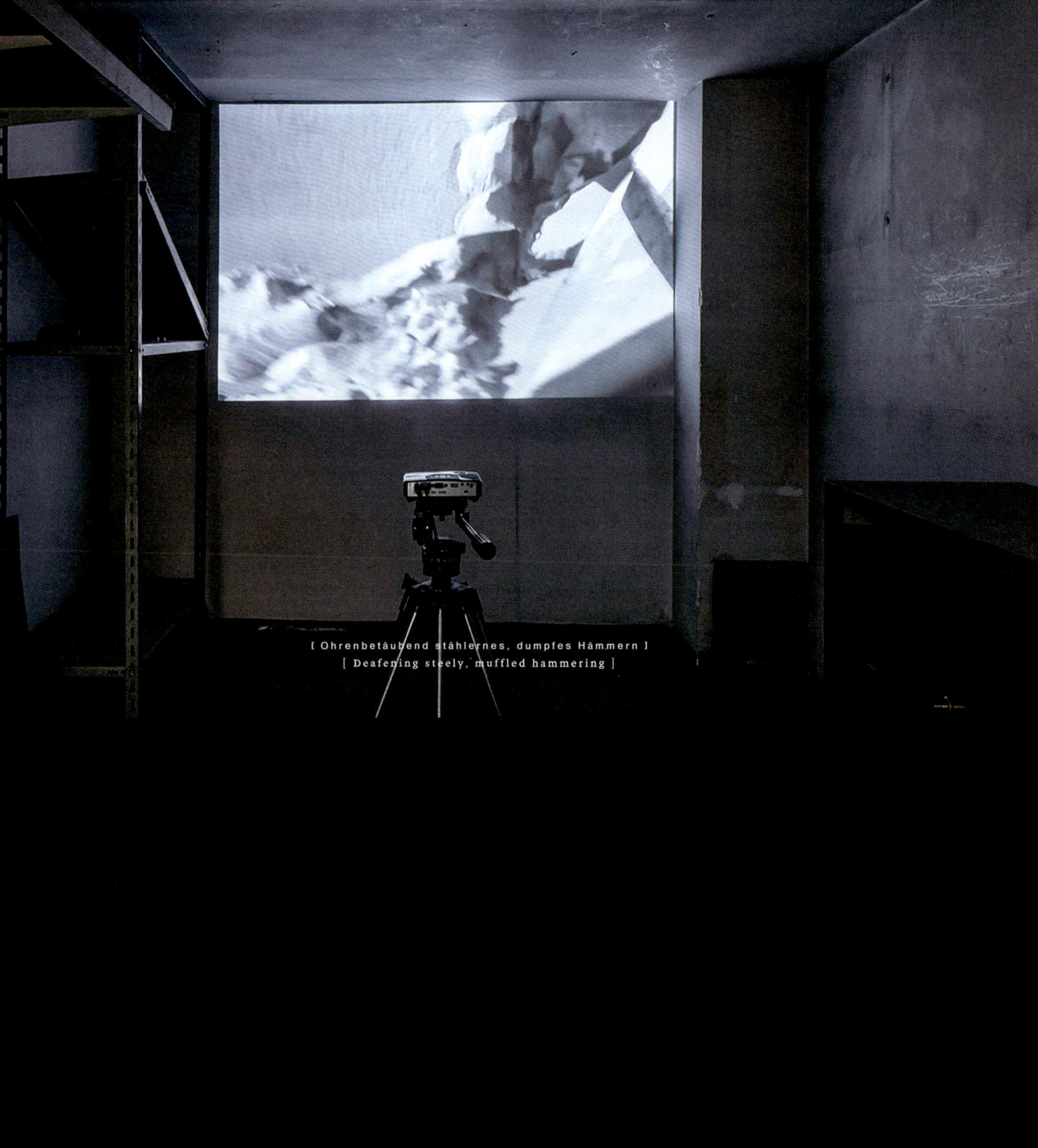

[Ohrenbetäubend stählernes, dumpfes Hämmern]
[Deafening steely, muffled hammering]

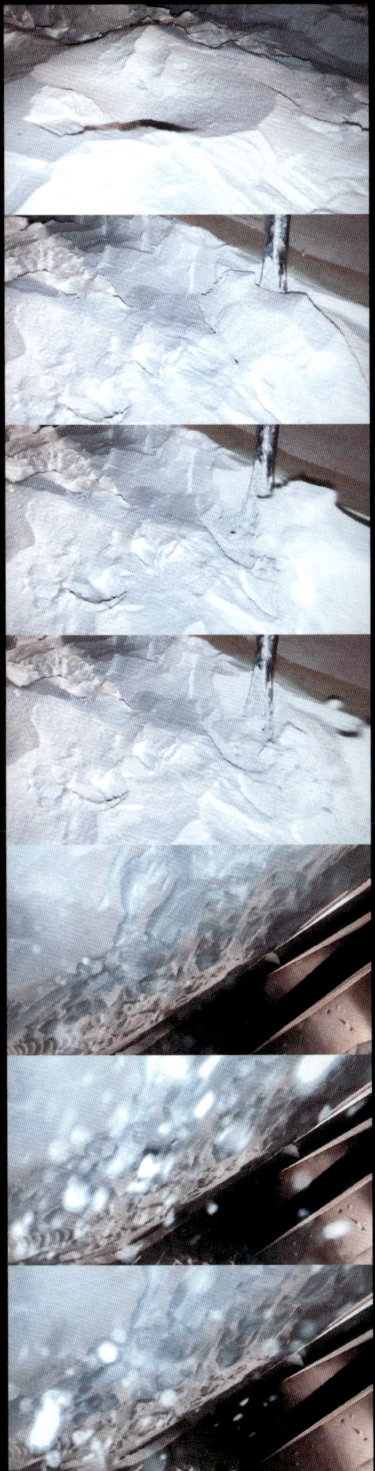

Video: ***MINING: Filmhaus – Kleiner Videosaal***, 2020 / 13:13 min
Video: 'MINING: Filmhaus – Small video room', 2020 / 13:13 min

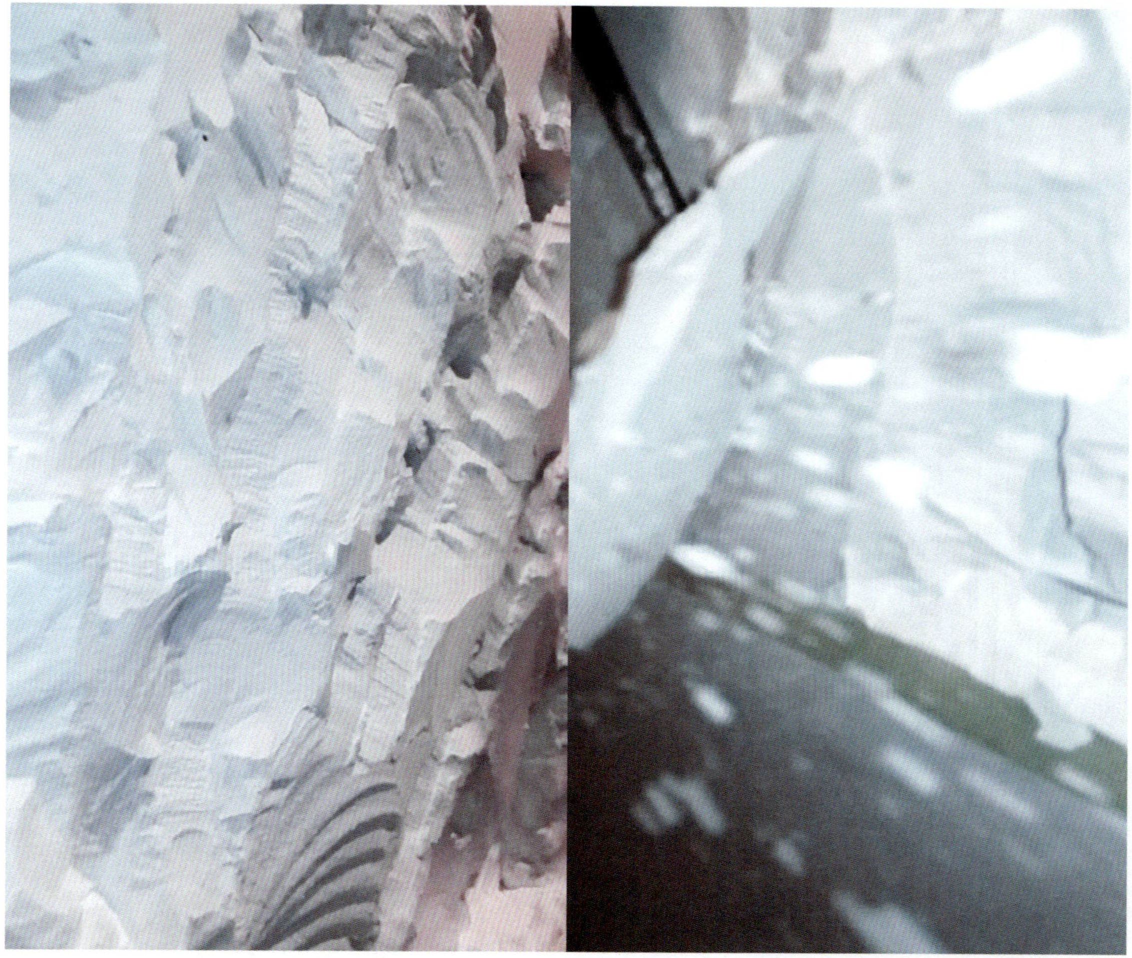

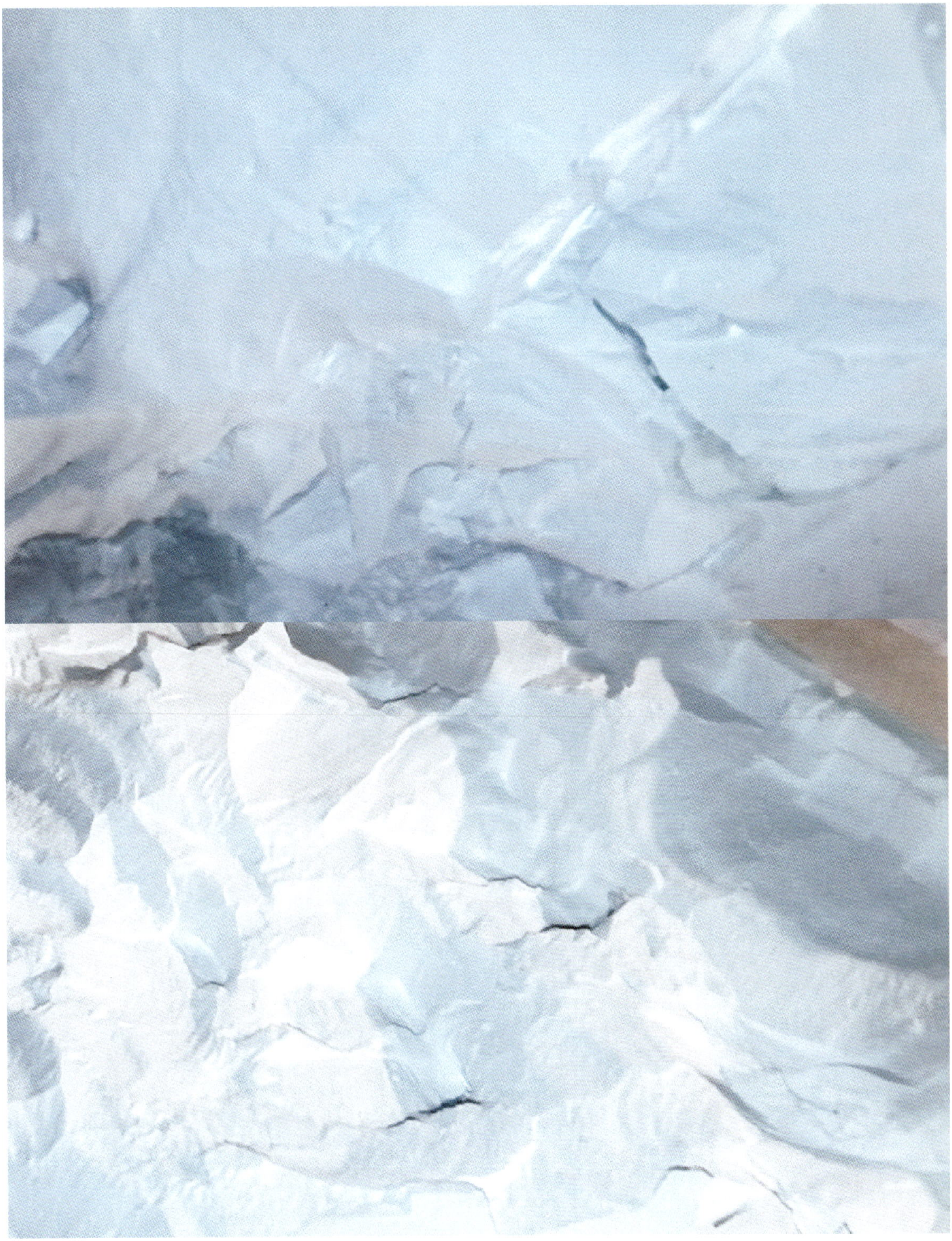

Video: ***MINING: Filmhaus –***
Kleiner Videosaal, 2020 / 13:13 min
Video: 'MINING: Filmhaus –
Small video room', 2020 / 13:13 min

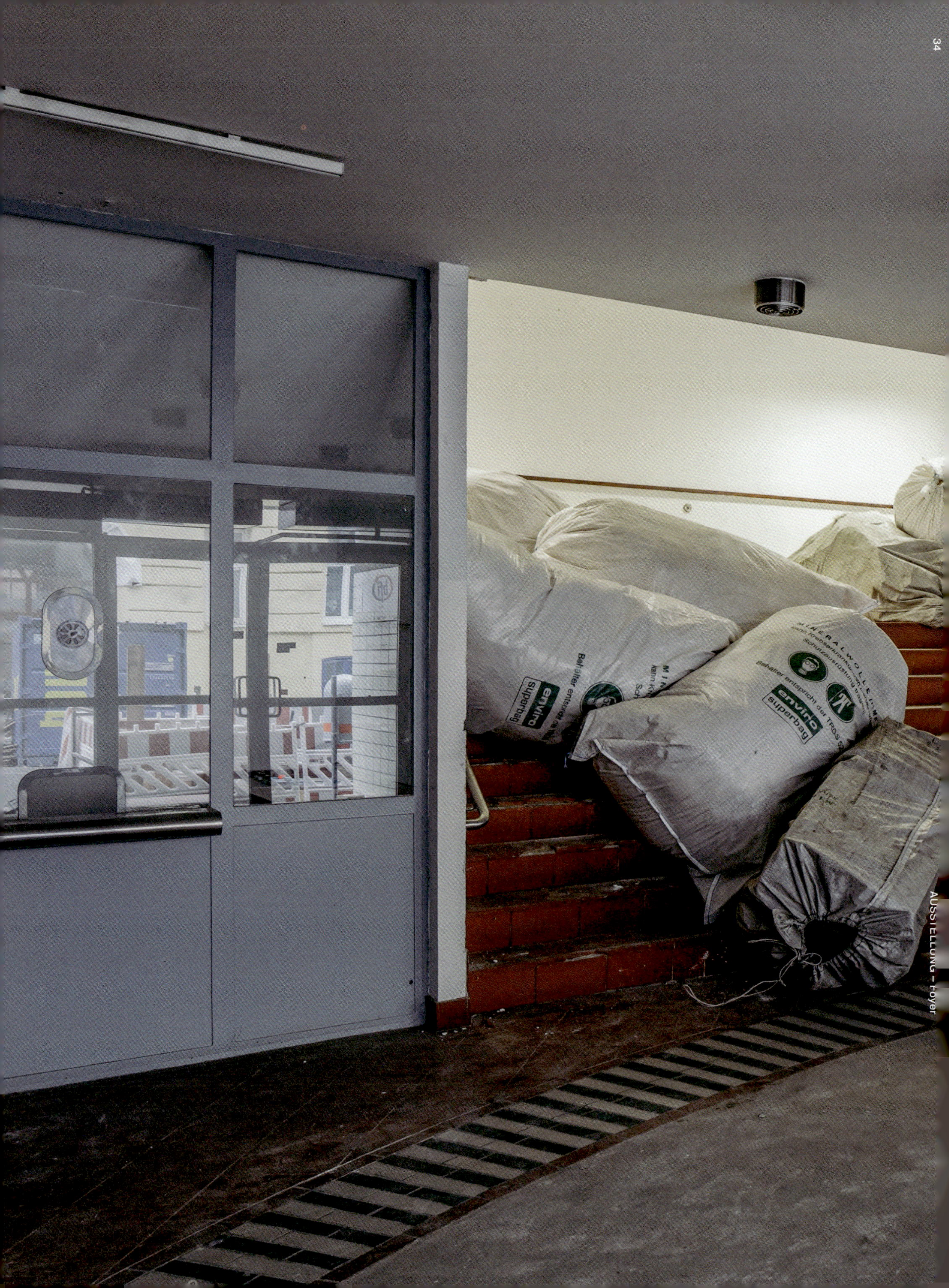
MINERALWOLLE
enviro
superbag

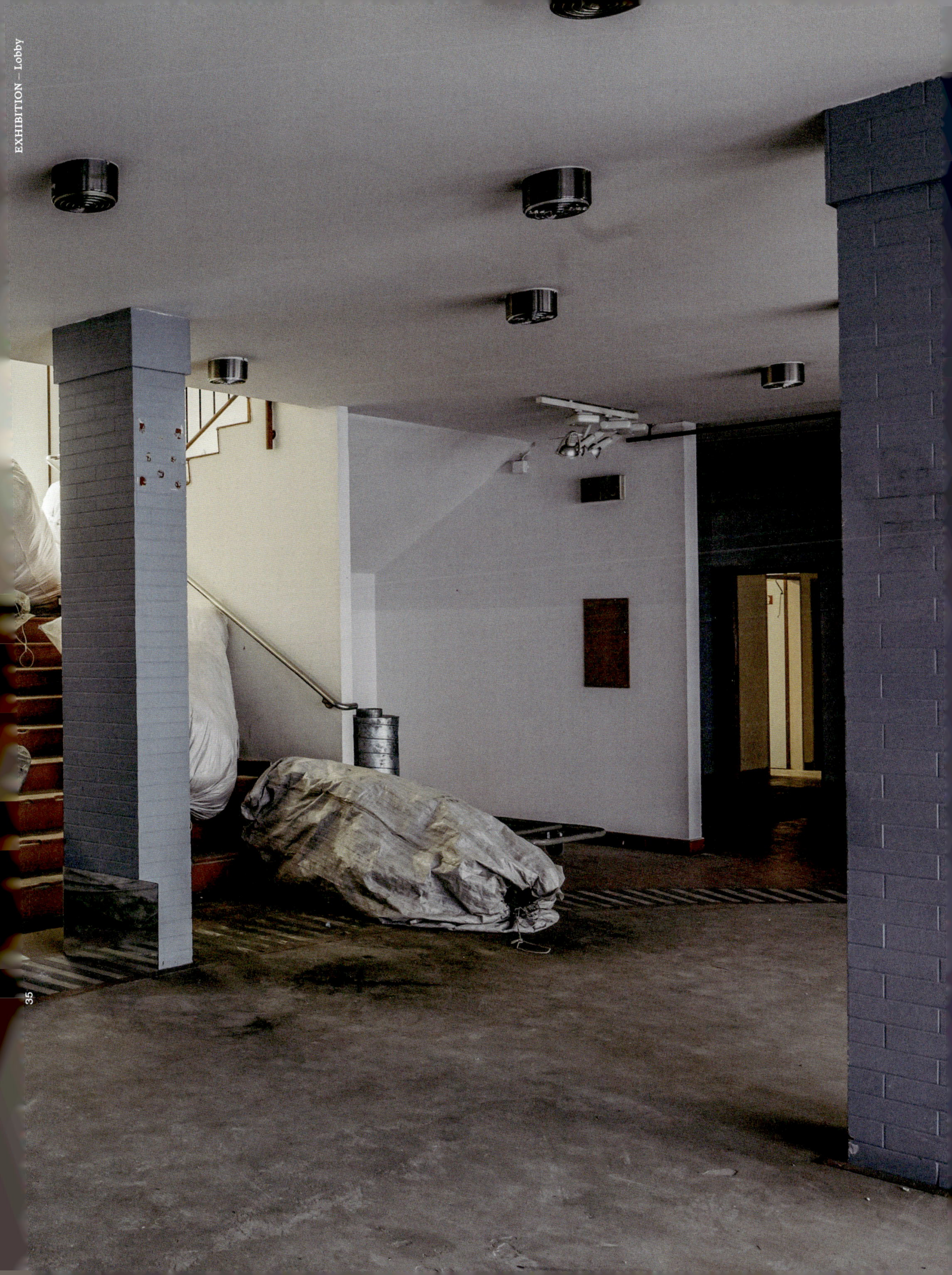

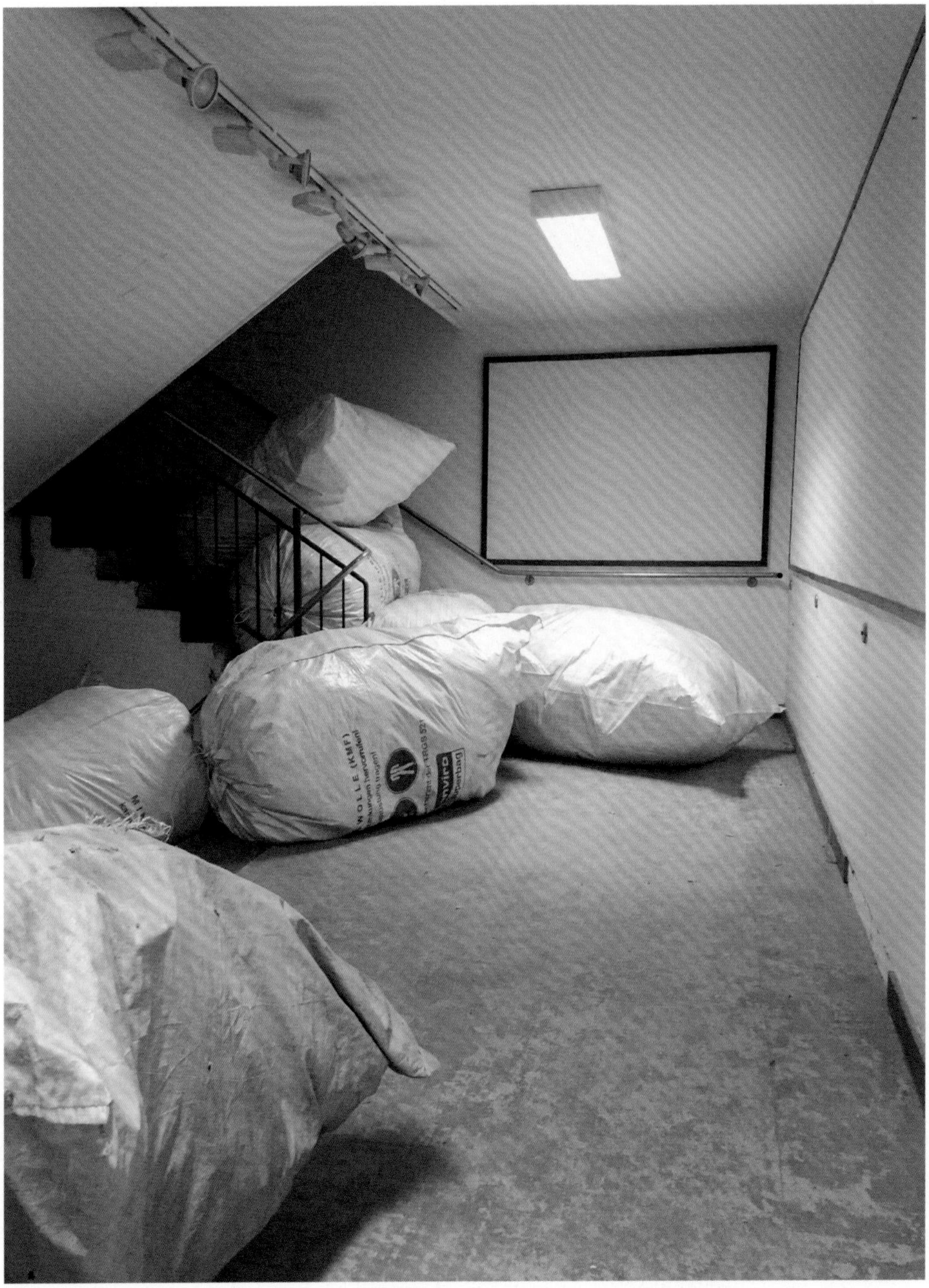

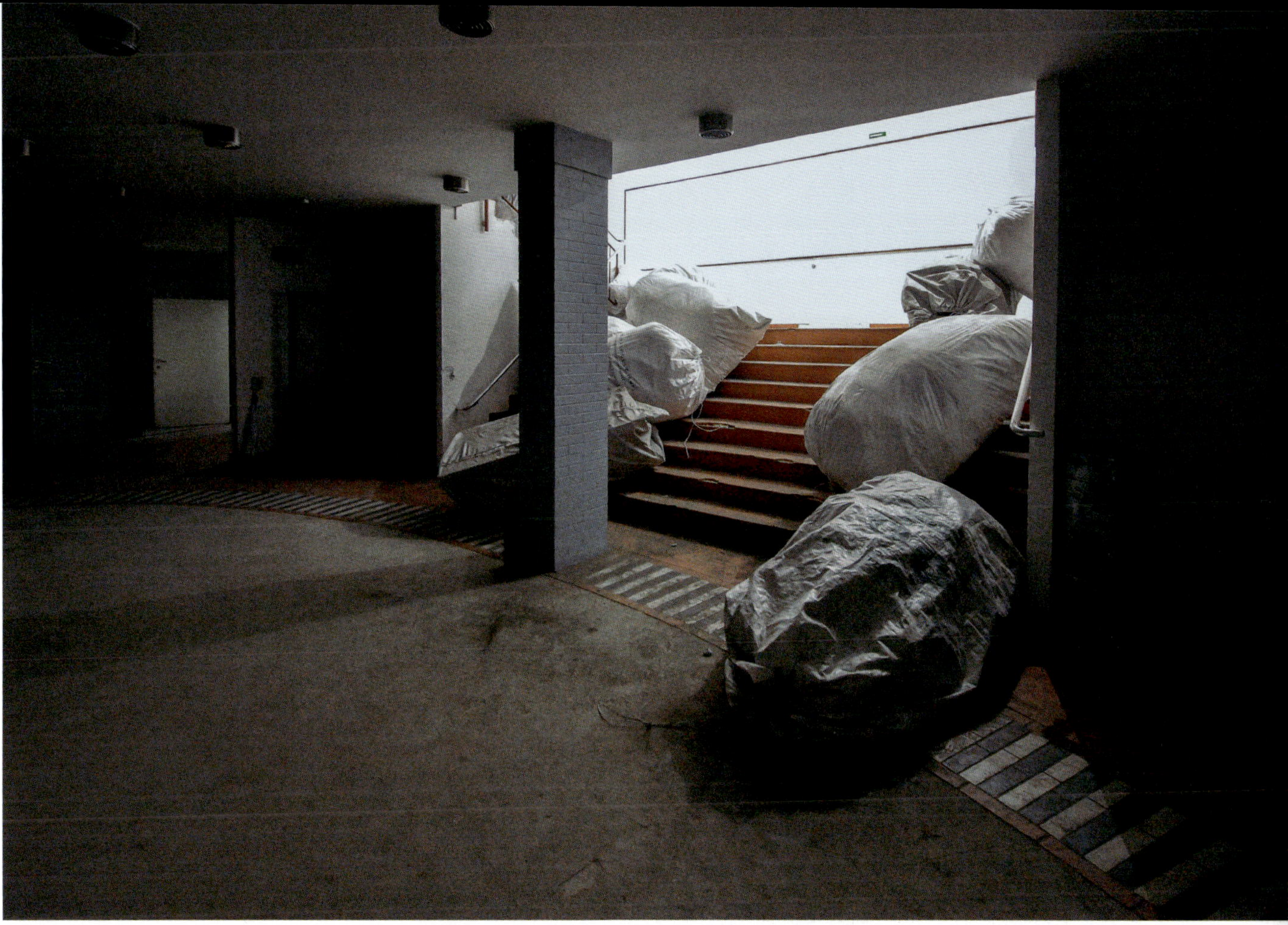

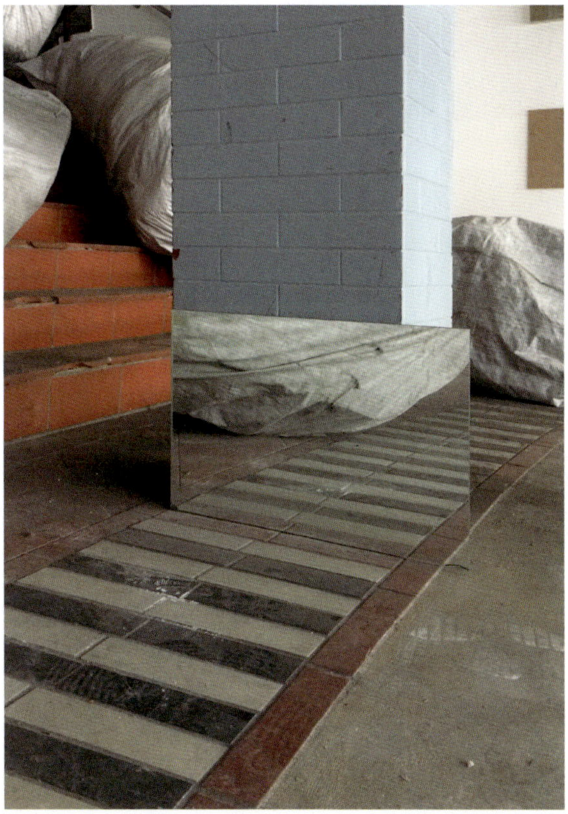

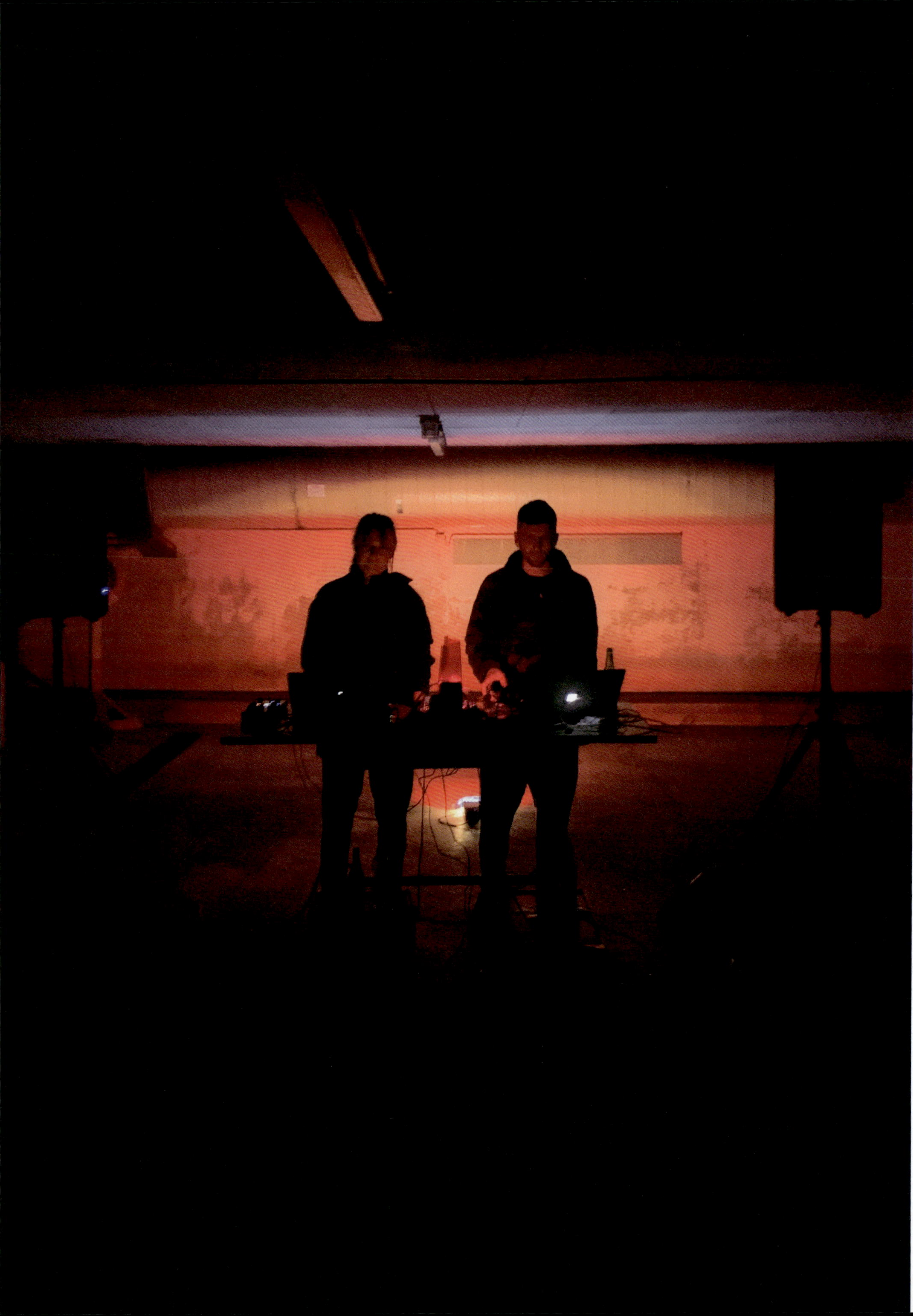

AUSSTELLUNG – Garage – Soundperformance von / by Pandora

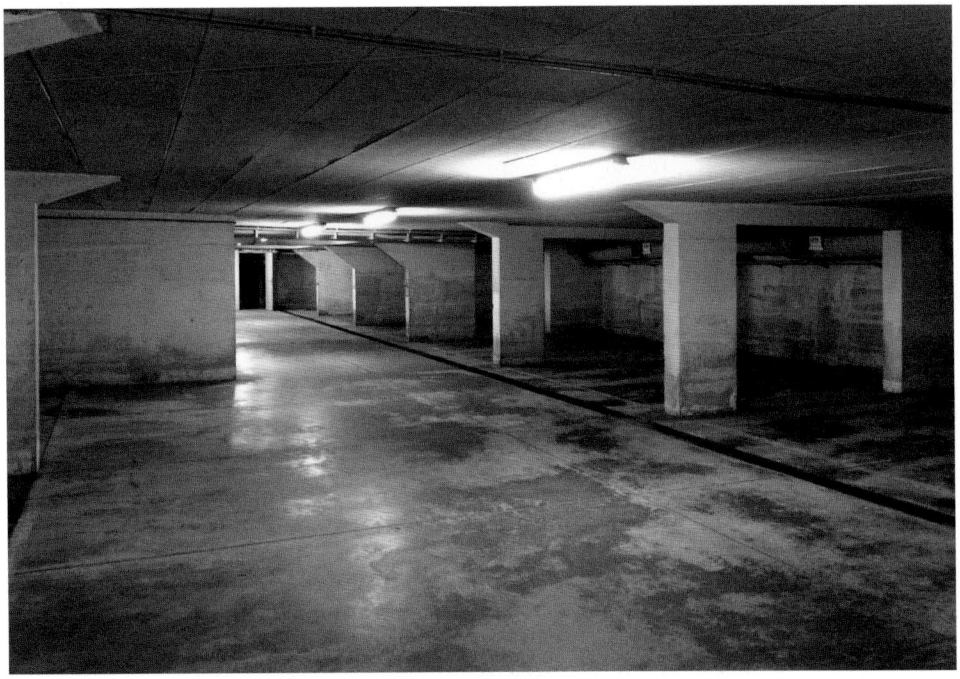

PROZESS
(Exposition)

PROCESS
(Exposition)

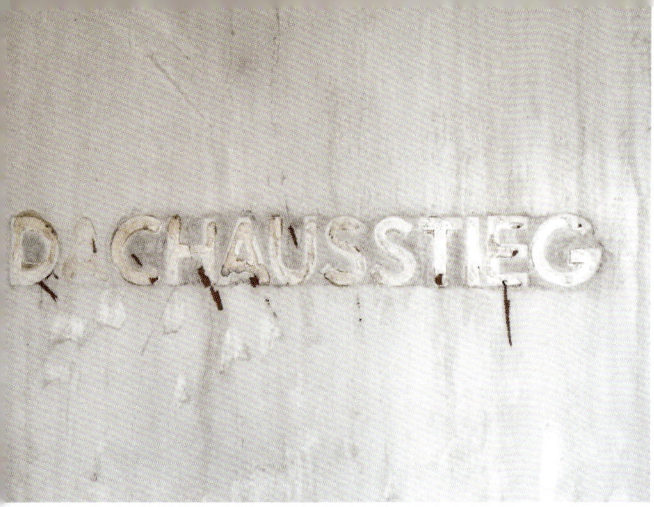
D CHAUSSTIEG

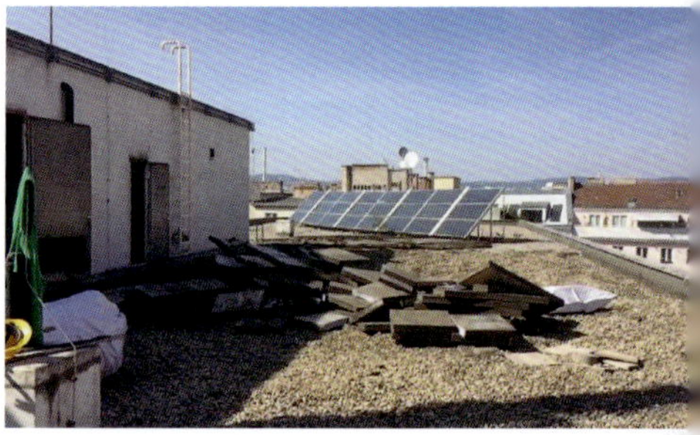

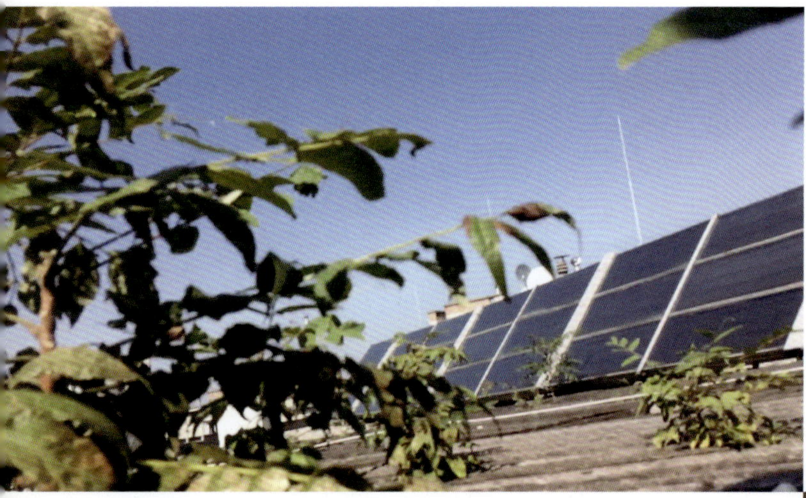

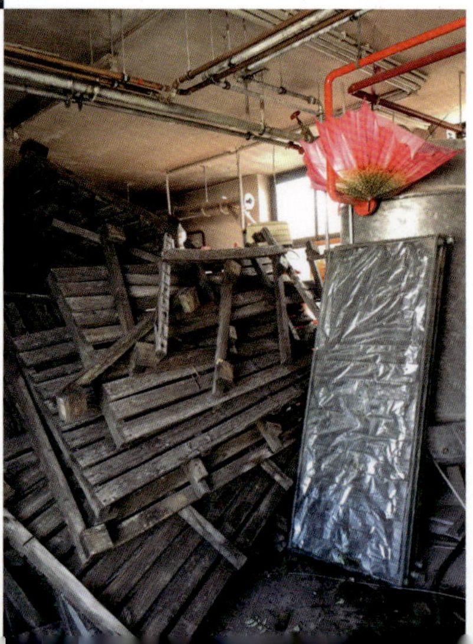

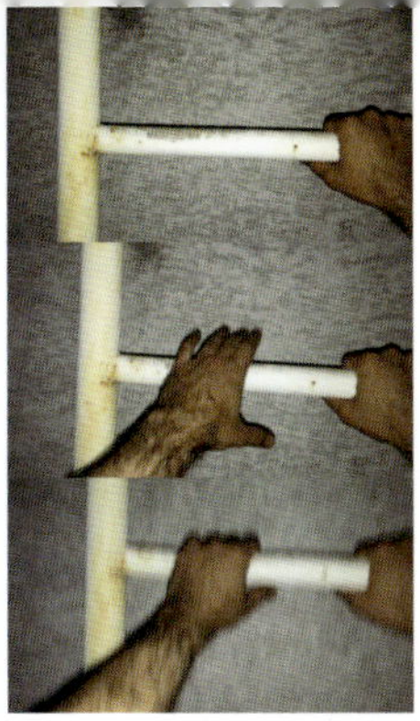

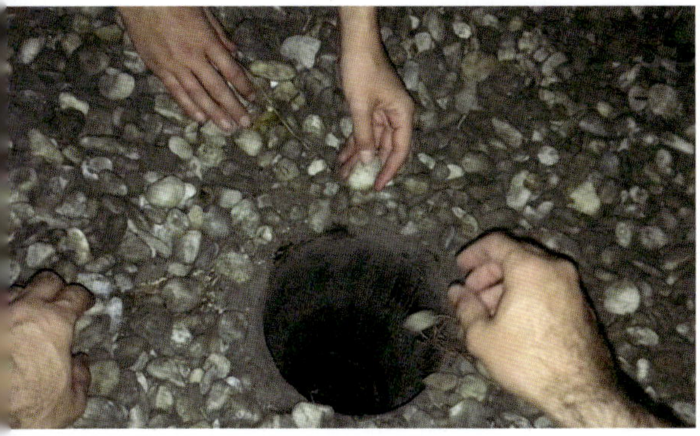

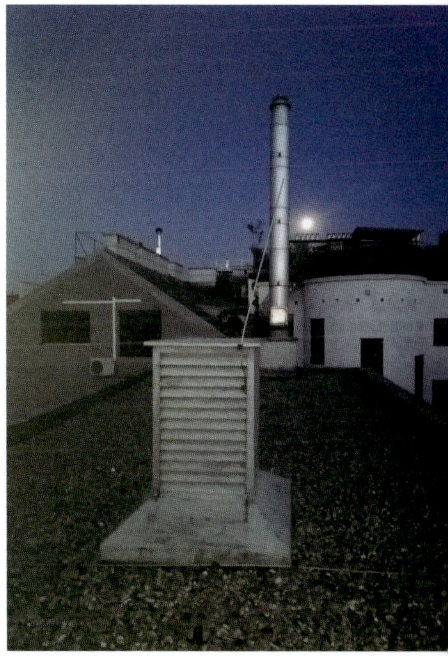

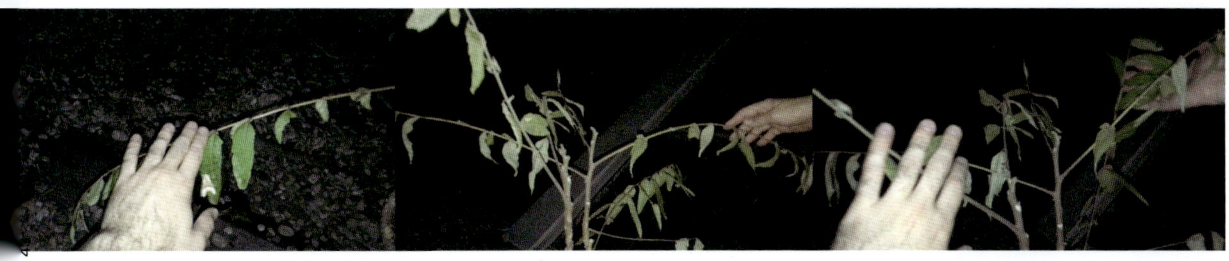

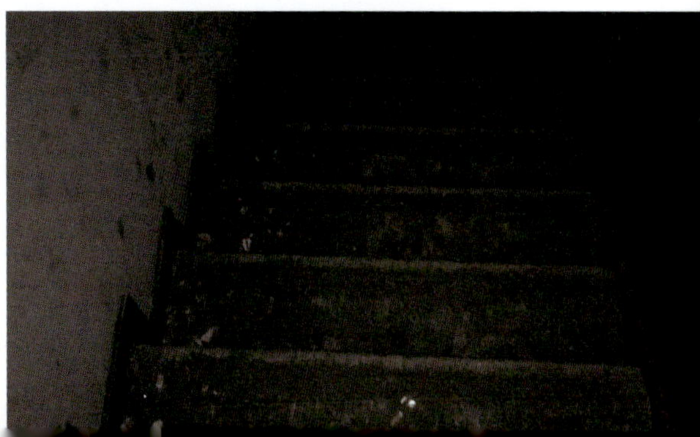

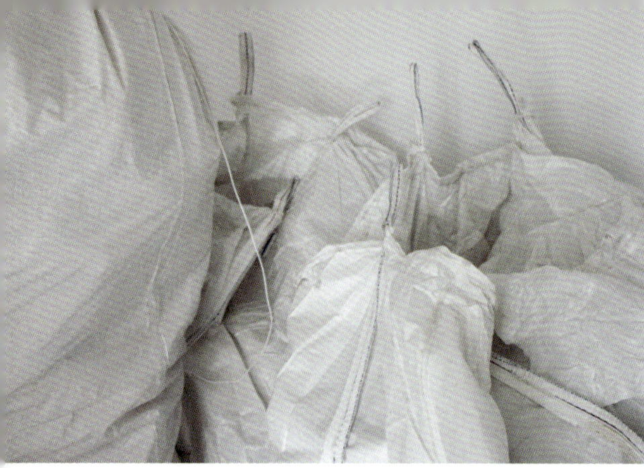

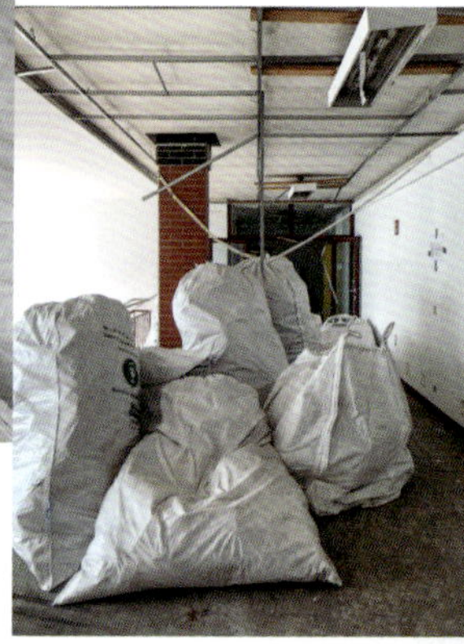

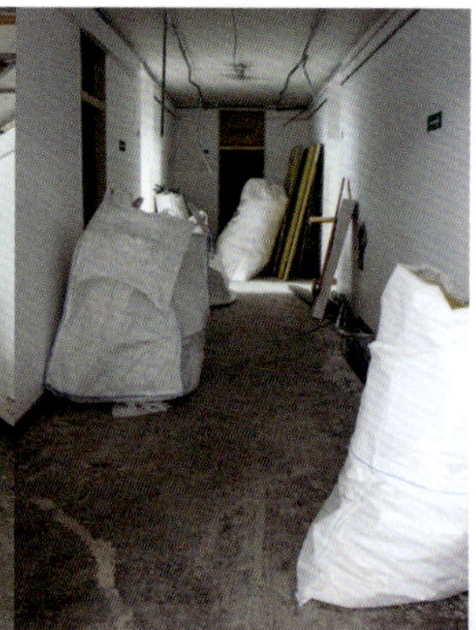

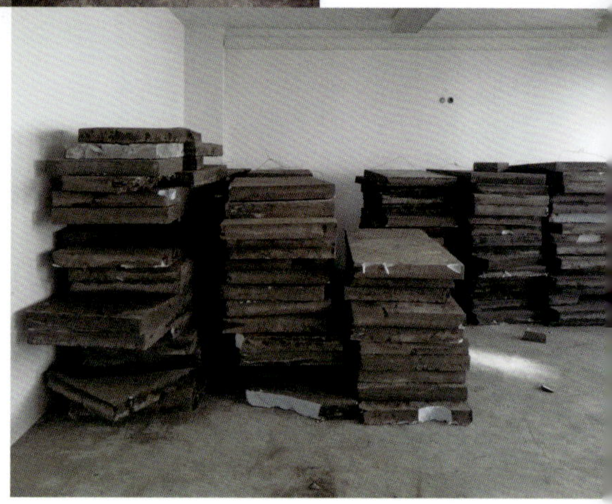

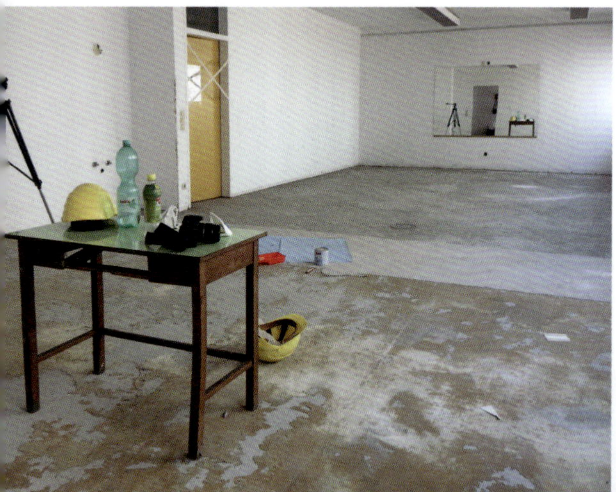

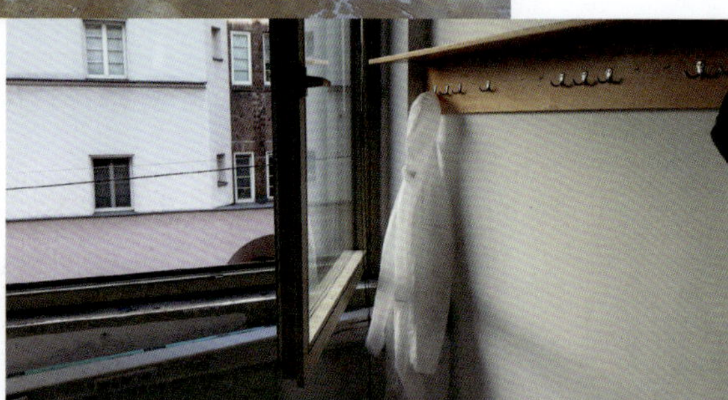

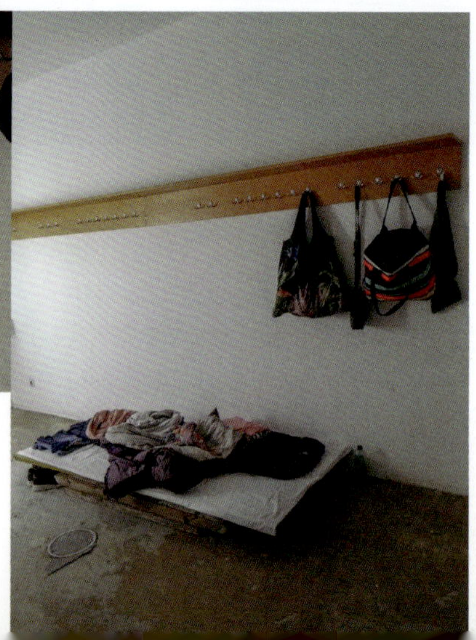

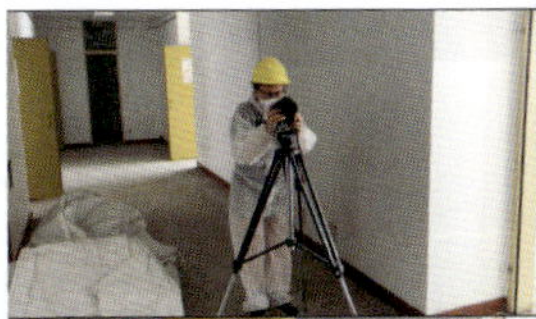

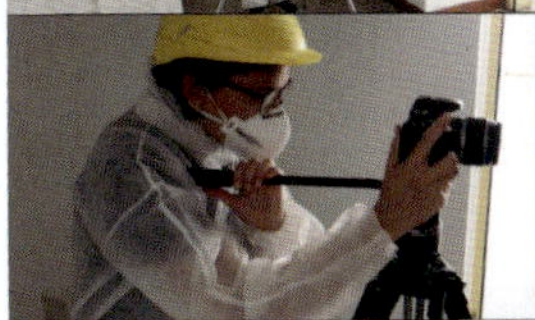

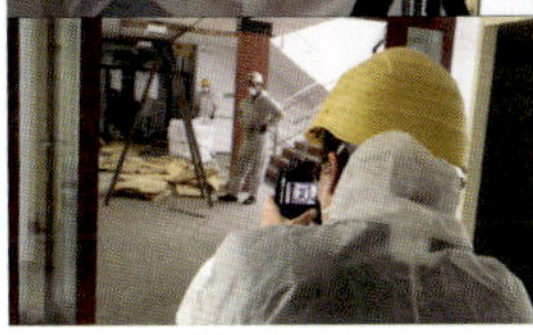

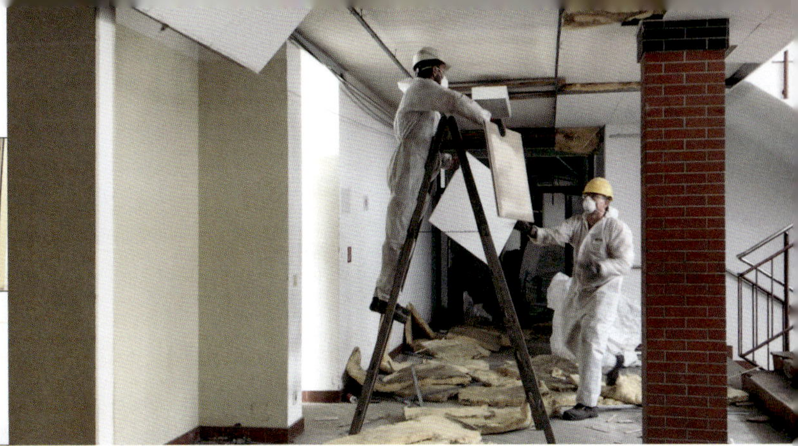

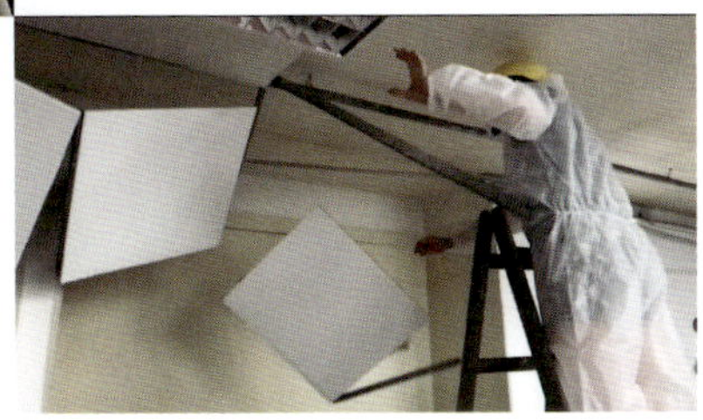

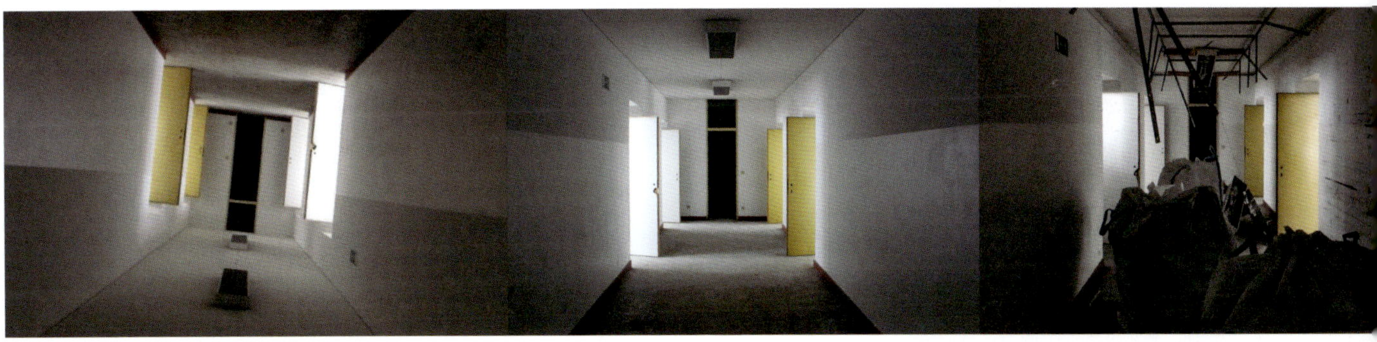

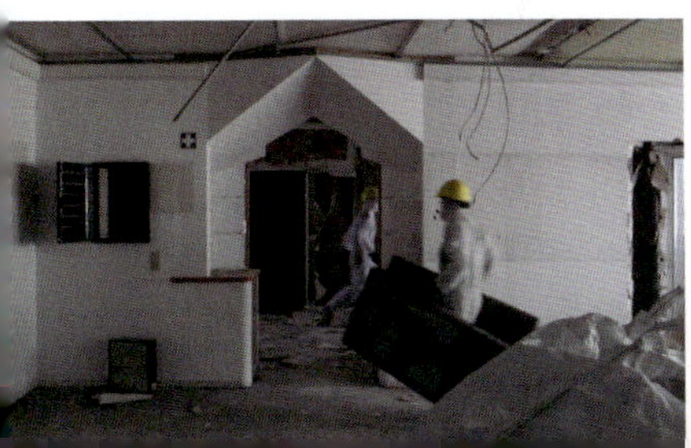

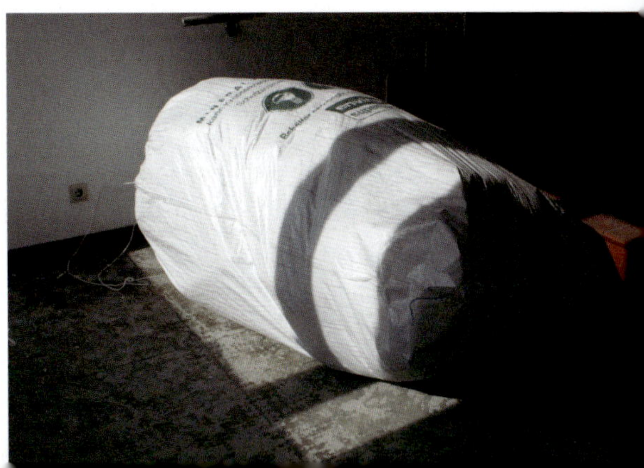

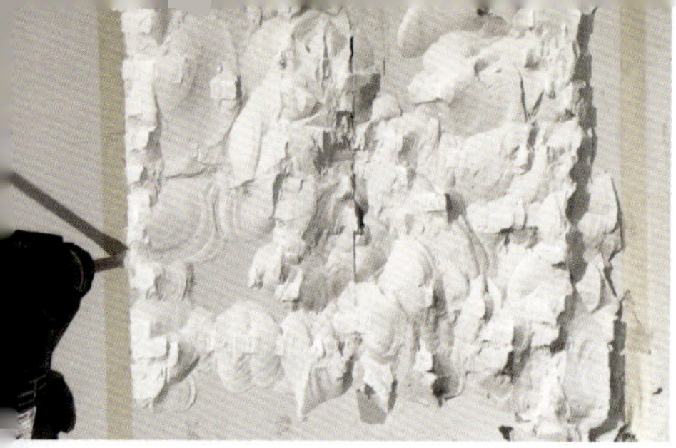

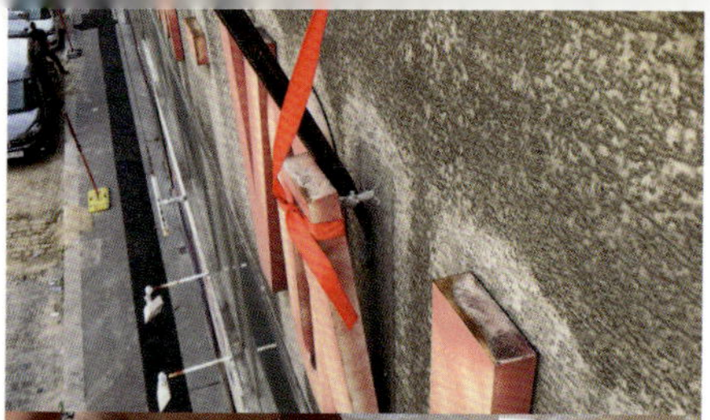

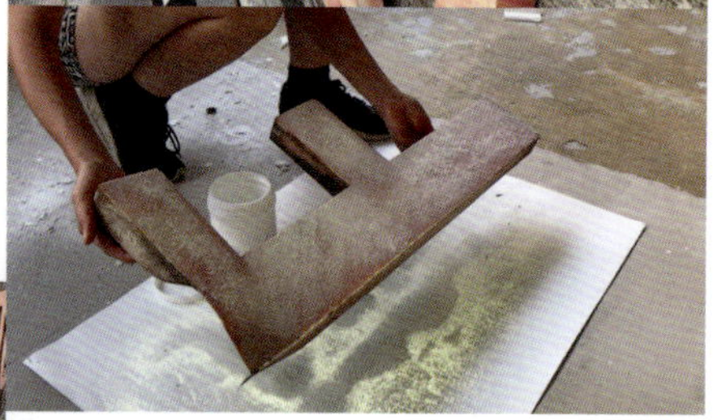

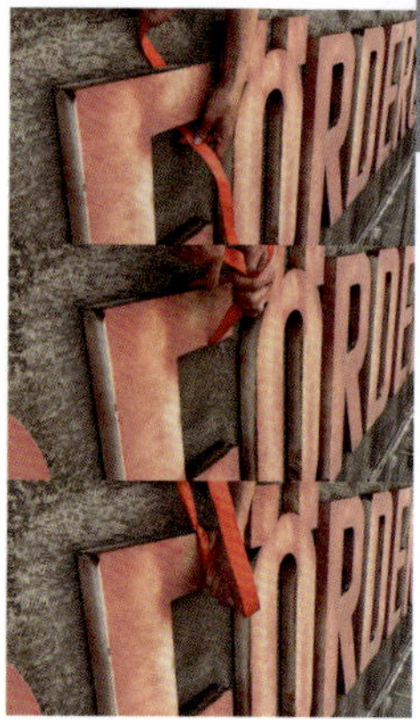

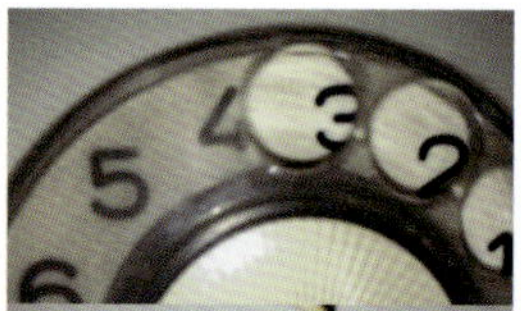

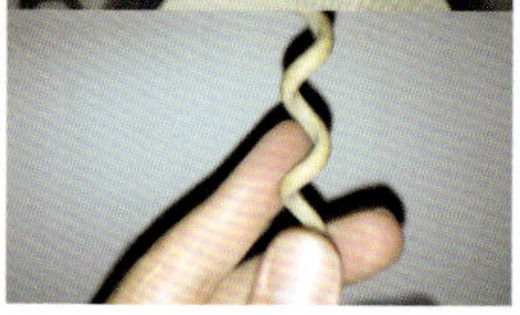

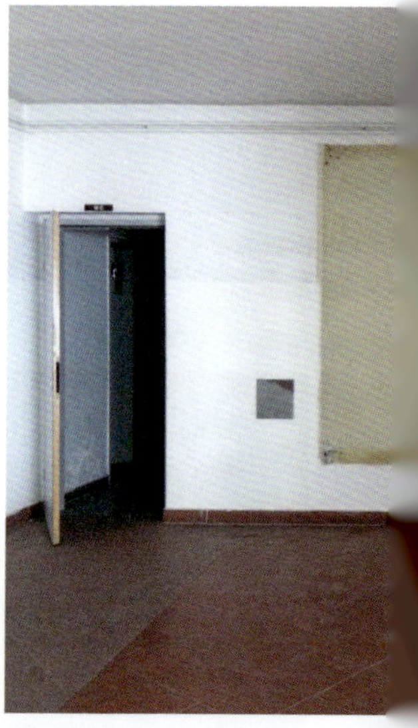

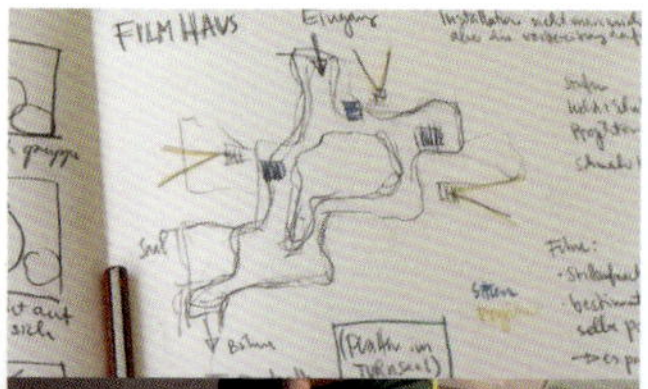
FILM HAUS

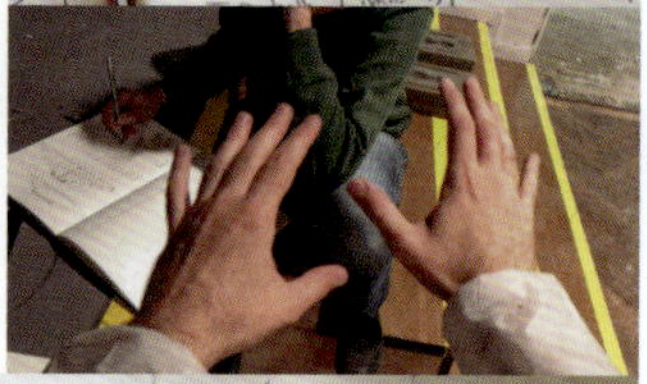

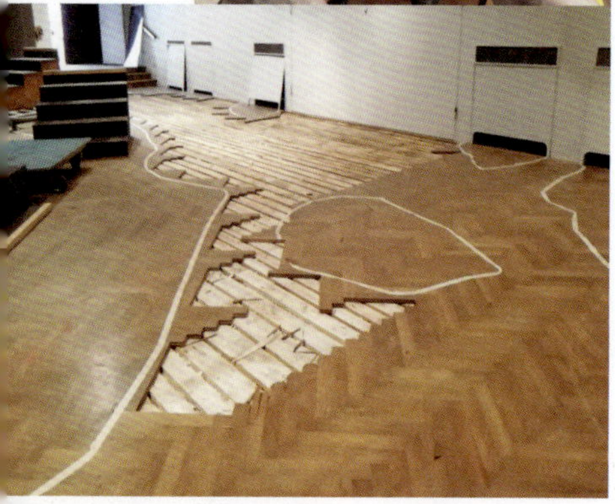

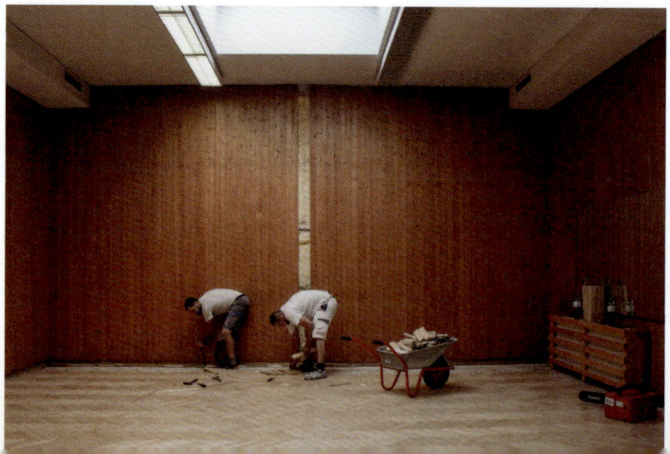

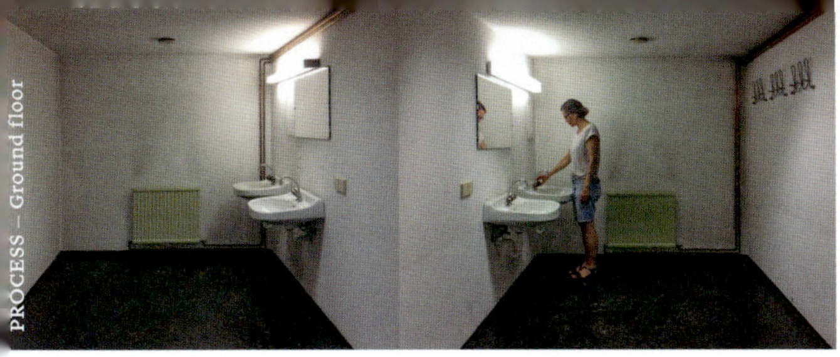

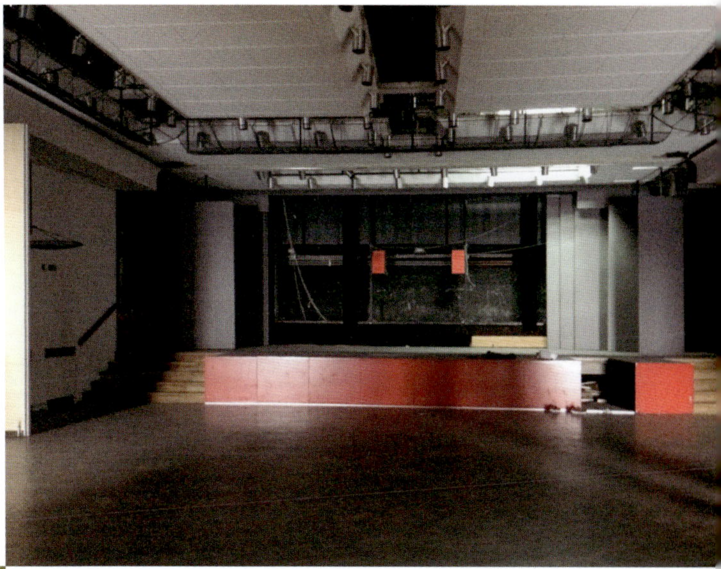

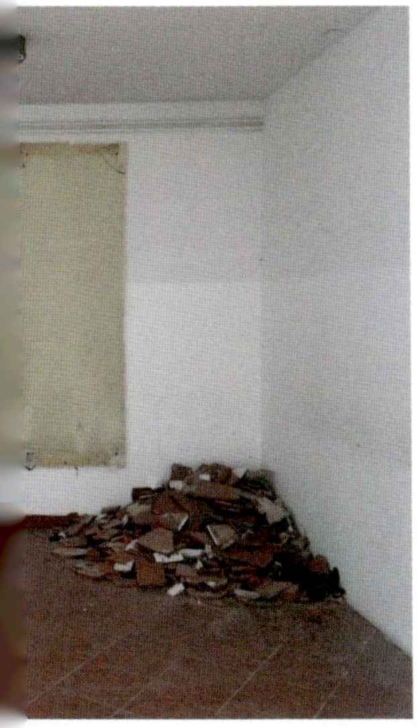

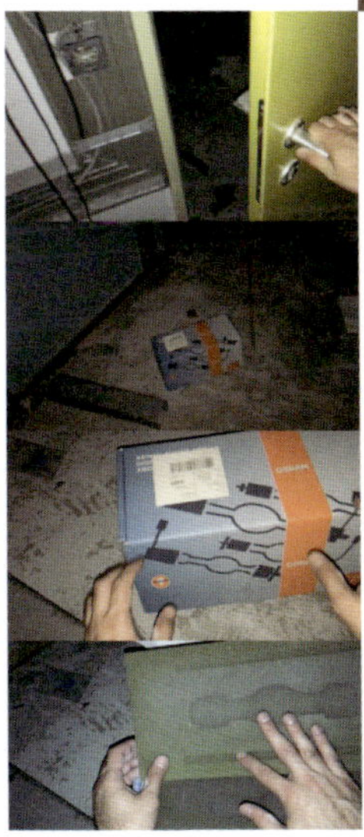

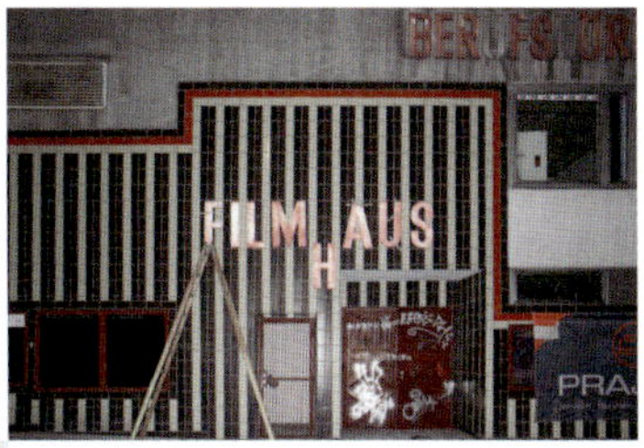
FILM AUS
H

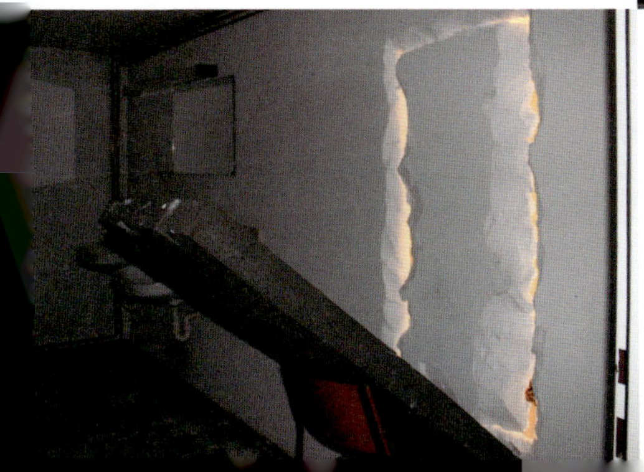

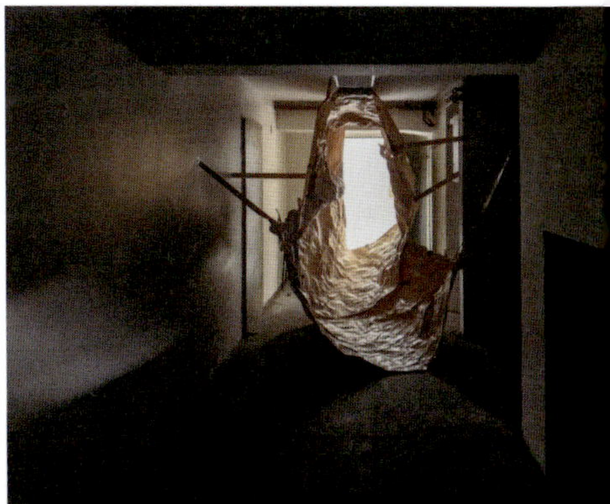

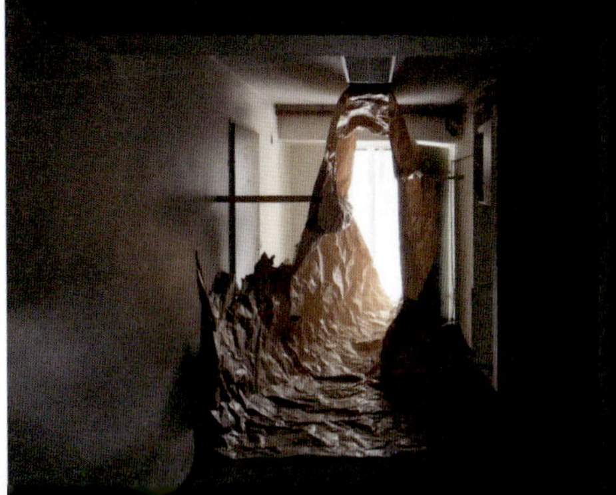

DEMOLIERUNG
(Auflösung)

DEMOLITION
(Resolution)

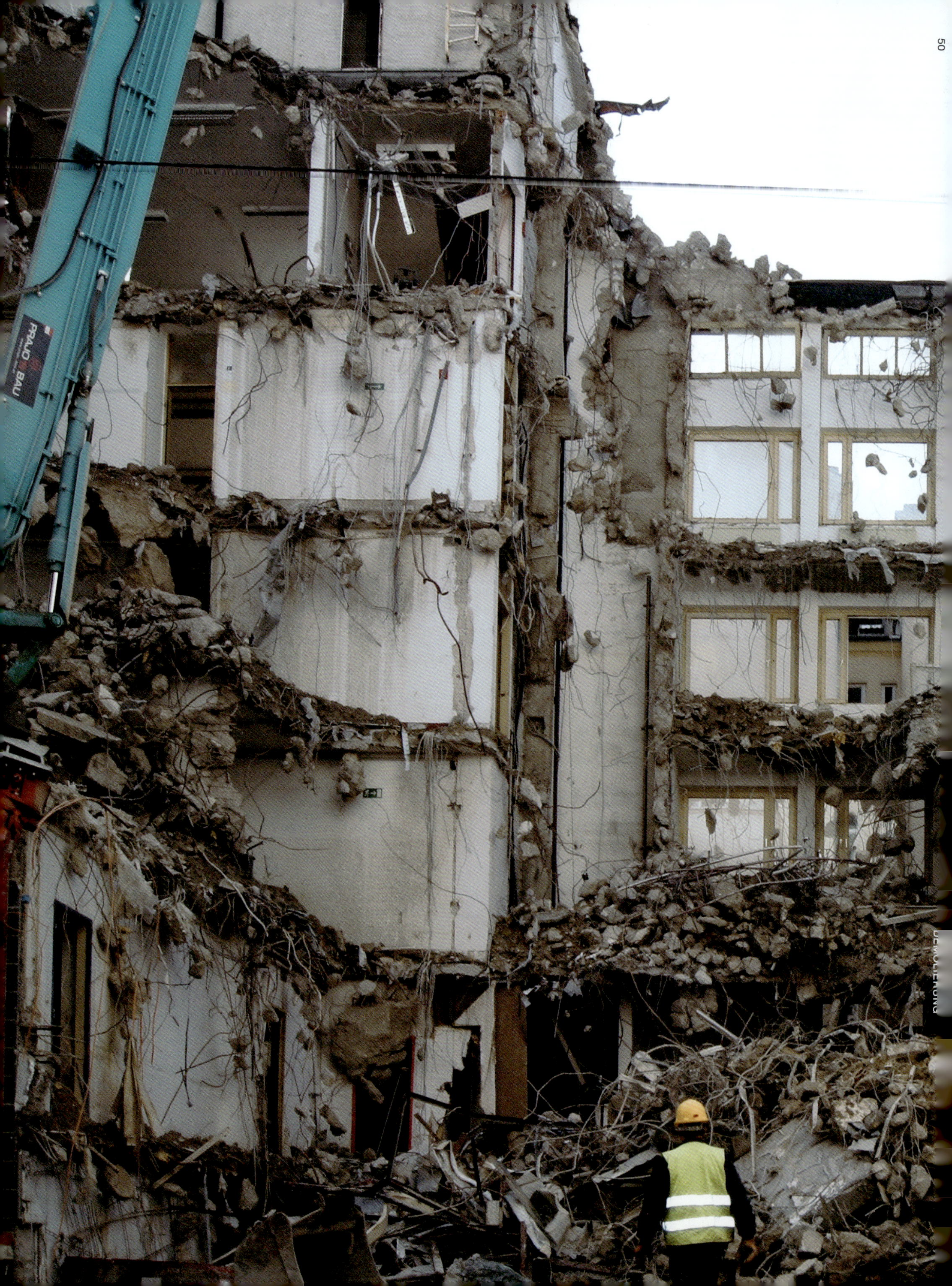

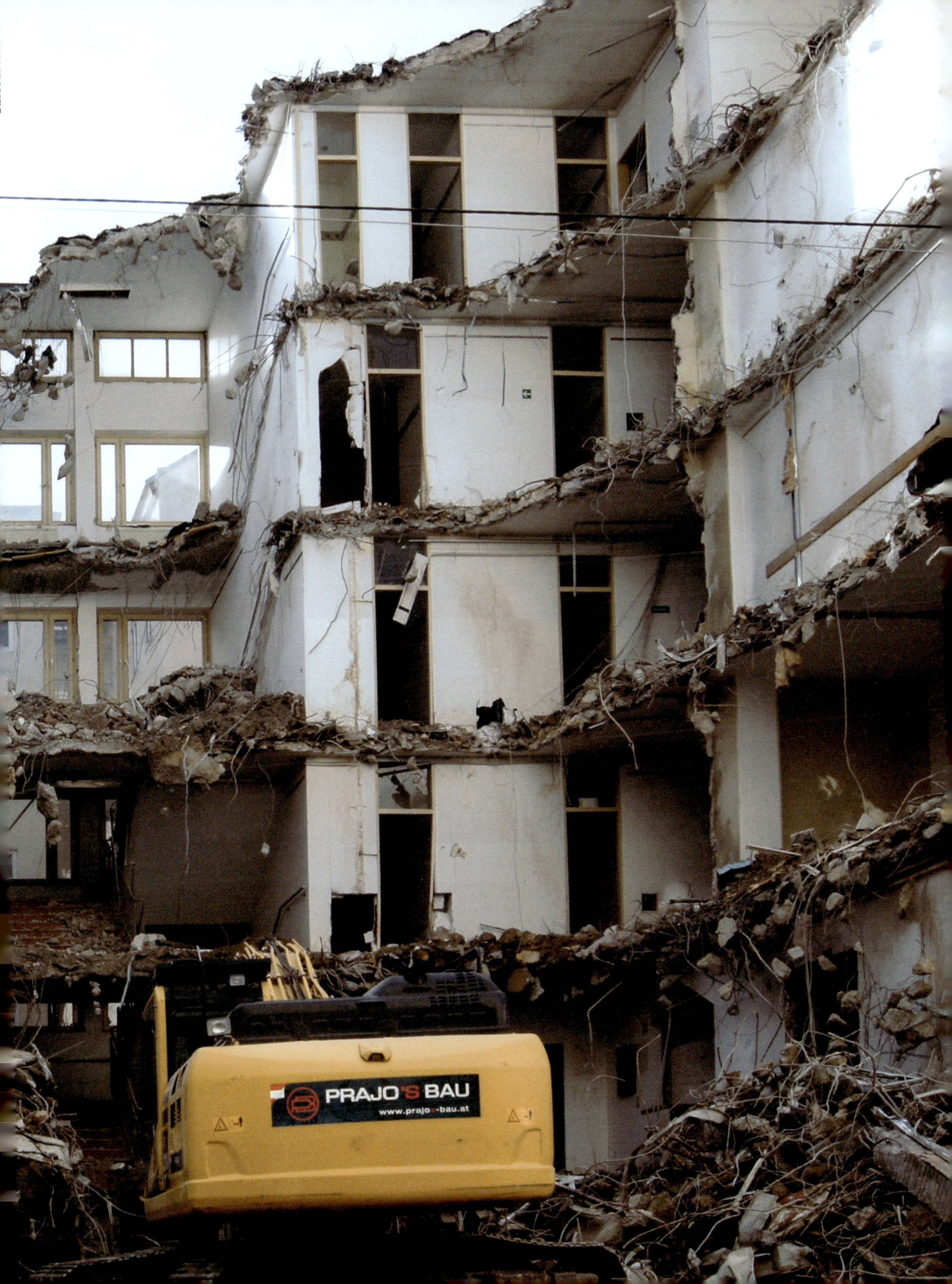
PRAJO'S BAU

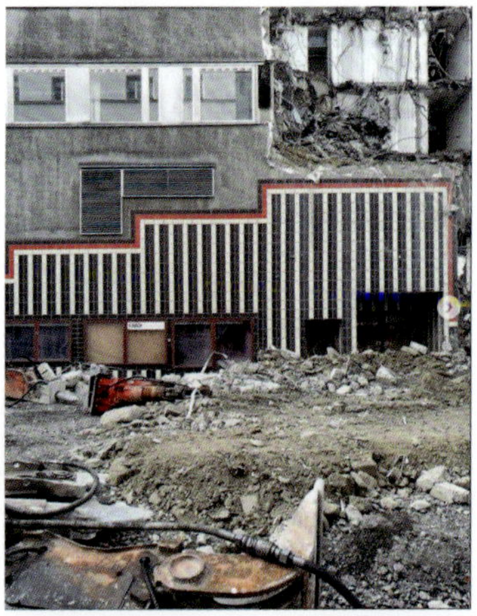

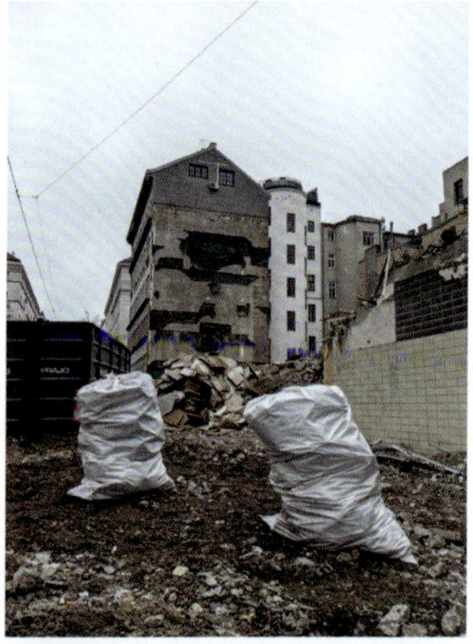

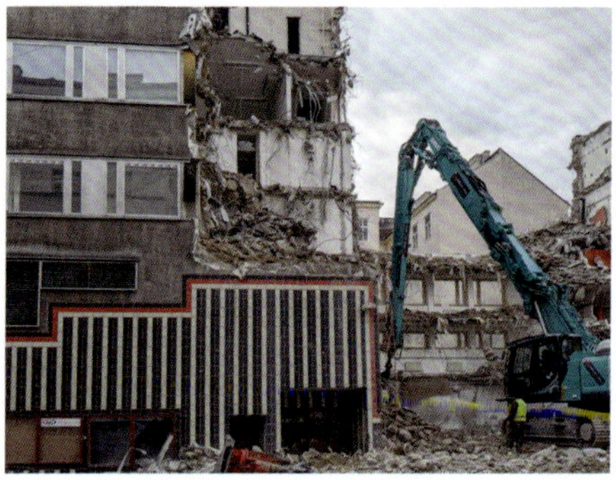

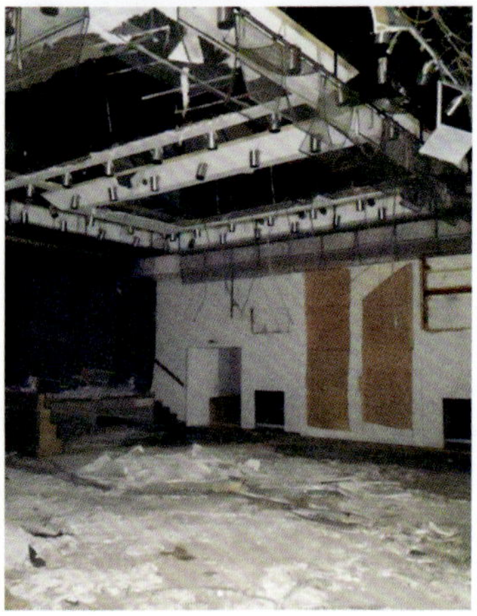

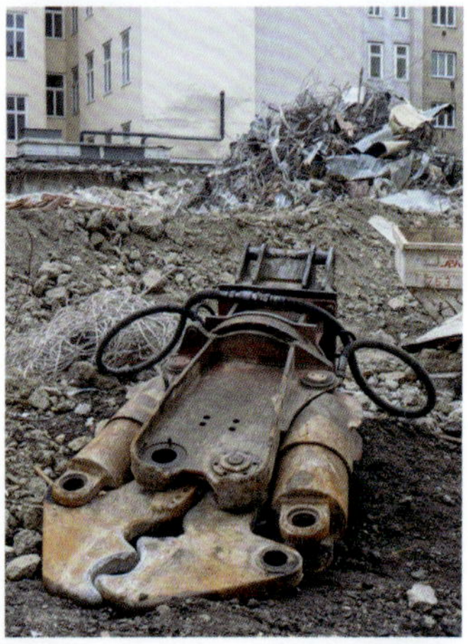

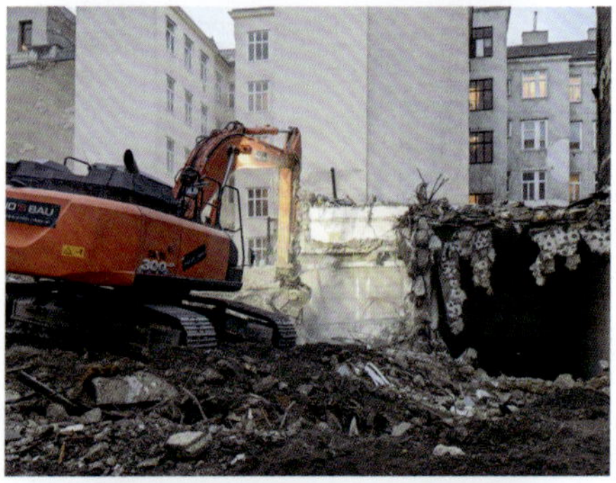

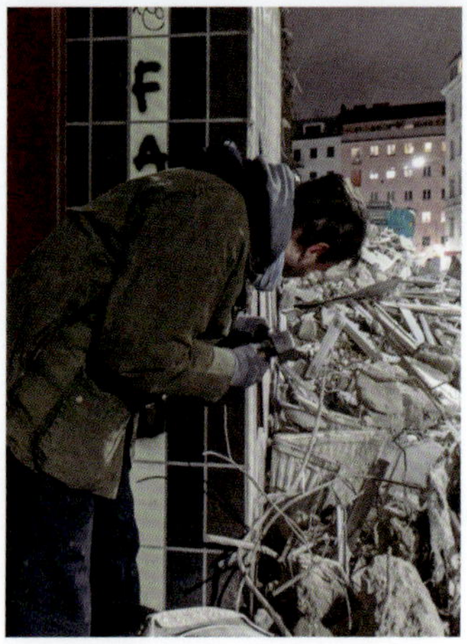

Andreas Fogarasi

Nikola Winkler

Michaela Schwaiger

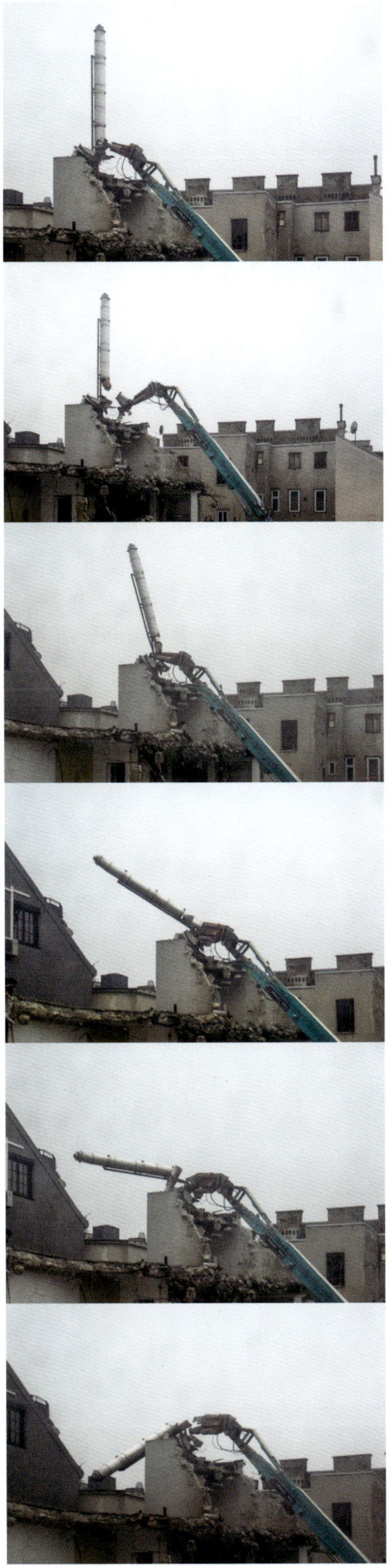

Erich Weber

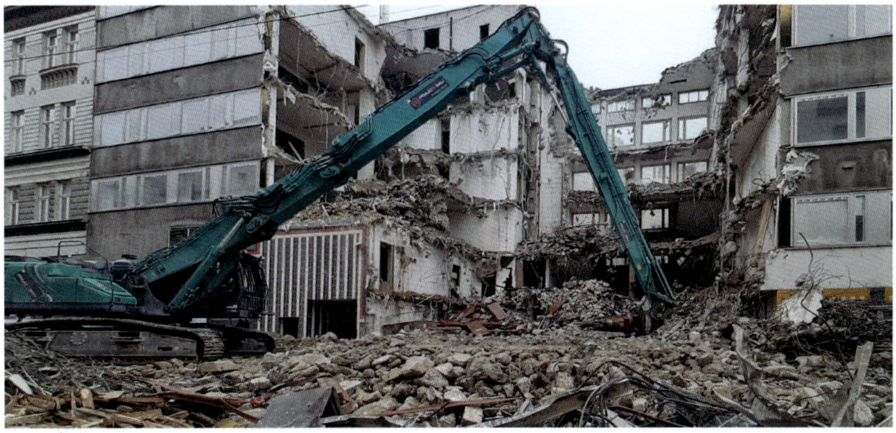

Sophie Yin

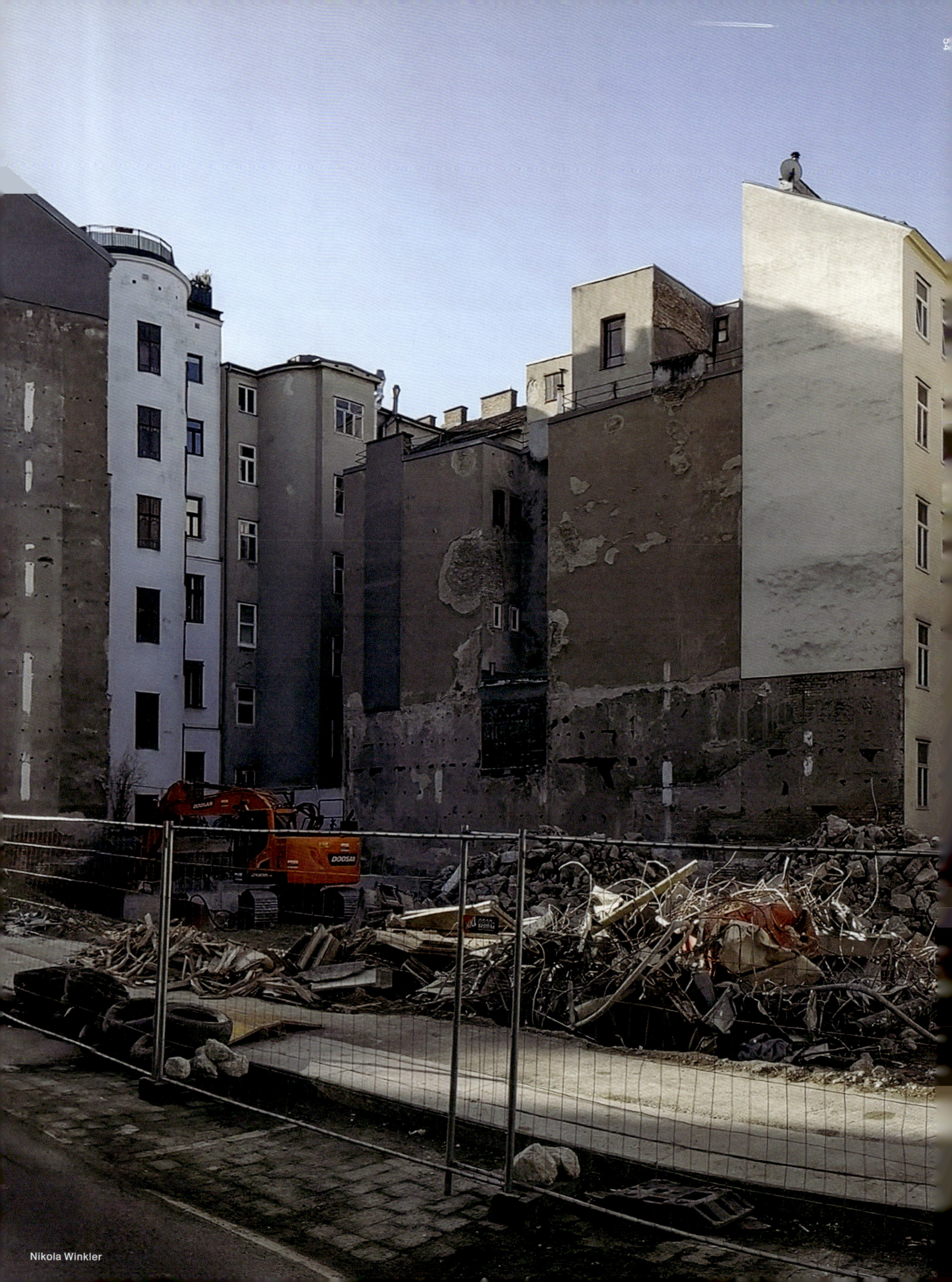

Nikola Winkler

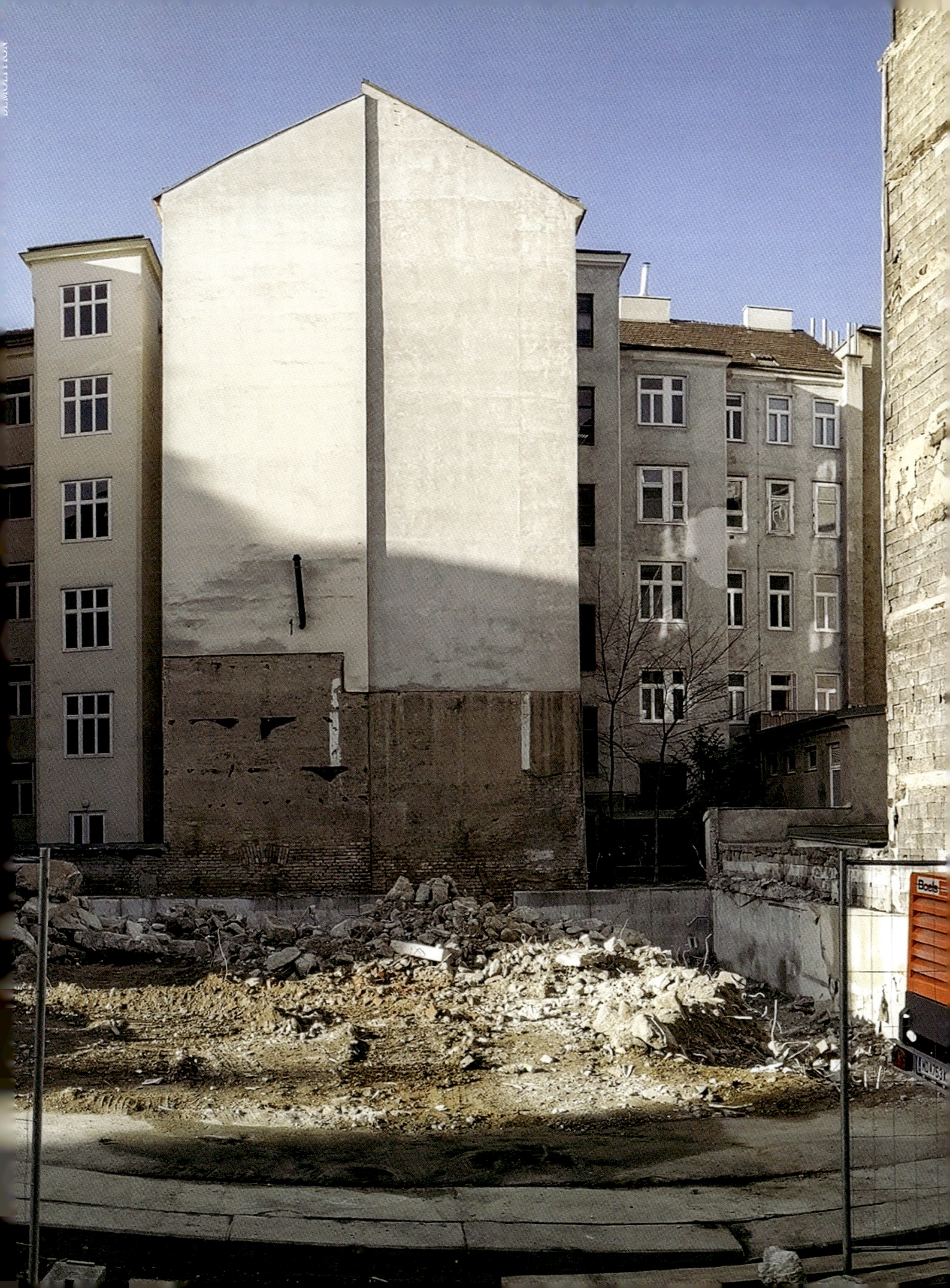
Boels

APPENDIX

mining

erinnerung an schweigeminuten im abbruchdüster. es roch und die wände waren still. wenige scheinwerferkegel. gestapeltes parkettzickzack. aufgerissenes – innehalten – bröckelndes. videos lichteten in einer ausgetrockneten nasszelle. styroporriesen lagen stiegenabwärts gestolpert.

gaisbauer + engl werkten sich als grubenarbeiter durch urbane ablagerungen, verschoben einiges im abrissfilmhaus – eine ausstellung, hieß es!

gratwanderung (kunst?) zwischen archäologie und zerstörungswut, freikämpfen von überdruss. und nun?

endlich durchbrechen zum ersten tageslichtstrahl!!… was wird man geblendet sehen?

künstler als erste?!

doch bis dahin bleibt noch viel zu tun… jedenfalls die ausrüstung verbessern:

schutzhelm, stirnlampe, spitzhacke, bohrmaschine, trennscheibe, kabeltrommel, hämmer, meissel, sicherheitsschuhe, atemschutz, schlafsäcke, wasserflaschen, teleskopanlegeleiter, seile, schaufel, spitzkelle, pinselset…

in erschöpfungspausen immer wieder erinnerungen an kunst (giotto, matisse, maulbertsch in halbturn) und die frage: wo ansetzen für künftige bohrungen?

im naturhistorischen museum wien, in stift göttweig?… in der werft in monfalcone liegen drei kreuzfahrtschiffe zur überholung.

Mario Terzic, Landschaftsdesigner

mining

memories of minutes of silence in the demolition gloom. it smelled and the walls were silent. several spotlight cones. stacked parquet zigzag. torn up—still—crumbling. videos illuminated in a dried out wet room. styrofoam giants stumbled down the stairs.

gaisbauer + engl worked their way through urban debris as miners, shifted things in the demolition film house—an exhibition it was called!

a balancing act (art?) between archaeology and destructive rage, fighting free from weariness. and now?

finally breaking through to the first ray of daylight!!… what will be seen dazzled?

artists first?!

but until then there is still a lot to do… certainly improving the equipment:

safety helmet, headlamp, pickaxe, drill, cutting disc, cable drum, hammers, chisel, safety shoes, breathing protection, sleeping bags, water bottles, telescopic single ladder, ropes, shovel, pointed trowel, set of brushes…

during breaks of exhaustion, memories of art (giotto, matisse, maulbertsch in halbturn) and the question: where to start for future drillings?

in the natural history museum vienna, in göttweig abbey?... in the shipyard in monfalcone there lie three cruise ships for overhaul.

Mario Terzic, landscape designer

A01_M_FH_92020

Gelbgrüne Türe mit Buchstaben und Aufhängung, Türgriff, ein S und Schloss fehlen / Yellow-green door with letters and hinge, lock and handle missing

Material / Material:	Holz / Wood
Maße / Dimensions:	200 × 85 × 4 cm
Fundort / Discovery site:	Korridor / Corridor

A02_M_FH_92020

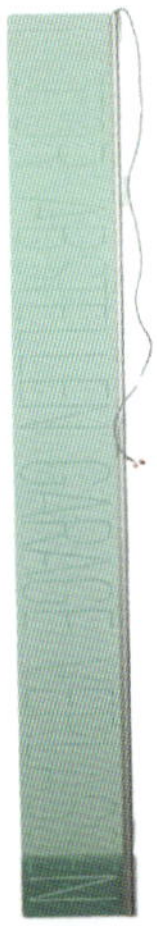

Türkises Leuchtschild, transparent, mit eingraviertem Schriftzug und Elektrokabelanschluss
Turquoise-transparent illuminated sign, with engraved lettering and electric cable connection

Material / Material:	Aluminium, Acrylglas, Kabel Aluminium, acrylic glass, cable
Maße / Dimensions:	200 × 26 × 2 cm
Fundort / Discovery site:	Garage

A03_M_FH_92020

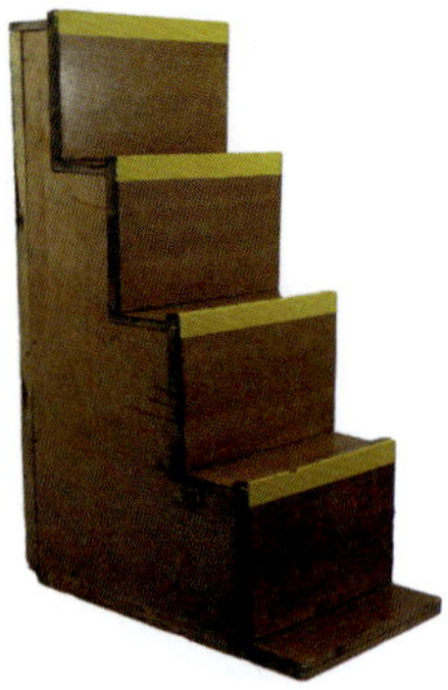

Bühnenelement, treppenförmig, vier Stufen, Holz lackiert mit gelben Aufmerksamkeitsstreifen
Stage element, stair-shaped, four steps, lacquered wood with yellow attention stripes

Material / Material:	Holz, lackiert / Wood, lacquered
Maße / Dimensions:	80 × 55 × 125 cm
Fundort / Discovery site:	Kinosaal / Cinema hall

A04_M_FH_92020

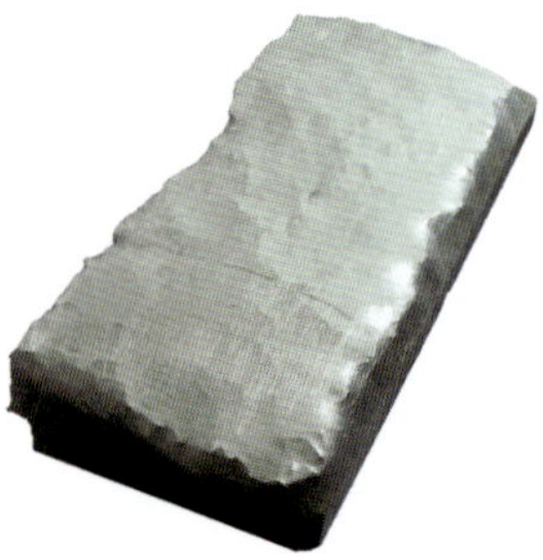

Tafel aus Gips mit Folie auf XPS-Platte gebunden
Tablet made of gypsum with foil bound on XPS board

Material / Material:	XPS-Platte, Gips, Frischhaltefolie XPS board, plaster, cling film
Maße / Dimensions:	125 × 60 × 19 cm
Fundort / Discovery site:	Dach und Garderoben Roof and dressing rooms

A05_M_FH_92020

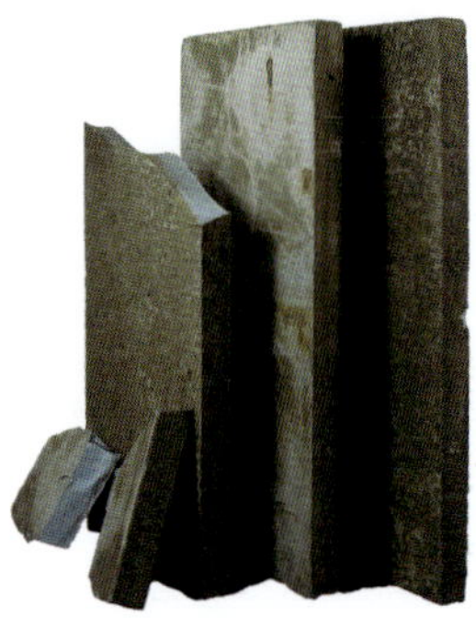

Drei XPS-Platten, schmutzig, mit Abdrücken von Kies und Wurzeln, eine davon ist in drei Teile gebrochen, eisblaue Bruchkanten / Three XPS boards, dirty, with marks of gravel and roots, one of them is broken into three parts, ice-blue broken edges

Material / Material:	XPS-Platte / XPS board
Maße / Dimensions:	je / each 125 × 60 × 8 cm
Fundort / Discovery site:	Dach / Roof

A06_M_FH_92020

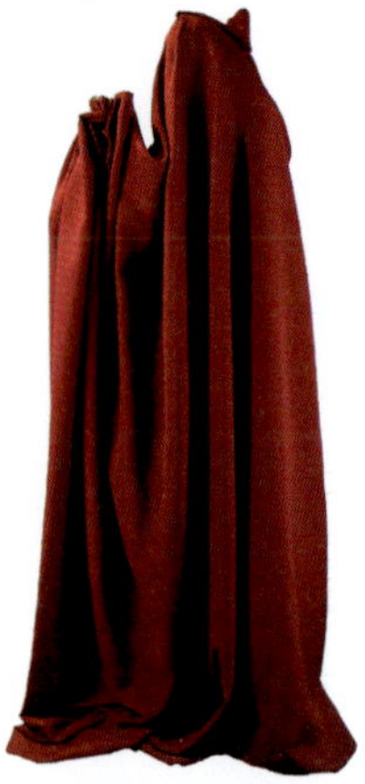

Roter Vorhangstoff / Red curtain fabric

Material / Material:	Polyester
Maße / Dimensions:	271 × 233 cm
Fundort / Discovery site:	Großer Videosaal / Big video room

A07_M_FH_92020

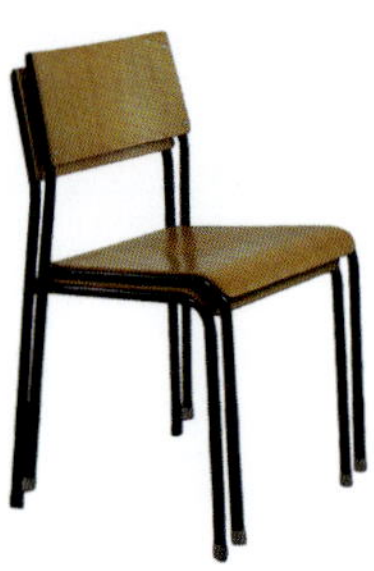

Zwei gestapelte Stühle mit schwarzem Metallgestell, Sitzfläche und Lehne aus Holz, Gummifüße
Two stacked chairs with black metal frame, wooden seat and backrest, rubber feet

Material / Material:	Holz, Metall, Gummi Wood, metal, rubber
Maße / Dimensions:	46 × 42 × 77 cm
Fundort / Discovery site:	Kinosaal / Cinema hall

A08_M_FH_92020

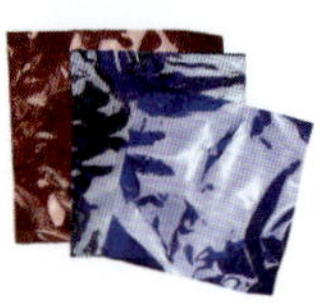

Drei Farbfolien in Rot, Dunkelblau und Mittelblau
Three colour foils in red, dark blue and medium blue

Material / Material:	Farbfolie / Colour foil
Maße / Dimensions:	26 × 25, 24 × 22, 22 × 22 cm
Fundort / Discovery site:	Kinosaal Cinema hall

A09_M_FH_92020

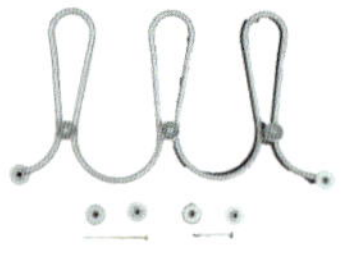

Geschwungene Metallgarderobe mit drei Haken, vier Beilagscheiben und zwei unterschiedlichen Schrauben
Curved metal coat rack with three hooks, four washers and two different screws

Material / Material:	Metall / Metal
Maße / Dimensions:	38 × 20 × 5 cm
Fundort / Discovery site:	Garderoben Dressing rooms

A10_M_FH_92020

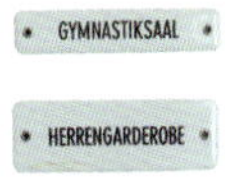

Zwei emaillierte Türschilder mit vier Schrauben
Two enamelled door plates with four screws
Material / Material: **Metall** / Metal
Maße / Dimensions: **15 × 3 + 15 × 5 cm**
Fundort / Discovery site: **Korridore** / Corridors

A11_M_FH_92020

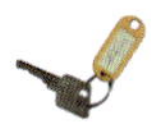

Generalschlüssel mit orangem Anhänger, beschriftet, sperrt jede Türe auf / Master key with orange tag, labelled, unlocks any door
Material / Material: **Metall und Plastik** Metal and plastic
Maße / Dimensions: **6 × 3 + 5 × 2 cm**
Fundort / Discovery site: **Büro der Sozialbau AG** / Office of Sozialbau AG

A12_M_FH_92020

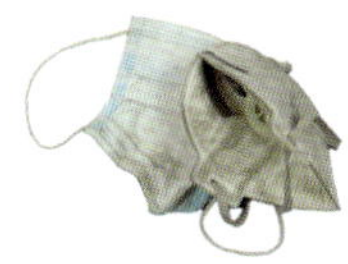

Medizinische Maske und FFP3-Maske, stark verschmutzt
Medical mask and FFP3 mask, heavily soiled
Material / Material: **Kunststoff** / Plastic
Maße / Dimensions: **18 × 10 + 16 × 12 cm**
Fundort / Discovery site: **1 Euro-Shop**

A13_M_FH_92020

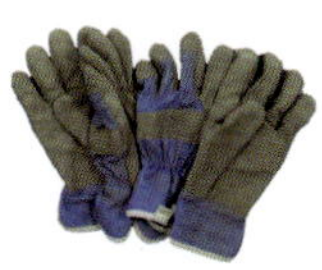

Zwei Paar Universal-Kunstlederhandschuhe, blau, dreckig
Two pairs of universal synthetic leather gloves, blue, dirty
Material / Material: **Baumwolle, Kunstleder** Cotton, faux leather
Maße / Dimensions: **je** / each **25 × 12 × 2 cm**
Fundort / Discovery site: **Baumarkt** / DIY market

A14_M_FH_92020

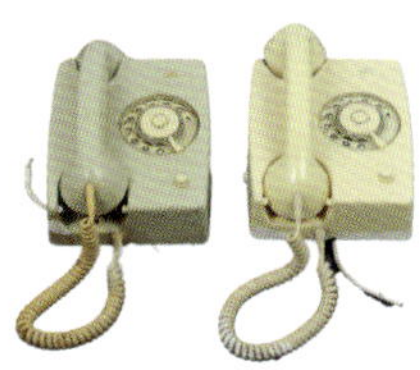

Zwei Wandtelefone in Khaki und Beige, mit Wählscheibe, Schnur und Hörer / Two wall phones in khaki and beige, with dial, cord and receiver
Material / Material: **Kunststoff** / Plastic
Maße / Dimensions: **26 × 15 × 11 cm**
Fundort / Discovery site: **Garderoben** Dressing rooms

A15_M_FH_92020

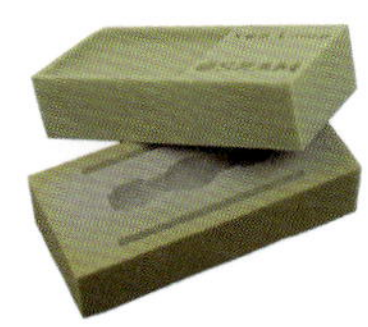

Schutzverpackung aus Schaumstoff für eine Xenon-Bogenlampe, grün / Foam protective packaging for one xenon arc lamp, green
Material / Material: **Schaumstoff** / Foam
Maße / Dimensions: **37 × 17 × 17 cm**
Fundort / Discovery site: **Projektionsraum** Projection room

A16_M_FH_92020

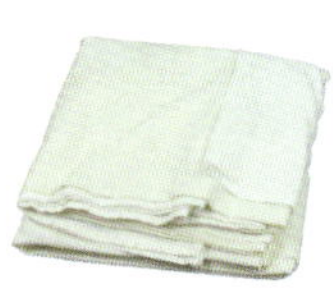

Weißes Bettlaken, vergilbt / White bed sheet, yellowed
Material / Material: **Baumwollstoff** / Cotton cloth
Maße / Dimensions: **212 × 205 cm**
Fundort / Discovery site: **Tanzsaal, 1. Stock** Dance hall, 1st floor

A17_M_FH_92020

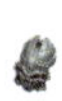

Plastikfigur, silbrig, außerirdisch / Plastic figure, silvery, extraterrestrial
Material / Material: **Kunststoff** / Plastic
Maße / Dimensions: **3 × 3 × 4 cm**
Fundort / Discovery site: **Turnsaal** / Gym

A18_M_FH_92020

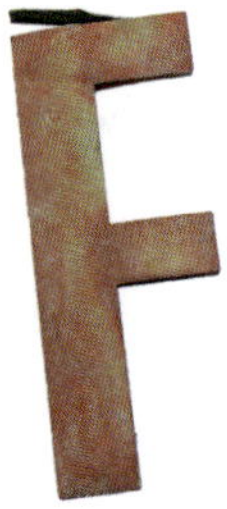

Buchstabe F aus rotem Metall, zum Teil oxidiert, lackiert, reflektierend, zerdellt, mit Montageschrauben auf der Rückseite / Letter F made of red metal, partly oxidised, lacquered, reflective, battered, with mounting screws on the backside

Material / Material:	Metall, Lack, Reflexperlen Metal, lacquer, reflective glass beads
Maße / Dimensions:	74 × 28 × 11 cm
Fundort / Discovery site:	Korridor / Corridor

A19_M_FH_92020

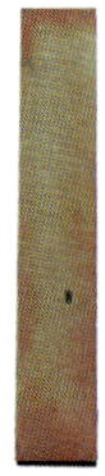

Buchstabe I aus rotem Metall, zum Teil oxidiert, lackiert, reflektierend, zerdellt, mit Montageschrauben auf der Rückseite / Letter I made of red metal, partly oxidised, lacquered, reflective, battered, with mounting screws on the backside

Material / Material:	Metall, Lack, Reflexperlen Metal, lacquer, reflective glass beads
Maße / Dimensions:	70 × 12 × 11 cm
Fundort / Discovery site:	Korridor / Corridor

A20_M_FH_92020

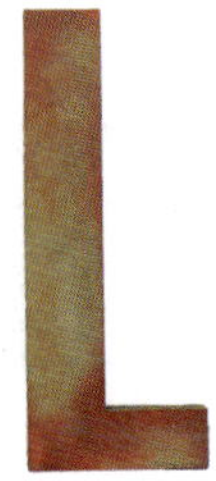

Buchstabe L aus rotem Metall, zum Teil oxidiert, lackiert, reflektierend, zerdellt, mit Montageschrauben auf der Rückseite / Letter L made of red metal, partly oxidised, lacquered, reflective, battered, with mounting screws on the backside

Material / Material:	Metall, Lack, Reflexperlen Metal, lacquer, reflective glass beads
Maße / Dimensions:	70 × 28 × 13 cm
Fundort / Discovery site:	Korridor / Corridor

A21_M_FH_92020

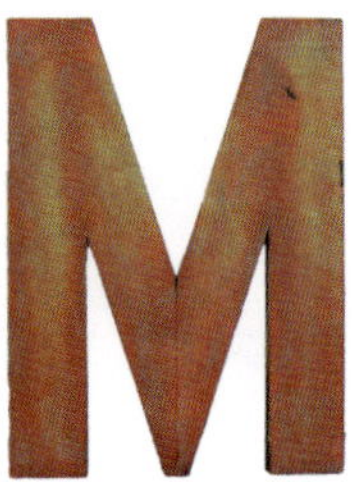

Buchstabe M aus rotem Metall, zum Teil oxidiert, lackiert, reflektierend, zerdellt, mit Montageschrauben auf der Rückseite / Letter M made of red metal, partly oxidised, lacquered, reflective, battered, with mounting screws on the backside

Material / Material:	Metall, Lack, Reflexperlen Metal, lacquer, reflective glass beads
Maße / Dimensions:	70 × 53 × 10 cm
Fundort / Discovery site:	Korridor / Corridor

A22_M_FH_92020

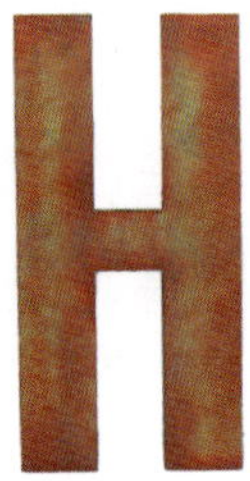

Buchstabe H aus rotem Metall, zum Teil oxidiert, lackiert, reflektierend, zerdellt, mit Montageschrauben auf der Rückseite / Letter H made of red metal, partly oxidised, lacquered, reflective, battered, with mounting screws on the backside

Material / Material:	Metall, Lack, Reflexperlen Metal, lacquer, reflective glass beads
Maße / Dimensions:	70 × 36 × 11 cm
Fundort / Discovery site:	Korridor / Corridor

A23_M_FH_92020

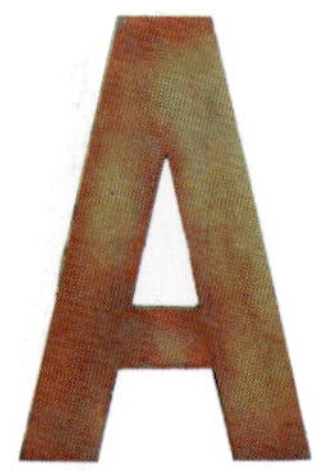

Buchstabe A aus rotem Metall, zum Teil oxidiert, lackiert, reflektierend, zerdellt, mit Montageschrauben auf der Rückseite / Letter A made of red metal, partly oxidised, lacquered, reflective, battered, with mounting screws on the backside

Material / Material:	Metall, Lack, Reflexperlen Metal, lacquer, reflective glass beads
Maße / Dimensions:	70 × 47 × 12 cm
Fundort / Discovery site:	Korridor / Corridor

A24_M_FH_92020

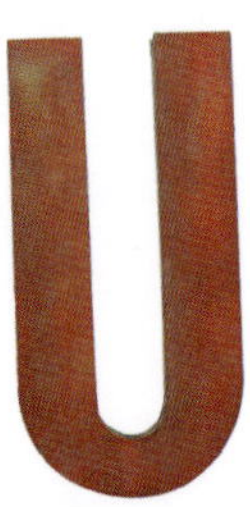

Buchstabe U aus rotem Metall, zum Teil oxidiert, lackiert, reflektierend, zerdellt, mit Montageschrauben auf der Rückseite / Letter U made of red metal, partly oxidised, lacquered, reflective, battered, with mounting screws on the backside

Material / Material:	Metall, Lack, Reflexperlen Metal, lacquer, reflective glass beads
Maße / Dimensions:	70 × 35 × 11 cm
Fundort / Discovery site:	Korridor / Corridor

A25_M_FH_92020

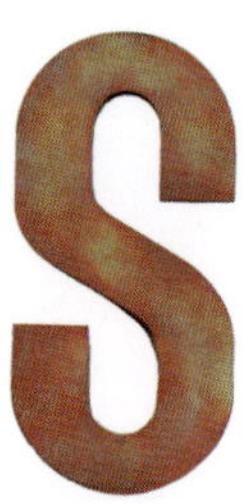

Buchstabe S aus rotem Metall, zum Teil oxidiert, lackiert, reflektierend, zerdellt, mit Montageschrauben auf der Rückseite / Letter S made of red metal, partly oxidised, lacquered, reflective, battered, with mounting screws on the backside

Material / Material:	Metall, Lack, Reflexperlen Metal, lacquer, reflective glass beads
Maße / Dimensions:	70 × 35 × 12 cm
Fundort / Discovery site:	Korridor / Corridor

A26_M_FH_92020

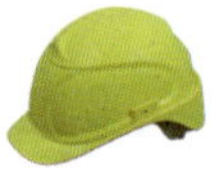

Bauhelm in Gelb / Safety helmet in yellow

Material / Material:	Plastik / Plastic
Maße / Dimensions:	29 × 22 × 17 cm
Fundort / Discovery site:	Baustelle Construction site

A27_M_FH_92020

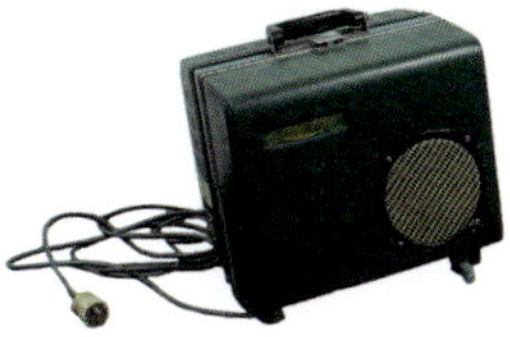

Alter 16mm-Filmprojektor in türkisgrüner Verschalung mit Griff und goldenem Lüftungsnetz und Stromkabel
Old 16mm film projector in turquoise green casing with handle and golden ventilation net and power cable

Material / Material:	Metall, versch. Materialien Metal, various materials
Maße / Dimensions:	35 × 29 × 37 cm
Fundort / Discovery site:	Regieraum / Control room

A28_M_FH_92020

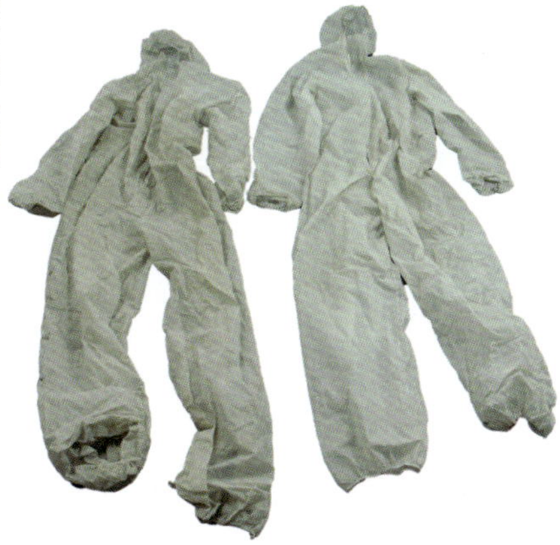

Zwei Schutzanzüge in Weiß, löchrig, staubig und gebraucht / Two protective suits in white, threadbare, dusty and worn

Material / Material:	Polypropylen Polypropylene
Maße / Dimensions:	170 × 96 cm
Fundort / Discovery site:	Geschenk der Abbrucharbeiter Gift from the demolition workers

A29_M_FH_92020

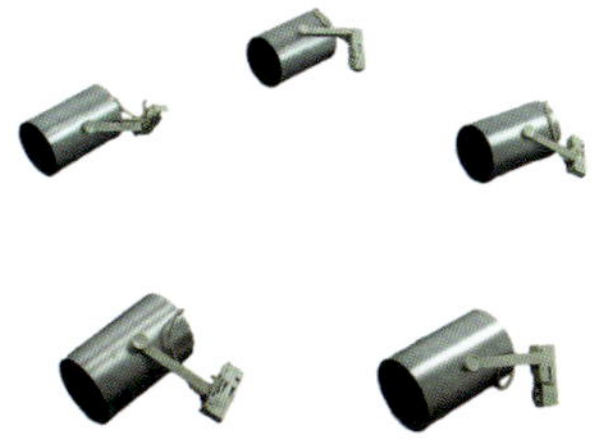

Fünf Strahler, röhrenförmig, silbern, teilweise mit Leuchtmittel / Five spotlights, tubular, silver, partly with illuminant

Material / Material:	Aluminium, Leuchtmittel Aluminium, illuminants
Maße / Dimensions:	30 × 14 × 14 cm
Fundort / Discovery site:	Kinosaal / Cinema Hall

A30_M_FH_92020

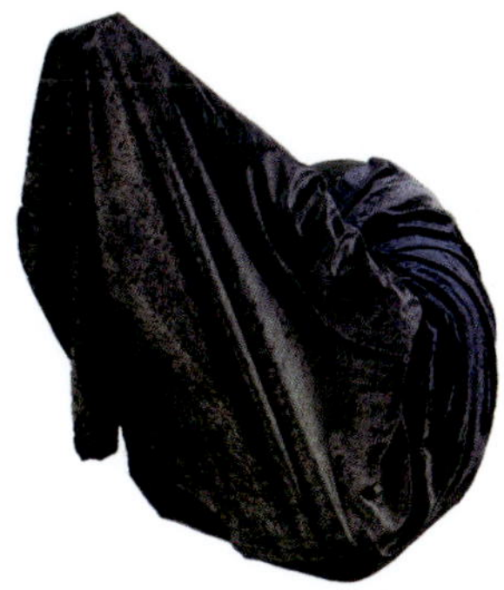

Violetter Samtstoff aus der Anschlagtafel, verblichen, Abzeichnungen von Filmplakaten / Purple velvet fabric from notice board, faded, markings from movie posters

Material / Material:	Samtstoff / Velvet cloth
Maße / Dimensions:	191 × 104 cm
Fundort / Discovery site:	Fassade / Façade

A31_M_FH_92020

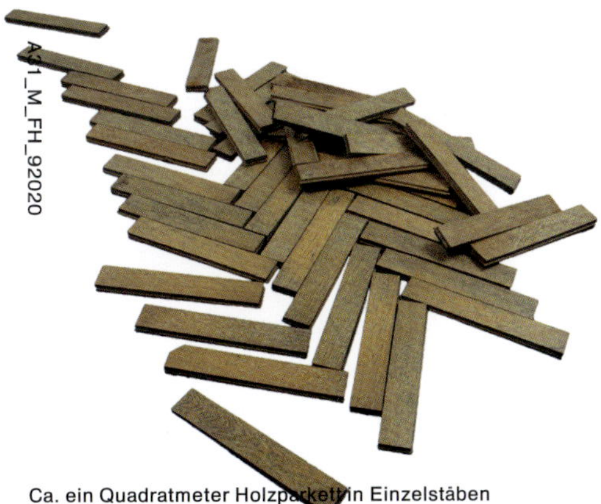

Ca. ein Quadratmeter Holzparkett in Einzelstäben
Approx. one square metre of wooden parquet in single strips

Material / Material:	Holz / Wood
Maße / Dimensions:	je / each 36 × 6 × 2 cm
Fundort / Discovery site:	Kinosaal / Cinema hall

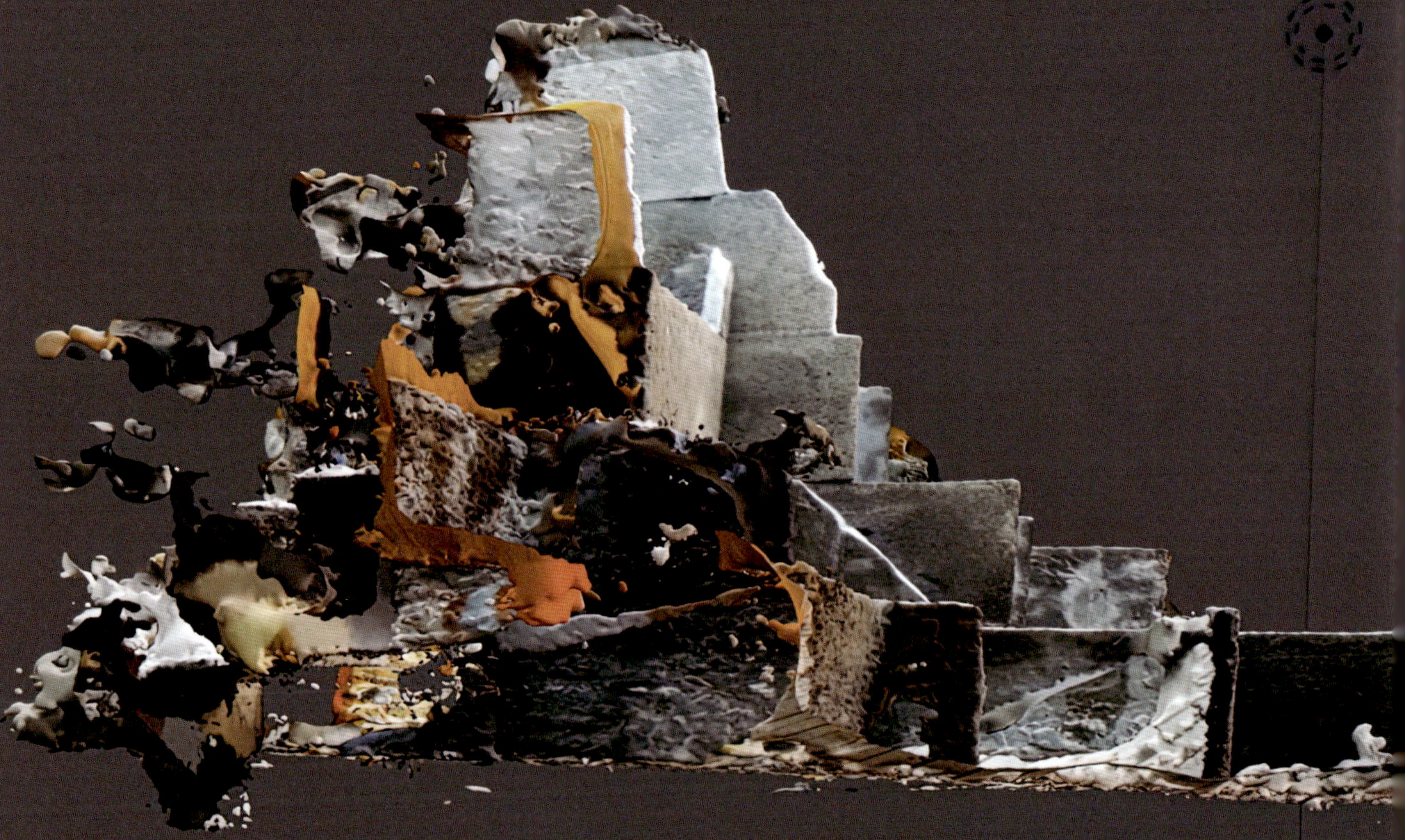

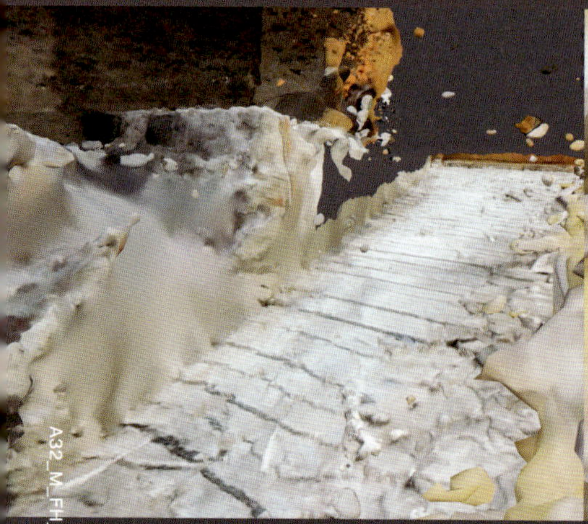

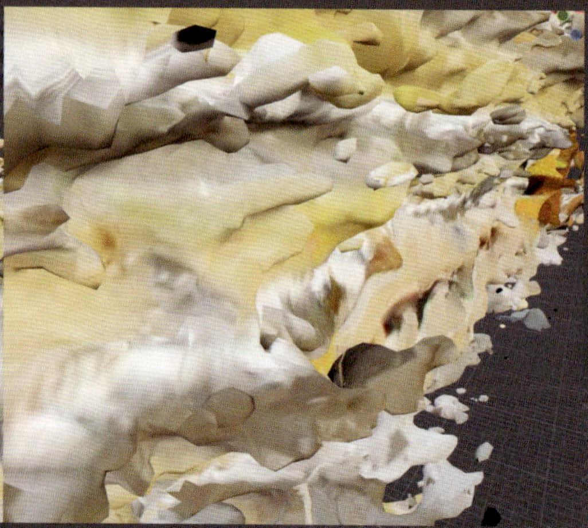

A32_M_FH_92020

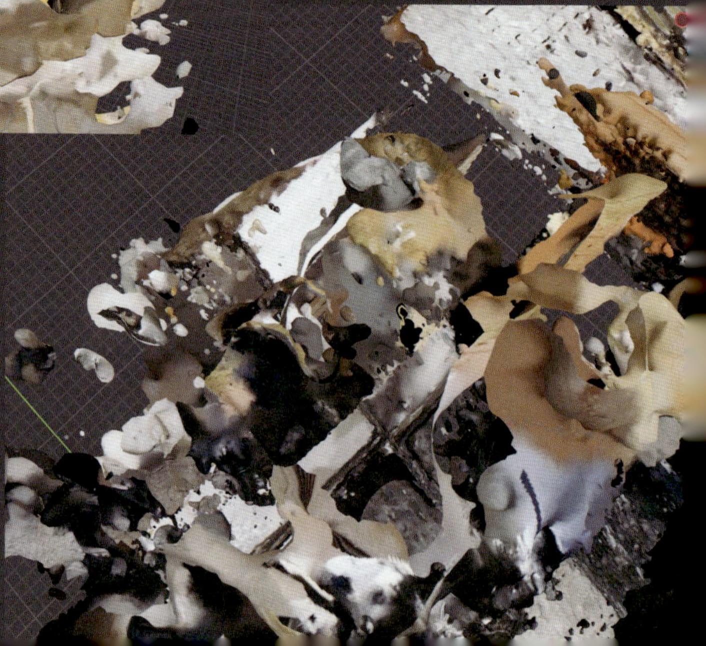

Aus Fotos von Besucher*innen fotogrammetrisch rekonstruiertes 3D-Objekt des Turnsaals mit Spiegelung, löst sich nach hinten hin wegen fehlender Daten auf
3D object of the gym with reflection, photogrammetrically rebuilt from photos of visitors, fades towards the back due to missing data

Material / Material:	Digitale Rekonstruktion, .blend-Datei Digital reconstruction, .blend file
Maße / Dimensions:	Beliebig skalierbar Scalable as desired
Fundort / Discovery site:	Turnsaal / Gym

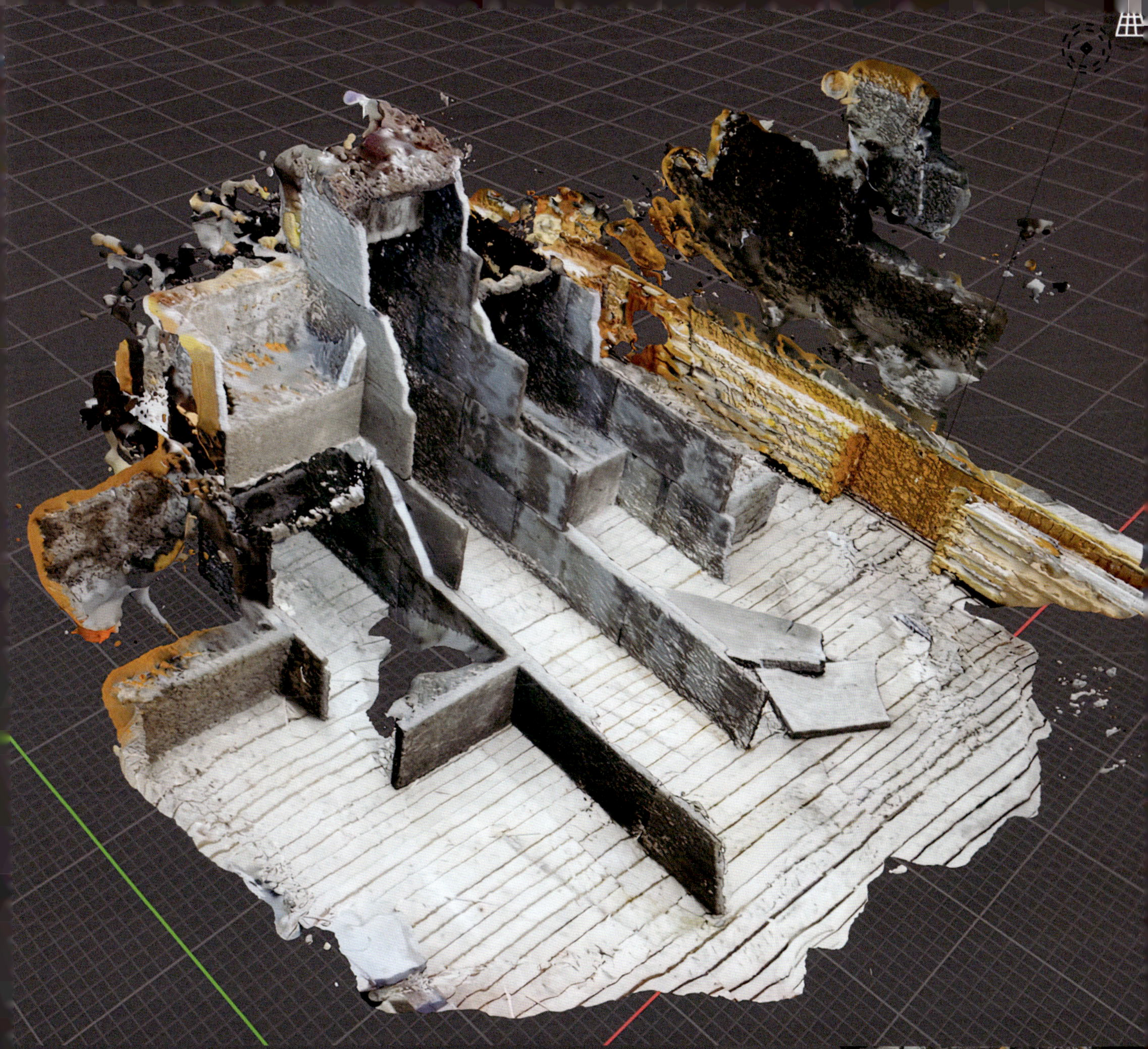

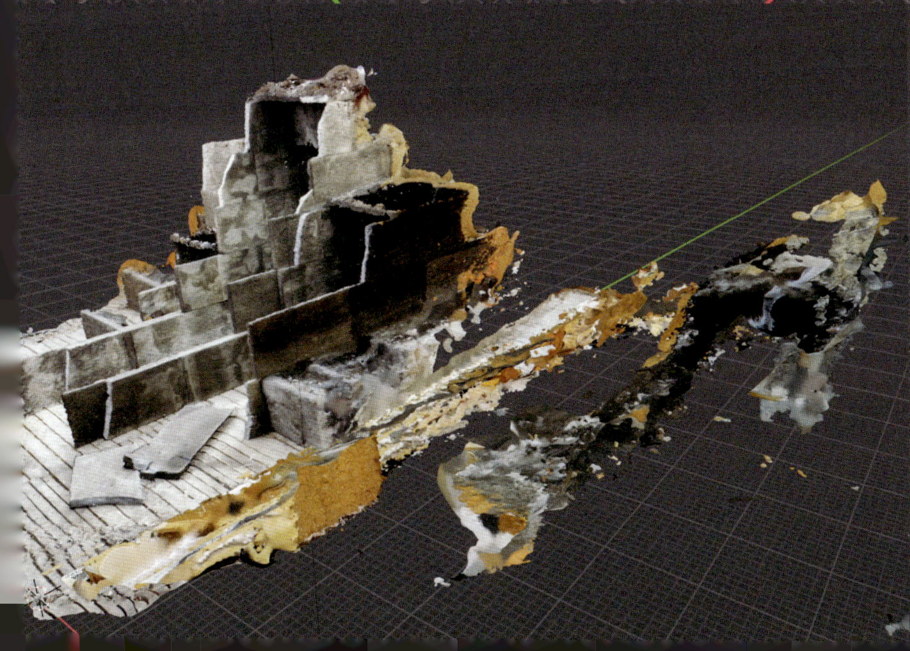

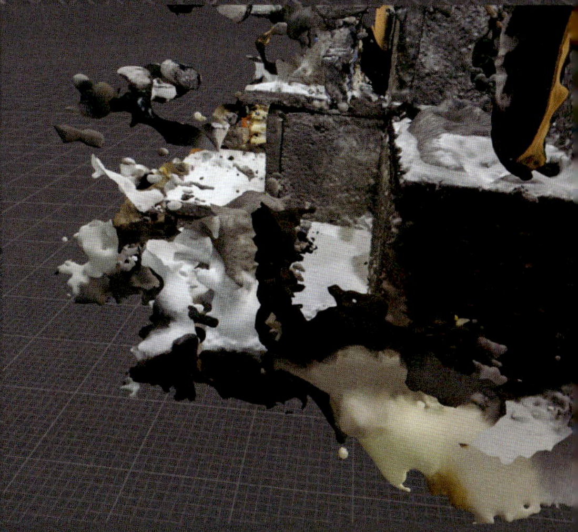

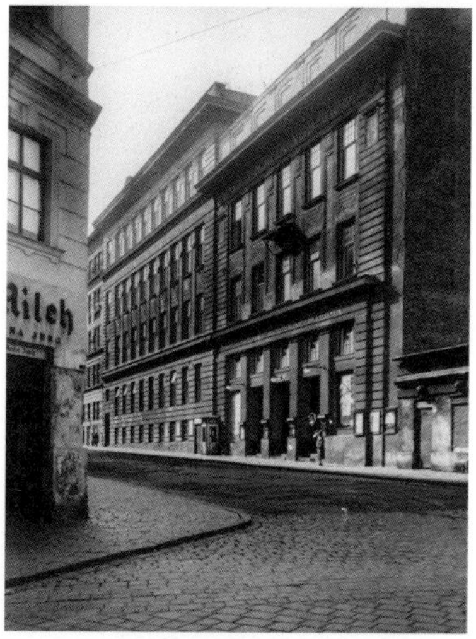

Der Wiener Volksbildungsverein errichtet am 22. Jänner 1911 in der Stöbergasse ein Volksbildungshaus mit modernster Ausstattung.

On 22nd January 1911, the Wiener Volksbildungsverein association erected an adult education centre in Stöbergasse with the most modern equipment.

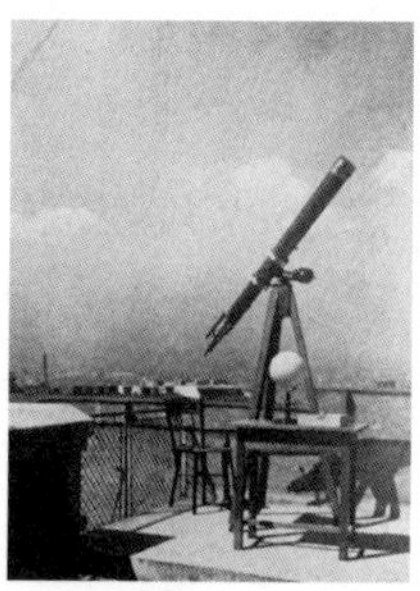

Astronomisches Observatorium
Astronomical Observatory

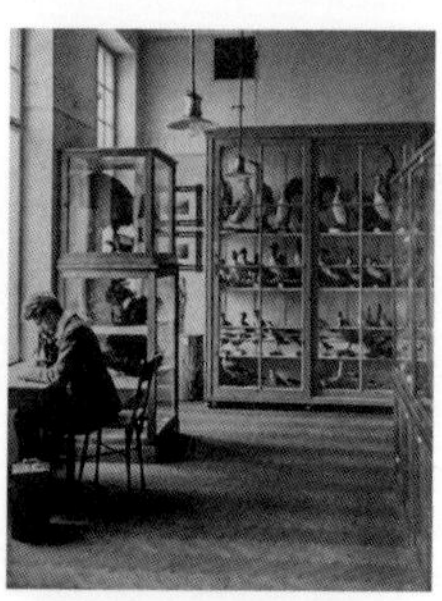

Naturwissenschaftliches Kabinett
Natural Science Cabinet

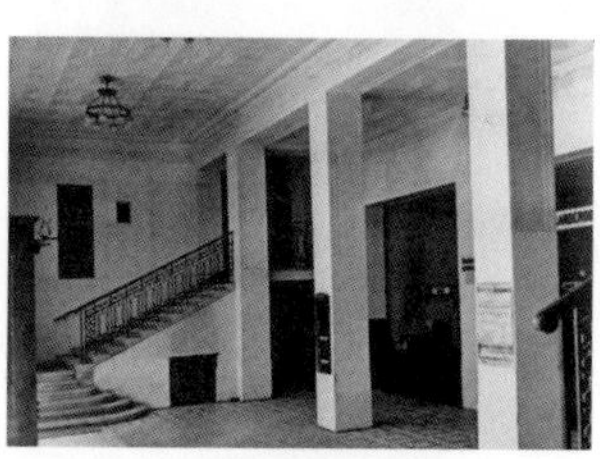

Vestibül
Vestibule

Unter dem austrofaschistischen Regime dient das Haus als „Volksbildungsstätte“ der nationalsozialistischen Indoktrination. Der Volksbildungsverein wird aufgelöst.

Under the Austrofascist regime, the house served as a "People's Education Centre" for National Socialist indoctrination. The Volksbildungsverein was dissolved.

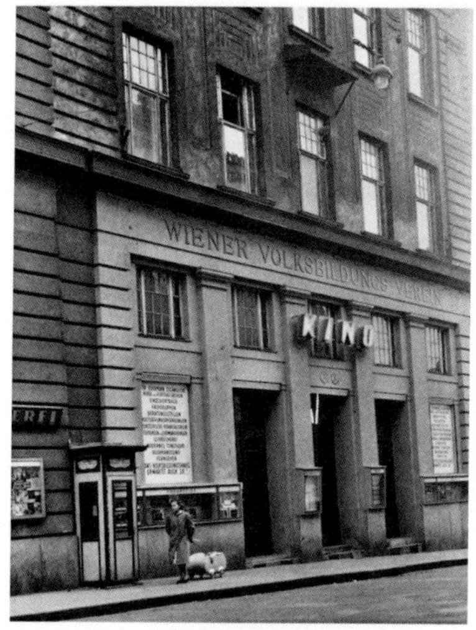

Nach dem Zweiten Weltkrieg nimmt der Wiener Volksbildungsverein seine Tätigkeit wieder auf. Im Jahr 1950 wird im Haus ein Filmstudio eingerichtet und es werden eigene Filme produziert, vor allem Expeditionsfilme. Das Haus wird zu einem kleinen, auf Schmalfilm spezialisierten Filmzentrum.

After the Second World War, the Wiener Volksbildungsverein resumed its activities. In 1950, a film studio was set up in the house and its own films, mainly expedition films, were produced. The house became a small film centre specialising in cine film.

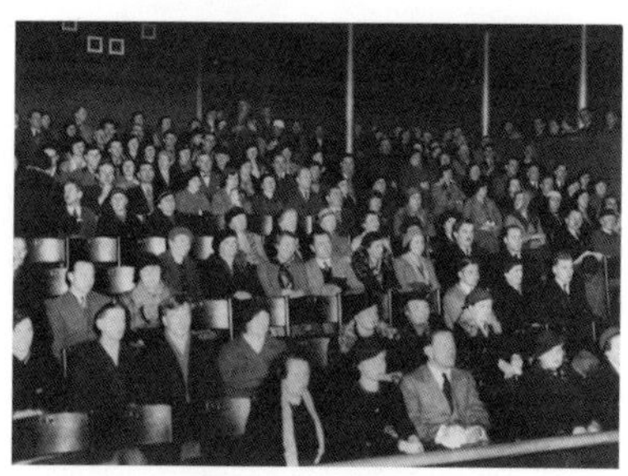

Kino- und Theatersaal
Cinema and theatre hall

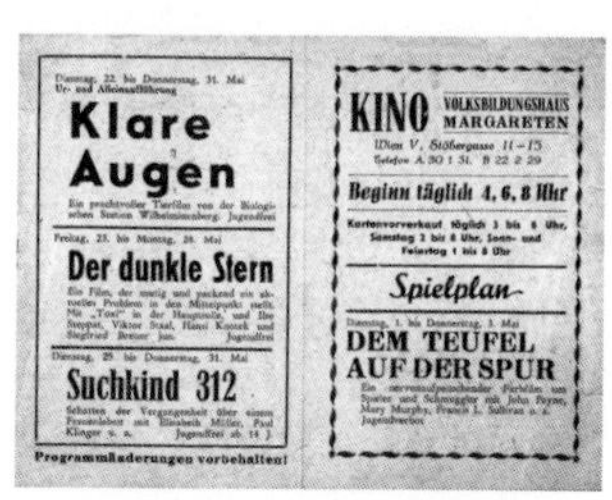
Klare Augen

Der dunkle Stern

Suchkind 312

Programmänderungen vorbehalten!

KINO VOLKSBILDUNGSHAUS MARGARETEN

Beginn täglich 4, 6, 8 Uhr

Spielplan

DEM TEUFEL AUF DER SPUR

Filmprogramm
Film programme

1975 wird das alte Bildungszentrum abgerissen und vom Volksbildungsverein in Kooperation mit dem Berufsförderungsinstitut (BFI) 1978 neu gebaut. Der Vorentwurf des neuen Gebäudes stammt von Fred Freyler, den Innenausbau und die Fassadengestaltung übernimmt die Planungs- und Ateliergemeinschaft Igirien (Werner Appelt, Franz Eberhard Kneissl und Elsa Prochazka).

Direktor Viktor Billek baut das Polycollege in der Stöbergasse zur größten Volkshochschule Österreichs aus.

In 1975 the old education centre was demolished and rebuilt in 1978 by the Wiener Volksbildungsverein in cooperation with the Berufsförderungsinstitut (BFI). The preliminary structure of the new building was designed by Fred Freyler. The interior and façade were designed by the planning and studio collective Igirien (Werner Appelt, Franz Eberhard Kneissl and Elsa Prochazka).

Director Viktor Billek turned the Polycollege in Stöbergasse into the largest adult education centre in Austria.

1911 1938 1950 1975

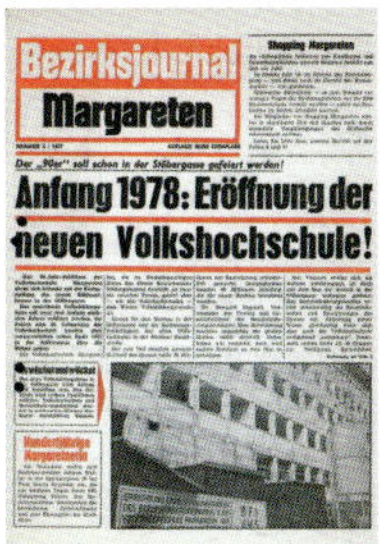
Bezirksjournal Margareten

Anfang 1978: Eröffnung der neuen Volkshochschule!

Artikel aus der Lokalzeitung
Article from the local newspaper

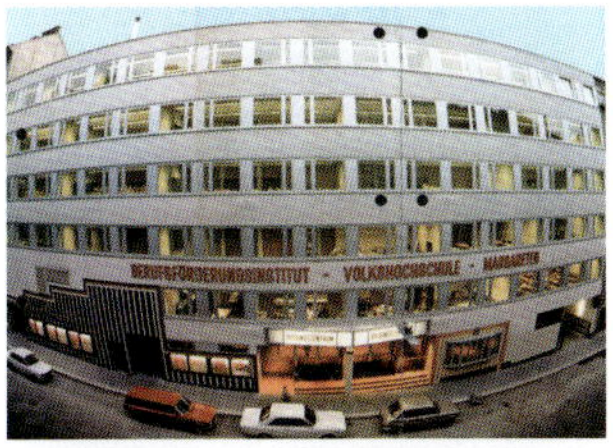

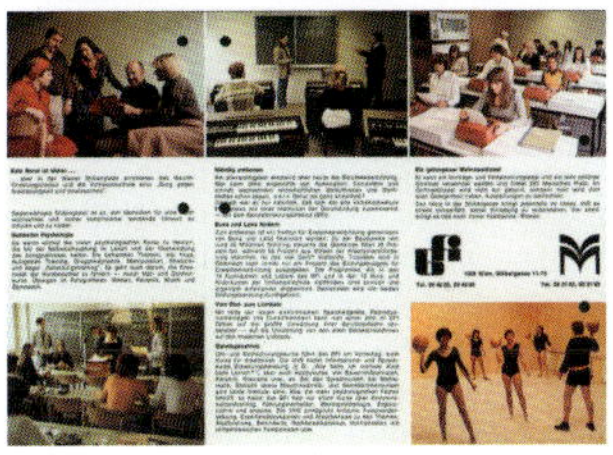

Flugblatt zur Eröffnung
Flyer for the inauguration

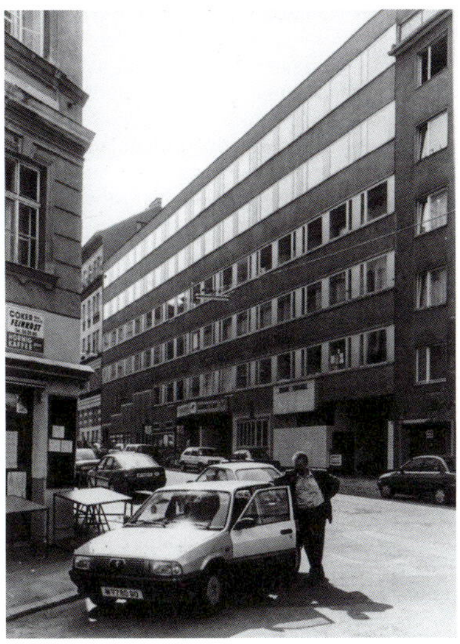

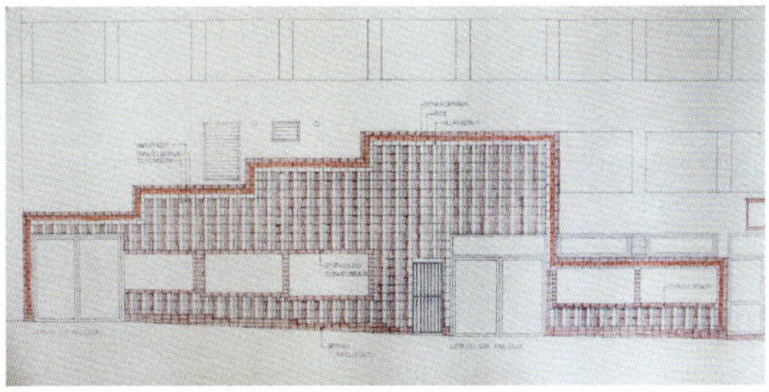

Technische Handzeichnung der Fassade von dem Kollektiv Igirien (Ausschnitt)
Technical hand drawing of the façade by the collective Igirien (detail)

„Baugestalterisch bewies das Team sein Können beim jüngst eröffneten Komplex des Berufsförderungsinstitutes mit angeschlossener Volkshochschule in Margareten. Da übernahmen sie es, den konventionellen Emmentaler-Rohbau eines anderen Architekten durch lebhafte Erdgeschoß-Fassadengestaltung und ansprechenden Innenausbau zu verschönern.

Tatsächlich präsentiert sich jetzt die weiße Front in braun-rot-gelb-weißem Streif unterschiedlicher Höhe einladend, freundlich und originell zugleich. An der – ursprünglich durch Gänge und Türen zerfransten und ungemütlichen – Eingangshalle vollbrachten sie durch schlichte Tricks wahre Wunder. So gelang ihnen durch Kombination unterschiedlicher Bodenbeläge und einem riesigen Bodenoval aus heller Keramik, den Eindruck eines großzügigen, zentralen Raums herzustellen.

Einfallsreich auch die Konzeption eines Mehrzwecksaals: Bewegliche Klapp-Wandelemente können konträre Atmosphäre schaffen; je nach Bedarf präsentiert sich der Raum einmal dunkel tapeziert als Kinosaal, einmal weiß als Vortrags- und Ausstellungslokalität. Daneben beharrten sie auf gepolsterten Holzsesseln gegenüber Stahlrohrsitzen: ‚Wir haben gefragt, ob man haben will, daß die Zuhörer bei Vorträgen glauben, das Gehörte sei schlecht, obwohl sie in Wirklichkeit nur schlecht sitzen. Daraufhin hat man sich für die besseren Stühle entschieden.'"

"In terms of building design, the team demonstrated their skills in the recently opened complex of the Berufsförderungsinstitut with the associated Volkshochschule in Margareten. There they took on the task of embellishing the conventional Emmentaler shell of another architect's building with a lively ground floor façade design and appealing interior fittings.

Indeed, the white façade in brown-red-yellow-white stripes of different heights now presents itself as inviting, friendly and original at the same time. In the entrance hall – originally perforated by corridors and doors and uncomfortable – they performed true miracles by using simple tricks. For example, by combining different floor coverings and a huge oval floor made of light-coloured ceramics, they succeeded in creating the impression of a spacious, central room.

The concept of the multipurpose hall is also imaginative: Movable folding wall elements can create contrasting atmospheres; depending on requirements, the room presents itself once darkly wallpapered as a cinema hall, conversely white as a lecture hall and exhibition venue. In addition, they insisted on upholstered wooden armchairs as opposed to tubular steel seats: 'We asked if they wanted the audience to think that what they heard was bad, when in fact they were just sitting badly. As a result, the better chairs were chosen.'"

Rudolf John, Kurier, 29.10.1978

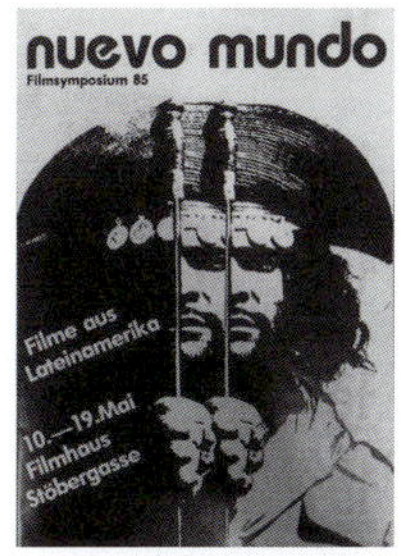

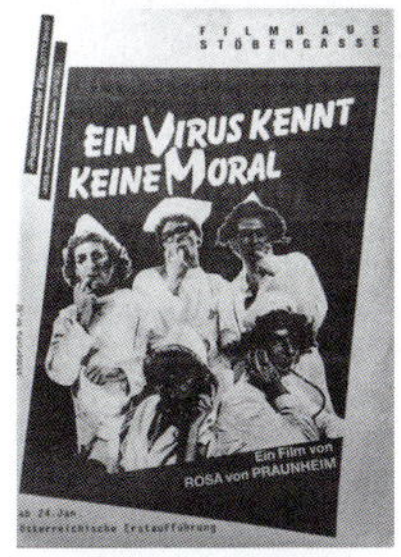

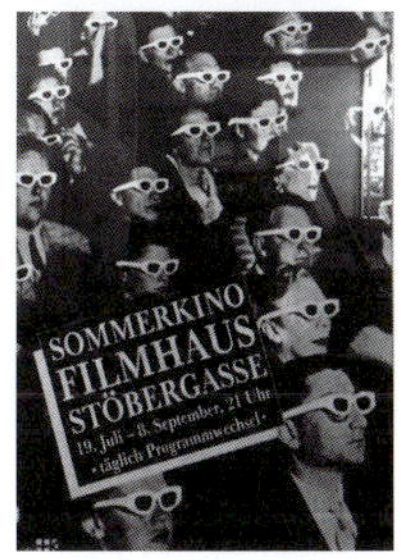

Programmheft und Festivalplakate
Programme booklet and festival poster

Das Filmhaus Stöbergasse avanciert ab 1981 zum anspruchsvollen Programm- und Schwerpunkt-Kino mit eigenem Filmverleih. Bis 2002 zeigt man im hauseigenen Mehrzwecksaal künstlerisches Kino abseits des kommerziellen Films, bevorzugt in Originalsprache mit Untertiteln. Das Filmhaus Stöbergasse spielt eine bedeutende Rolle bei der Vermittlung von Filmkultur in Wien.

From 1981 on, the Filmhaus Stöbergasse advanced to become a sophisticated arthouse and focal point cinema with its own film distribution. The multipurpose hall served until 2002 as a movie theatre, which showed artistic non-commercial films, preferably in the original version with subtitles. The Filmhaus Stöbergasse played a significant role in promoting film culture in Vienna.

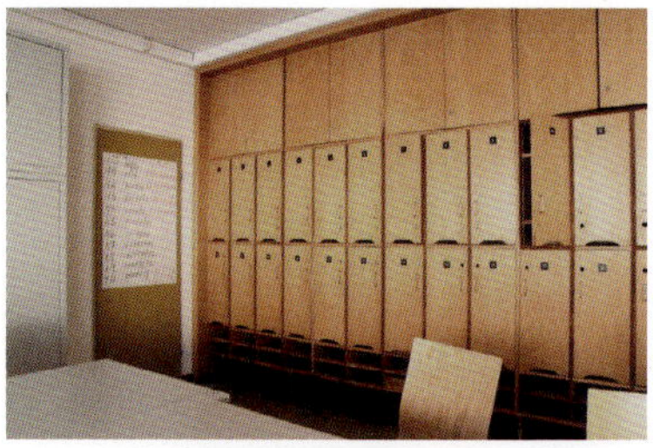

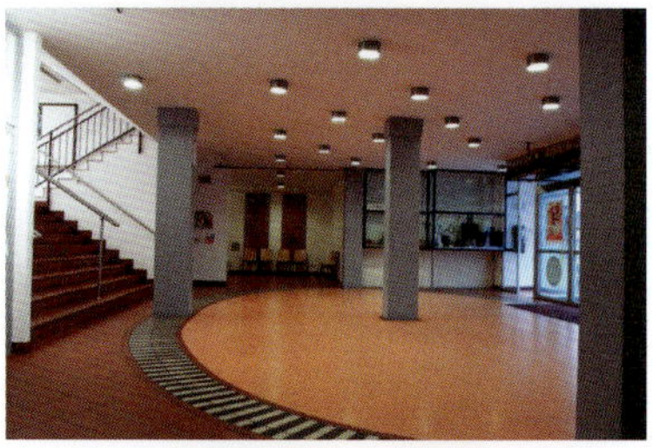

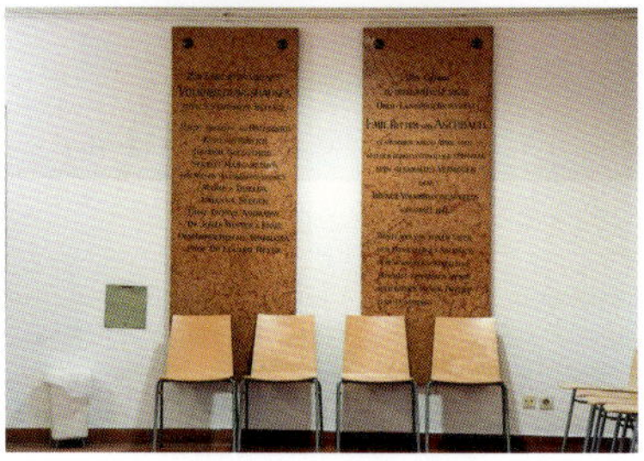

Das Haus 2016
The house in 2016

Mit 16. Februar 2019 stellt das Polycollege seine Aktivitäten in der Stöbergasse ein. Das Haus wird geschlossen und soll abgerissen werden.

As of 16th February 2019, the Polycollege ceased its activities at this location. The house closes and is to be demolished.

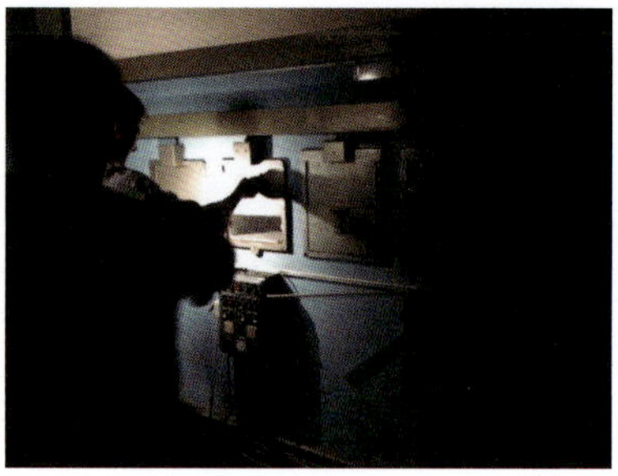

Besichtigung
On-site visit

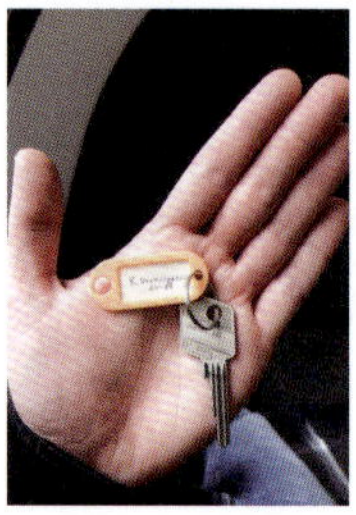

Übergabe des Generalschlüssels im Büro der Sozialbau AG
Picking up the master key at the Sozialbau AG office

„Das Thema Kreislaufwirtschaft, und damit auch Überlegungen im Zusammenhang mit Recycling und der Wiederverwendung von Rohstoffen, ist auch in der Baubranche längst angekommen. Im Zuge der Abbrucharbeiten des Bestandsgebäudes [in der Stöbergasse, Anm.] wurde in Zusammenarbeit mit BauKarussell Urban Mining mit sozialem Mehrwert durchgeführt. Re-Use-fähige Bauteile wurden ausgebaut und im Sinne einer Kreislaufwirtschaft einer weiteren Verwendung zugeführt.

Diesen Prozess mit künstlerischen Interventionen zu unterstreichen fanden wir eine sehr interessante Idee. Die Arbeit von Ursula Gaisbauer und Friedrich Engl ermöglichte den Besuchenden der Ausstellung einen eindrucksvollen Einblick in das Thema."

"The topic of circular economy, and thus also considerations related to recycling and the reuse of raw materials, has long since arrived in the construction industry as well. In the course of demolishing the existing building [in Stöbergasse, note], urban mining with social-added-value was carried out in cooperation with BauKarussell. Re-usable components were removed and reused in the sense of a circular economy.

We found it a very interesting idea to underline this process with artistic interventions. The work of Ursula Gaisbauer and Friedrich Engl gave visitors to the exhibition an impressive insight into the subject."

Hannes Stangl, Technischer Direktor / Technical director (Sozialbau AG)

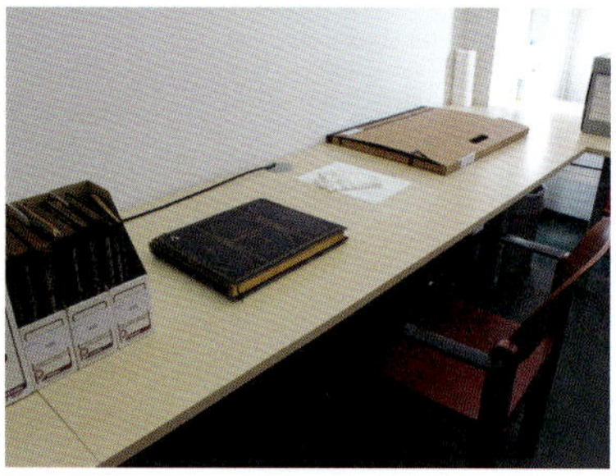

Recherche
Research

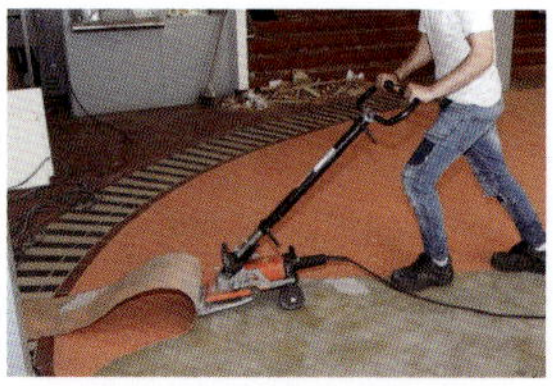

Social Urban Mining – Kooperation mit BauKarussell und Die Kümmerei
Social Urban Mining–Cooperation with BauKarussell and Die Kümmerei

„Urbane Minen, Städte als Rohstofflager, lösen natürliche Lagerstätten in ihrer Bedeutung ab. Wir müssen neue Wege finden zur Bewirtschaftung dieser Berge, die sich im Gebäudebestand aufgetürmt haben. Denn unsere planetaren Ressourcen sind gezählt. Dabei unterscheiden wir Ressourcen und Reserven: Reserven sind der Anteil an Ressourcen, also dem gesamten Vorkommen, der nach dem Stand der Technik noch wirtschaftlich gefördert werden kann. Die Reserven an Kupfer sind ab 2054 zu Ende. Kupfer ist aber die Basis für Energiewende und E-Mobilität. Die wichtigste Ressource ist aber weder das Kupfer noch die intelligente Wiederverwendung von Gebäuden. Eine lebenswichtige Ressource ist die Hoffnung, die aus sinnvoller Beschäftigung erwächst. Auch aus der eigenen."

"Urban mines, cities as raw material depots, are replacing natural deposits in importance. We need to find new ways to farm these mountains that have piled up in the building stock because our planetary resources are numbered. We distinguish between resources and reserves: Reserves are the share of resources, i.e. the total deposit, that can still be extracted economically according to current methods and technologies. The reserves of copper will run out from 2054. However, copper is the basis for the energy transition and e-mobility. The most important resource, however, is neither copper nor the intelligent reuse of buildings. A vital resource is the hope that comes from meaningful employment. Even from our own."

Thomas Romm, Architekt / Architect (BauKarussell)

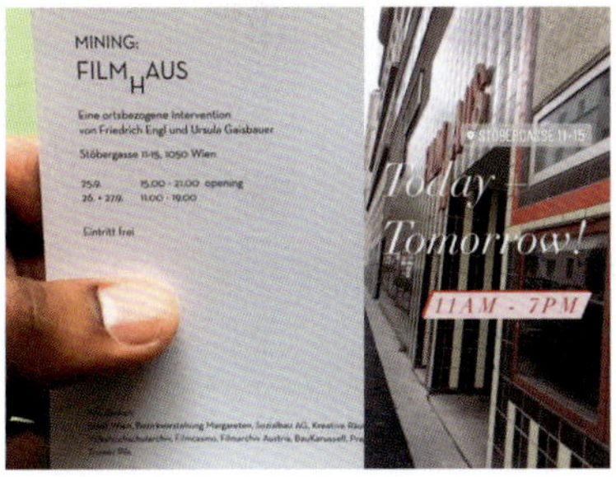

Einladung zur Ausstellung
Invitation to the exhibition

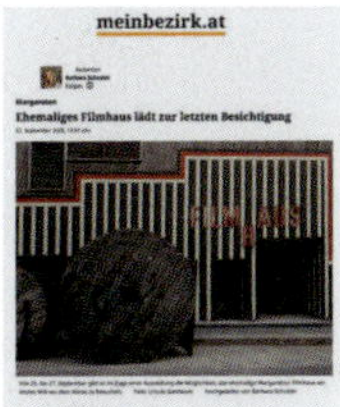

Artikel aus der Lokalzeitung
Article from the local newspaper

Im September 2020 bespielt das MINING Kollektiv das Gebäude parallel zu den Abbruchvorbereitungen. Vom 25. bis 27. September wird das Filmhaus Stöbergasse für drei Tage ein letztes Mal der Öffentlichkeit zugänglich gemacht.

In September 2020, the MINING Kollektiv occupied the building alongside the demolition preparations. For three days, between the 25th and the 27th of September, the Filmhaus Stöbergasse opened its doors to the public for the very last time.

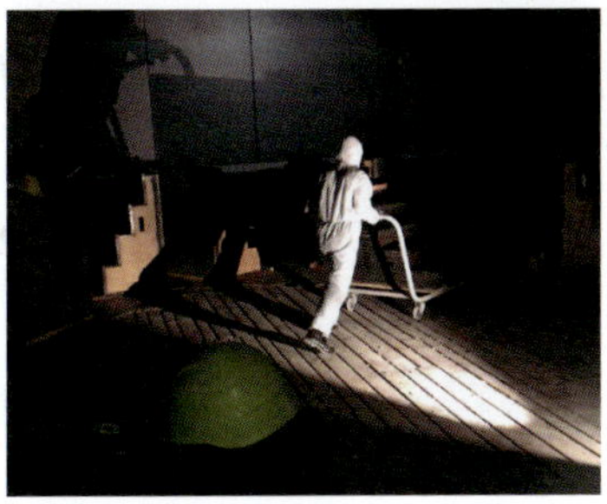

Intervention
Intervention

„Die Kreativen Räume Wien standen den Künstler*innen bei der Projektentwicklung zur Seite. So freuen wir uns besonders, dass das Gebäude dekonstruktivistisch erschlossen werden konnte, was die Vergänglichkeit der gebauten Umwelt auf spannende Weise aufzeigt.

Die VHS Stöbergasse betrieb einst ein in Wien einzigartiges Kino. Daran erinnerte ich mich wieder, als ich die Stöbergasse auf dem Weg zur Ausstellung suchte. Die minimalen künstlerischen Eingriffe an der Fassade der VHS und im Inneren des Gebäudes waren für mich eine intensiv empfundene körperlich-sinnliche Begegnung mit Raum und Materialität, mit Körper im Raum. Eine beinahe meditative Konfrontation mit dem Ort, in der ich die Zeit nicht als Bewegung, sondern als Stillstand empfand."

"Kreative Räume Wien assisted the artists with the development of the project. We are particularly pleased that the building could be approached through a lens of deconstructivism, which demonstrated the transience of the built environment in an exciting way.

The VHS Stöbergasse once ran a cinema that was unique in Vienna. I remembered this again when I was looking for the Stöbergasse street on my way to the exhibition. The minimal artistic interventions on the façade of the VHS and inside the building were for me an intensely felt physical-sensual encounter with space and materiality, with body in space. An almost meditative confrontation with the place, in which I felt time not as movement but as standstill."

Ula Schneider, Künstlerische Leitung / Artistic director SOHO STUDIOS / Kreative Räume Wien

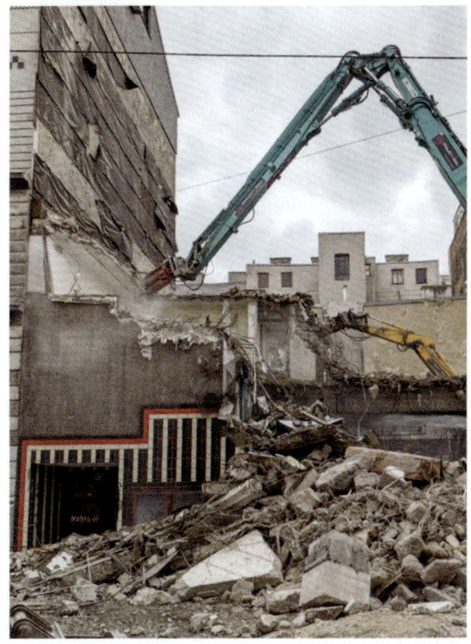

Im Oktober 2020 wird das Gebäude abgerissen. An derselben Stelle entsteht ein von der Stadt Wien gefördertes Wohnbauprojekt. Auch die Volkshochschule zieht wieder ein.

The building was demolished during the month of October 2020. A housing project, funded by the City of Vienna, was erected on the same site. The Volkshochschule moves back in.

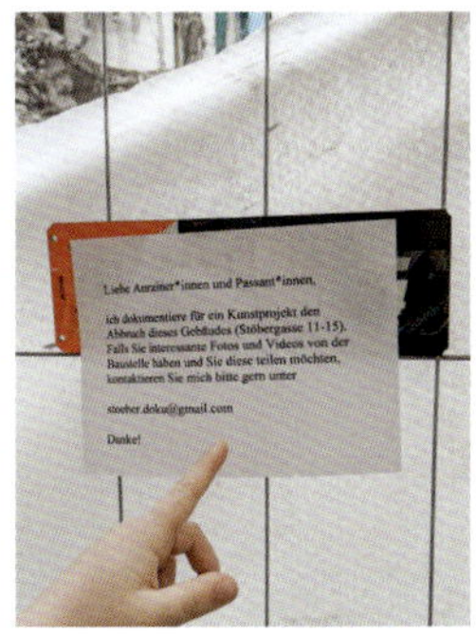

Aufruf an Nachbar*innen und Passant*innen, uns ihre Fotos des Abrisses zu schicken.

Call on neighbours and passers-by to send us their photos documenting the demolition.

MINING ist ein sich fortlaufend weiter entwickelndes Konzept des MINING Kollektivs und setzt sich mit ‚Spaces in Transition' bzw. Architektur und Orten im Um- oder Abbruch künstlerisch auseinander.

MINING transformiert Räume, die sich in einem Übergangszustand befinden. Diese Orte werden vorübergehend von Bedeutung und Zweck befreit und können in diesem kurzen Zeitfenster stark verändert werden.

MINING arbeitet mit den Materialien, die bei Umbau- oder Abbrucharbeiten zum Vorschein kommen. Durch das Entfernen, Sortieren und Anordnen dieser Materialien wird der Raum schrittweise umgeformt.

MINING spielt mit kinematografischen Stimmungen und kollektiven Erinnerungen, die Assoziationen hervorrufen und Emotionen wecken.

MINING will nichts Dauerhaftes schaffen, es schlägt keine Alternative oder neue Nutzung von Räumen vor.

Innerhalb der vorgegebenen räumlichen, materiellen und historischen Verhältnisse schafft MINING mithilfe von Skulptur, Video, Sound und Performance eine immersive und archiskulpturale Raumerfahrung von ephemerer Dauer und ermöglicht Teilnahme und Interaktion durch Erkundung/Entdeckung des Ortes.

In experimentellen Arbeitsprozessen entstehen auf der Baustelle Synergien mit anderen Akteur*innen.

Die künstlerische Methode beinhaltet die Dekonstruktion und Neukonstruktion der Räumlichkeiten sowie die Begleitung der Schließung, Zerstörung oder Auflösung des Ortes.

MINING sucht nach neuen Schnittstellen zwischen Kunst, Architektur, Film, Archäologie, Erinnerungskultur und nachhaltigem Bauen.

MINING is a continuously developing concept of the MINING Kollektiv that engages artistically with 'Spaces in transition' or architecture and places in conversion or demolition.

MINING transforms spaces that are in a transitional state. These places are temporarily liberated from their original purpose and intended meaning allowing them to be reshaped within a short timeframe.

MINING transmutes and utilizes the materials that are exposed through the renovation or demolition process. The space is gradually reshaped by removing, sorting and arranging these materials.

MINING plays with cinematographic moods and collective memories that evoke associations and awake emotions.

MINING does not intend to create anything permanent and does not propose any alternative or new use of spaces.

Within the given spatial, material and historical conditions, MINING uses sculpture, video, sound and performance to create an immersive and archisculptural spatial experience of ephemeral duration, enabling participation and interaction through exploration/discovery of the site.

Through experimental processes, synergies with other acteurs emerge on the construction site.

The artistic method involves actions of deconstruction and reconstruction of and on the premises that accompany the closure, destruction or dissolution of the site.

MINING seeks new intersections between art, architecture, film, archaeology, culture of remembrance and sustainable building.

INTERVIEW

vom 16. Oktober 2021
from October 16th, 2021

ÜBER DAS ARBEITEN MIT SPACES IN TRANSITION
WORKING WITH SPACES IN TRANSITION

Ein Gespräch zwischen Ulrike Payerhofer
und dem MINING Kollektiv
A conversation between Ulrike Payerhofer
and the MINING Kollektiv

UP Ulrike Payerhofer
UG Ursula Gaisbauer FE Friedrich Engl

Über viele Stufen geht es hinab in den Bauch des ehemaligen Sandleiten-Kinos. In diesem verschachtelten Kellerlabyrinth in Wien-Ottakring hat sich das MINING Kollektiv temporär eingerichtet. Im Warteraum unter der Treppe läuft die Videodokumentation zu *MINING: Untertage*. Vorbei an einem Empfangstisch gelangt man über einen dunklen Gang in einen fensterlosen, mit Neonröhren hell erleuchteten Raum. An der Wand lehnen schmutzige Dämmplatten, teiloxidierte Metallbuchstaben und eine grüne Tür. Auf dem Boden sind staubige Schutzanzüge, ein roter Vorhang, Wählscheibentelefone und andere Kuriositäten systematisch angeordnet. An einer Werkbank in der Mitte des Raumes sitzen Ursula Gaisbauer und Friedrich Engl und versehen die Objekte mit dem Buchstaben ‚M'.

UP Beginnen wir mit *MINING: Filmhaus* und dem ursprünglichen Zweck des bereits abgerissenen Gebäudes in der Stöbergasse. Einerseits war es eine Bildungseinrichtung für Bürger*innen, aber eben auch ein ambitioniertes Programmkino bis in die 2000er Jahre. Wie kam es zu dieser intensiven Auseinandersetzung mit dem Ort?

UG Am Anfang des Projekts stand eine große Recherche über ehemalige Kinos in Wien. Dazu haben wir uns zunächst im Internet informiert, dann haben wir uns die Räume in situ angesehen und diese in ganz unterschiedlichen Zuständen vorgefunden. Teilweise waren sie renoviert, teilweise fanden wir uns mitten auf einer Baustelle wieder. Bei manchen konnten wir gar keine Kontakte mehr ausfindig machen.

FE Viele waren z.B. als Supermarkt schon total entcharakterisiert, manche wenige schlummern allerdings noch im Originalzustand. Vom Filmhaus Stöbergasse haben wir zufällig erfahren. Im April 2020 erzählte ich einer Bekannten von meinem Filmscreening-Projekt in São Paulo, und dass Ursula und ich in Wien nach ehemaligen Kinos für eine MINING-Intervention suchen. Sofort erwähnte sie das Filmhaus Stöbergasse, welches demnächst abgerissen werden sollte. „Fragt doch einmal dort nach…"

UG Die ehemaligen Nutzer*innen des Gebäudes, die Volkshochschule und das BFI (Berufsförderungsinstitut), haben uns an die neue Eigentümerin – die Sozialbau AG – vermittelt. Da sind wir gleich auf offene Ohren gestoßen. Wir wurden von einem ganzen Planungsteam empfangen, um das Gebäude zu besichtigen und über die Idee zu sprechen, Kunst in den Rückbauprozess zu integrieren.

UP Wie ging es von da an weiter? Wurde euch ein gewisses Zeitfenster zugesprochen, um eure Intervention umzusetzen?

FE Ja, zunächst erhielten wir den Generalschlüssel für drei Tage und konnten uns schon einmal umsehen. Parallel dazu haben wir uns durch die Recherche in diversen Archiven mit der Geschichte und der film- und soziokulturellen Bedeutung des Ortes auseinandergesetzt.

Many steps lead down into the belly of the former Sandleiten cinema. The MINING Kollektiv has temporarily settled in this labyrinthine cellar in Vienna's Ottakring district. In the waiting room under the stairs, the video documentary on 'MINING: Untertage' is playing. Past a reception desk, one passes a dark corridor into a windowless room brightly lit with neon tubes. Dirty insulation boards, partially oxidised metal letters and a green door lean against the wall. On the floor, dusty protective overalls, a red curtain, dial telephones and other curiosities are systematically arranged. Sitting at a workbench in the middle of the room, Ursula Gaisbauer and Friedrich Engl label the objects with the letter 'M'.

UP Let's start with 'MINING: Filmhaus' and the original purpose of the now already demolished building in Stöbergasse. On the one hand, it was an educational institution for the public, but it was also an ambitious art house cinema until the 2000s. How did this intensive engagement with the space come about?

UG At the beginning of the project we did a lot of research on former movie theatres in Vienna. To do this, we searched on the internet, and then we looked at each spaces in situ finding them in vastly different conditions. Some of them had been completely renovated, while in others we found ourselves in the middle of a construction site. In some cases we could no longer find any contacts at all.

FE Many had already been converted into something different, supermarkets, for example, but a few still lie dormant in their original state. We discovered the Filmhaus Stöbergasse by chance. In April 2020, I told an acquaintance about my film screening project in São Paulo and that Ursula and I were looking for former cinemas in Vienna for a MINING intervention. She immediately mentioned the Filmhaus Stöbergasse, which was soon to be demolished. "Why don't you ask there…"

UG The former users of the building, the VHS (Adult Education Centre) and the BFI (Vocational Training Institute), put us in touch with the new owner and property developer—Sozialbau AG. We immediately found open ears there. We were welcomed by a whole planning team to visit the building and talk about the idea of integrating art into the deconstruction process.

UP What happened from there onward? Were you given a certain amount of time to realise your intervention?

FE Yes, first we received the master key for three days and were able to check out the place. At the same time, we looked into the history and the cinematic and socio-cultural significance of the place by digging through various archives.

UG During the first three days, BauKarussell—a social urban mining project for the reuse of building

UG An diesen ersten drei Tagen war auch das BauKarussell – ein Social Urban Mining Projekt zur Wiederverwendung von Baumaterialien – vor Ort. Sie haben PVC-Böden abgezogen, Möbel ausgebaut, die verschiedensten Einbauten rausgetragen und für sie wertvolle Materialien entnommen. Das war für uns auch wie eine Art Bestandsaufnahme für unsere Arbeit. Wir hatten ursprünglich ein paar Ideen entwickelt, mit dem Stand vom Gebäude, den wir von dieser dreitägigen Besichtigung kannten. Gut einen Monat später, als wir mit der Umsetzung beginnen wollten, war von diesen Materialien aber nichts mehr da.

FE Es wurde uns buchstäblich der Boden unter den Füßen weggezogen (lacht). Was für die einen vielleicht Müll oder ein Problemstoff ist, ist für uns spannendes und brauchbares Baumaterial.

UP Das heißt, ihr musstet spontan umplanen und reagieren auf die neue Situation und den Zustand in dem das Gebäude zu diesem Zeitpunkt war.

UG Richtig. Für die tatsächliche Umsetzung hatten wir genau zwei Wochen Zeit. Als wir ankamen, war der nächste Schritt im Abbruchprozess, dass die Problemstoffe rausgenommen wurden. Da waren in etwa 20 Personen mit weißen Schutzanzügen und gelben Helmen von einem Abbruchunternehmen involviert. Es sind dadurch wieder ganz andere Materialien zum Vorschein gekommen, mit denen wir experimentieren konnten. Im ersten Moment waren wir jedoch etwas geschockt, weil das Gebäude so leer gewirkt hat.

UP Das ist ja auch eine ungewöhnliche Situation für die Firmen vor Ort. Eine temporäre Zusammenarbeit zwischen einem Abbruchunternehmen und Künstler*innen ist nicht gerade typisch.

UG Für uns war es auch ein Prozess. Wir hatten ja im Vorfeld schon überlegt und geplant was gut funktionieren könnte; am Ende hatte es seinen Reiz, dass wir vor Ort von Null beginnen mussten. Es haben sich wirklich täglich neue Sachen aufgetan. Zum Beispiel wurde der Parkettboden rausgerissen und zwei Tischler kamen den abholen, da sie ihn zur Wiederverwendung vom BauKarussell gekauft hatten. Hier haben wir es geschafft rechtzeitig in den Dialog mit den Tischlern zu treten, die das Fischgrätparkett entlang der von uns aufgeklebten Form entfernt haben.

FE Tatsächlich haben die Tischler durch ihre Interpretation der Markierung die Endform bis zu einem gewissen Grad mitbestimmt.

UP Ihr habt dieses Gebäude an einem ganz spezifischen Moment übernommen und interveniert – in der letzten Lebensphase. Die öffentliche Nutzung war schon längst vorbei, der Abbau begann, es ist ein Moment, der in der öffentlichen Wahrnehmung keine besondere Relevanz besitzt. Dieses letzte Kapitel des Gebäudes, in welches ihr euch mit eurer künstlerischen Arbeit eingeschrieben

materials—was also on site. They stripped PVC floors, removed furniture, took out all kinds of fixtures and removed materials that were valuable to them. For us, this was also like a kind of stocktaking for our work. We had originally developed a few ideas with the state of the building that we knew from this three-day visit. But a good month later, when we wanted to start with the implementation, none of these materials were left.

FE The rug was literally pulled out from under our feet (laughs). What might be rubbish or hazardous material for others is exciting and useful building material for us.

UP That means you had to adapt your plans spontaneously and react to the new situation and the condition of the building at that time.

UG Exactly. We had just two weeks for the actual realisation. When we arrived, the next step in the demolition process was to take out the problematic materials. There were about 20 people with white protective suits and yellow helmets from a demolition company involved. This revealed completely different materials that we could experiment with. At first we were a bit shocked because the building looked so emptied.

UP This is also an unusual situation for the local companies. A temporary collaboration between a demolition company and artists is not very common.

UG For us it was also a process. We had already thought about and planned in advance what could work well; in the end it was thrilling that we had to start from scratch. New things really came up every day. For example, the parquet floor was ripped out and two carpenters came to pick it up because they had bought it from BauKarussell for reuse. Here we managed to get into dialogue with the carpenters in time and they removed the herringbone parquet along the shape we had taped on.

FE In fact, the carpenters influenced the final shape to a certain extent through their interpretation of the marks we already made.

UP You took over and intervened in this building at a very specific moment—in the last phase of its life. The public use had long since ended, the dismantling began, it is a moment that has no particular relevance in the public perception. This last chapter of the building, in which you have made an entry with your artistic work—is this the specific transitional moment that is significant for you?

FE We would generally say that it doesn't necessarily have to be about the final phase, but we focus on 'Spaces in Transition'—places that are in a state of transformation. Compared to 'MINING: Filmhaus', where

habt – ist das jener spezifische Übergangsmoment, welcher für euch von Bedeutung ist?

FE Wir würden generell sagen, dass es nicht unbedingt um die letzte Phase gehen muss, sondern wir fokussieren auf ‚Spaces in Transition' – Orte die sich in einem Übergangszustand befinden. Im Vergleich zu *MINING: Filmhaus*, wo das Gebäude abgerissen wurde, war beim Vorgängerprojekt *MINING:Untertage* eine radikale Renovierung vorgesehen und der Raum war nur für kurze Zeit zweckbefreit.

UG Im Moment des Übergangs verwandelt sich etwas.

FE In diesem Zustand erlangt der Ort eine gewisse Art von Neutralität und eröffnet neue Möglichkeiten. Wir setzen die Materialien, die wir vorfinden, neu zusammen. Durch unsere Eingriffe und Formung des Raumes entsteht eine neue (Sur-)Realität für den Ort und er ist ganz anders wahrnehmbar.

UG Es fallen viele Baustoffe und Materialien an, die ihren Nutzen und Wert verloren haben. Die Besonderheiten des Ortes, seine Atmosphäre, und genau diese Materialien inspirieren uns zur jeweiligen künstlerischen Intervention.

UP Ein wichtiger Aspekt in eurer Arbeit ist das Kollektive: Ihr arbeitet als Künstlerduo, integriert euch in Arbeitsabläufe der Gewerke vor Ort und komponiert eure Interventionen aus verschiedenen Prozessen.

FE Im Grunde besteht das MINING Kollektiv nicht nur aus uns beiden, sondern setzt sich zusammen aus der Gesamtzahl der an der jeweiligen Baustelle beteiligten Akteur*innen. *MINING: Untertage* z.B. war eine Zusammenarbeit mit der irischen Künstlerin Rhona Byrne und acht Abbrucharbeitern. Das erweiterte Kollektiv entsteht ortsspezifisch und jedes mal neu.

UP Im Video, das im großen Videosaal gezeigt wurde beispielsweise, seid ihr in derselben Arbeitskleidung wie die Abbrucharbeiter zu sehen, scheinbar die gleiche Tätigkeit verrichtend. Hier verschwimmt die Rolle zwischen Künstler*in und Abbrucharbeiter*in auch visuell sehr stark. War die Zusammenarbeit vor Ort schon Teil des ersten Konzepts oder hat sich das erst entwickelt?

UG Wie die Zusammenarbeit vor Ort aussieht hat sich erst im Prozess entwickelt. In einem Video von *MINING: Filmhaus* schlüpfen wir in die Rolle der Abbrucharbeiter, kehren aber ihre Arbeitsschritte gewissermaßen um. Im Projekt *MINING: Untertage* ist diese Art von Interaktion bereits in Grundzügen vorhanden. Hier war das Ausräumen auch schon im vollen Gange und wir mussten das quasi anhalten und „Stopp, Stopp, Stopp!" rufen. Wir hätten es ohne die Hilfe der Arbeiter aber nicht so hinbekommen wie wir wollten. Dort hatten wir uns schließlich aber darauf geeinigt, dass sie nach Hause gehen, weil sie meinten, für sie bringt das gar nichts mehr. So hatten wir drei Tage unsere Ruhe.

the building was demolished, in the previous project 'MINING: Untertage', a radical renovation was planned and the space was only free of purpose for a short time.

UG In the moment of transition, something transforms.

FE In this state, the place acquires a certain kind of neutrality and opens up new possibilities. We reassemble the materials we find. Through intervention and shaping of the space, a new (sur-)reality is created for the place and it can be perceived in a completely different way.

UG There are many construction materials and resources that have lost their use and value. The particularities of the place, its atmosphere, and precisely these materials inspire us to the respective artistic intervention.

UP An important aspect of your work is the collective: You work as an artist duo, integrate yourselves into the various work processes of the trades/crafts already occurring on site and then compose your interventions in reaction.

FE Technically, the MINING Kollektiv is not just the two of us, but is made up of the total number of agents or acteurs involved in the respective construction site. 'MINING: Untertage', for example, was a collaboration with the Irish artist Rhona Byrne and eight demolition workers. The extended collective emerges site-specifically and newly each time.

UP In the video that was shown in the big video room, for example, you can be seen in the same work overalls as the demolition workers, apparently doing the same job. Here, the role between artist and demolition worker is also visually very blurred. Was the collaboration on site already part of the initial concept or did it develop along the way?

UG How the collaboration looks on site only developed during the process. In a video by 'MINING: Filmhaus' we slip into the role of the demolition workers, but in a way reverse their work steps. In the project 'MINING: Untertage', this kind of interaction is already present in its basic features. Here, the clearing out was already in full swing and we had to stop it and shout "stop, stop, stop!" We couldn't have done it the way we wanted without the help of the workers. We finally agreed that they should go home, because they thought it would be useless for them. So we had three days of peace.

FE A construction site is like a living organism. Many operations occur simultaneously. But often you don't even know what is happening. For example, the water was turned off from one day to the next and we were almost without electricity a few days before the opening. Some processes happen spontaneously, some we can plan and influence to a certain extent.

FE Eine Baustelle ist wie ein lebendiger Organismus. Es passieren viele Abläufe gleichzeitig. Oft weiß man aber gar nicht, was alles passiert. So wurde von einen Tag auf den anderen das Wasser abgedreht und wir waren wenige Tage vor Eröffnung beinahe ohne Strom. Manche Vorgänge entstehen spontan, manche können wir bis zu einem gewissen Grad planen und lenken.

UP Wie hat sich die Zusammenarbeit mit den Abbrucharbeitern angebahnt?

UG Im Filmhaus Stöbergasse waren es ca. 20 Leute. Am Anfang gab es schon irritierte Blicke und Fragezeichen in den Gesichtern. Dadurch, dass wir aber täglich da waren, haben sie mit uns Bekanntschaft geschlossen und wir haben den sehr wichtigen Vorarbeiter kennengelernt. Außerdem gab es vor allem mit zwei Personen mehr Kontakt, die waren sehr interessiert. Bei denen haben wir uns ein wenig drangehängt und es war schnell klar, dass wir nicht mit der normalen Kleidung rumlaufen können. Wir brauchten wirklich Schutz vor dem Staub und den Problemstoffen.

FE Wir haben hier noch die Anzüge und Masken (zeigt auf die ausgebreiteten löchrigen Schutzanzüge und die schmutzigen Atemschutzmasken). Da sieht man sehr gut, wie staubig und dreckig das Ganze werden kann.

UG Dadurch, dass wir täglich im Haus gefilmt haben, gewöhnten sich die Abbrucharbeiter – es waren tatsächlich nur Männer – an die Präsenz der Kamera und gaben ihr Einverständnis, bei verschiedenen Tätigkeiten gefilmt zu werden.

FE Wir spielen auch gern mit dem Zufall und Intention. Es gibt Arrangements und Situationen auf Baustellen, die einen (vermutlich) unbeabsichtigt künstlerischen und ästhetischen Charakter haben. Auch hier verschwimmen die Rollen.

UP Hier im *MINING: Office* zeigt ihr u. a. drei Dämmplatten vom Dach, die Teil eurer großen Skulptur im ehemaligen Turnsaal des Gebäudes waren. Diese Platten haben eine interessante Geschichte und verweisen exemplarisch auf den Moment des Übergangs.

UG Die XPS-Dämmplatten müssen ca. 30, 40 Jahre da oben gelegen haben und darauf war eine Kiesschicht, die sich abgedrückt hat. Außerdem wuchsen auf dem Flachdach kleine Götterbäume, deren Wurzeln sich auf der Unterseite der Platte eingedrückt haben. Diese Vorder- und Rückseiten waren bei unserer skulpturalen Umsetzung wichtig. Wir haben die Skulptur so konstruiert, dass sie vorne hin offen und aufgebrochen war, dann geht man rundherum und hinten ist sie sehr geschlossen. Wie eine aufgebrochene Pyramide.

FE Das Material sieht beinahe aus wie Marmor, wie sehr schwere Steinplatten. Viele Besucher*innen haben tatsächlich geglaubt, es handele sich um eine massive Steinskulptur. Mir gefällt dieses Spiel mit der Illusion, die Assoziation mit einer Filmkulisse.

UP How did the collaboration with the demolition workers unfold?

UG There were about 20 people at the Filmhaus Stöbergasse. At the beginning there were irritated looks and question marks on their faces. But because we were there every day, they got to know us and we got to know the chief foreman. There was also more contact with two people in particular, they were very interested. With them we hung around a bit and it was soon clear that we couldn't walk around with our normal clothes. We really needed protection from the dust and problematic substances.

FE We still have the suits and masks here (points to the spread-out, holey protective overalls and the dirty dust masks). You can see very well how dusty and dirty the whole thing can get.

UG Because we filmed in the building every day, the demolition workers—they were really only men—got used to the presence of the camera and gave their consent to be filmed during various actions.

FE We also like to play with coincidence and intention. There are haphazard material arrangements and situations on construction sites that have a (presumably) unintentional artistic and aesthetic character. Here, too, the roles become blurred.

UP Here in the 'MINING: Office' you show, among other things, three insulation boards from the roof that were part of your large sculpture in the former gym of the building. These panels have an interesting history and exemplify the moment of transition.

UG The XPS insulation boards must have been up there for about 30, 40 years and there was a layer of gravel on top of them that had imprinted. In addition, there were 'tree of heaven' saplings growing on the flat roof whose roots had grown through the underside of the board. These front and back sides were important in creating our sculpture. We constructed it in such a way that it was open and broken up at the front, then you walk around it and at the back it is closed, like a cracked pyramid.

FE The material looks almost like marble, like very heavy slabs of stone. Many visitors actually believed it was a massive stone sculpture. I like this play with illusion, the association with a film set.

UG Also the process before, this falling down from the roof into the gym...

FE ...as if it fell from the sky. In fact, the whole process took several steps. The demolition workers used crowbars to lift the slabs out of the flat roof on the 6th floor, carried them down the central main staircase to the 1st floor and stored them temporarily in a room. From there we moved them to another roof in the courtyard and from there we threw them down through a roof hatch into the gym. We documented this on film and integrated it into the exhibition.

UG Auch der Prozess davor, dieses Herabfallen vom Dach in den Turnsaal…

FE …wie vom Himmel gefallen. Tatsächlich waren das mehrere Arbeitsschritte. Die Platten wurden von den Abbrucharbeitern mit Brechstangen aus dem Flachdach im 6. Stock herausgestemmt, über die zentrale Hauptstiege in den 1. Stock runtergetragen und in einem Raum zwischengelagert. Von da haben wir sie auf ein anderes Dach im Hof verfrachtet und von dort aus durch eine Luke in den Turnsaal hinuntergeworfen. Das haben wir filmisch dokumentiert und in die Ausstellung integriert.

UP Diese begehbare Skulptur dominierte den Raum sehr und man wurde als Besucher*in auf verschiedenen Ebenen angesprochen: die Größe, das Begehen, der Geruch, Schmutz und Staub. Durch diese Intensität war der Prozess des Entstehens greifbarer Teil des Werks und verwies auch auf die zeitliche Dimension der Intervention.

FE Was zur beschriebenen Wirkung beigetragen hat, war sicherlich auch der stählerne Rhythmus des Meißelhammers, der von der Videoinstallation im kleinen Videosaal kam, der an den Turnsaal angrenzte. Dadurch wurden die Besucher*innen in den hinteren Teil der Ausstellung gelockt. Der laute Sound hat die monumentale Körperlichkeit der Skulptur unterstrichen. Man wird auditiv, visuell, olfaktorisch angesprochen: Man taucht in eine Art immersives Environment ein. Zentral war außerdem, dass sich alles miteinander verknüpft, mehrere Arbeiten fließen ineinander. Das Video vom kleinen Videosaal dokumentiert abstrahiert das Herausmeißeln eines Lochs in die Zwischenwand aus Gips in den Garderoben.

UG Das Format der Öffnung bezieht sich wiederum auf die Dämmplatten vom Dach, welches wir erst mit Hilfe eines der mobilen Treppenelemente aus dem Kinosaal gut erreichen konnten. Ein anderes Beispiel sind die großen weißen Säcke auf der Hauptstiege im Foyer. In den Gängen der oberen Stockwerke lagen überall Säcke voller Problemstoffe. Die Vorgabe seitens des Bauträgers war ursprünglich, dass wir nur im Erdgeschoss arbeiten dürfen und nicht in allen sechs Stockwerken. Wir haben diese Säcke dann hinuntergeworfen um das Stiegenhaus zu blockieren. Davon haben sich nicht alle aufhalten lassen, es war uns aber wichtig, dass es keine fixe Tour durch die Ausstellung gibt, sondern dass man sie selbst erkunden muss.

UP Eure Intervention stellt ein Angebot für die Besucher*innen dar. Ihr stellt Beziehungen zwischen den Räumen und Objekten her und schafft neue Verbindungen. Dadurch schafft ihr Architektur und Narration in bestehender Architektur, ein sehr wichtiger Moment in eurer künstlerischen Praxis. Einerseits seid ihr gebunden an das, was eben da ist, gleichzeitig bleibt immer Spielraum für Zufälliges. Wie geht ihr mit diesem Spannungsfeld zwischen Abstraktion und Manifestation um?

UP This walk-in sculpture dominated the room very much and as a visitor you were addressed on different levels: the size, walking into it, the smell, dirt and dust. Through this intensity, the process of creation was a tangible part of the work and also referred to the temporal dimension of the intervention.

FE What contributed to the effect described was certainly the metallic rhythm of the chisel hammer, which came from the video installation in the small video room adjacent to the gym. This lured the visitors to the rear of the exhibition. The loud sound underlined the monumental physicality of the sculpture. One is addressed aurally, visually, olfactorily: One is plunged into a kind of immersive environment. Another central aspect was that everything is interconnected, several pieces flow into each other. The video of the small video room documents in abstract form the chiselling of a hole in the plaster partition wall in the cloakrooms/dressing rooms.

UG The size of the opening again refers to the insulation panels from the roof, which we could only reach easily with the help of one of the mobile stair elements from the cinema hall. Another example are the large white sacks on the main staircase in the lobby. In the corridors of the upper floors, there were bags full of problematic materials everywhere. The property developer originally stipulated that we could only work on the ground floor and not on all six floors. We then threw these bags down to block the stairs. Not everyone let that stop them, but it was important to us that there was no fixed tour through the exhibition, but that you had to explore it on your own.

UP Your intervention is an offer to the visitors. You establish relationships between the spaces and objects and create new connections. In this way you create architecture and narration in existing structures, a very important moment in your artistic practice. On the one hand, you are bound to what is there, but at the same time there is always room for chance. How do you deal with this tension between abstraction and manifestation?

UG That's what makes it particularly exciting for me, because you have to feel your way along and new developments always emerge. That in itself is the attraction for me. You know that somewhere else it would be a completely different project. You have to respond to the given materials, situations and spaces in order to find a suitable intervention for them. Of course, it is also an extreme test of nerves. Until the day before the opening, you often don't know if and how it will succeed.

FE Most processes are experimental and the outcome is therefore very unpredictable.

UG Das macht es für mich besonders spannend, weil man sich herantasten muss und immer neue Entwicklungen entstehen. An sich ist das für mich der Reiz. Man weiß, woanders würde es eine komplett andere Arbeit sein. Man muss auf die vorhandenen Materialien, Situationen und Räume eingehen, um überhaupt eine passende Intervention dafür zu finden. Natürlich ist es auch eine extreme Nervenprobe. Bis zum Tag vor der Eröffnung weiß man oft nicht, ob und wie es gelingt.
FE Die meisten Prozesse verlaufen experimentell und das Resultat ist daher sehr unvorhersehbar.

UP Im ehemaligen Kinosaal habt ihr sehr szenografisch gearbeitet: Hier habt ihr einen unscheinbaren Gebrauchsgegenstand in den Vordergrund gerückt.
UG Der Filmprojektor, den wir versteckt in einem Regal im ehemaligen Regieraum gefunden haben, war ein zentrales Element. Wir haben die vorgefundenen Bühnenelemente, die auch als Treppen genutzt werden konnten, im Raum positioniert und mit Licht und Schatten in Szene gesetzt. Der Projektor hat beispielsweise zwei Treppenelemente, die knapp aneinander gestellt waren, so beleuchtet, dass deren übergroßer Schatten auf die ehemalige Bühne projiziert wurden, für mich ist das auf eine minimalistische Art und Weise, was Kino kann. Es werden auf eine sehr einfache Art und Weise Assoziationen geweckt.

UP Das gesamte Konzept nennt sich ‚MINING'. Das bezeichnet im klassischen Sinne einen invasiven und ausbeutenden Prozess im Umgang mit Rohstoffen und Materialien, wohingegen eure Praxis dem konträr gegenübersteht. Wie hat sich das entwickelt, mit vorhandenem und gebrauchtem Material zu arbeiten?
UG In meiner Diplomarbeitszeit haben Umbau- und Abrissprozesse bereits eine Rolle gespielt. Das Gebäude der Universität für angewandte Kunst am Oskar-Kokoschka-Platz wurde zu dieser Zeit umgebaut und viele mussten übersiedeln. Dementsprechend habe ich mit dem gearbeitet, was ich vorfand an Räumen und Materialien. Ich habe Holzwände unserer ehemaligen Klassenräume rausgenommen, woanders wieder eingebaut und so mit dem Raum perspektivisch gearbeitet. Das Arbeiten mit dem vorhandenen Material und der räumlichen Situation hat sich für mich sehr sinnvoll angefühlt. Warum soll ich in den Baumarkt einkaufen gehen, eine Ausstellung machen und danach kommt alles in den Müll?
FE Das gemeinsame Konzept hat sich während und im Anschluss an *Untertage* entwickelt. Das Projekt hat sich im Rahmen einer Artist Residency in São Paulo ergeben und markiert den Beginn unserer Zusammenarbeit. Der Raum, den wir bekamen, war ein Business-Center an der FAAP-Universität mit Schulklassencharakter. Uns war gleich klar, dass wir den stark verändern möchten. Wir hatten zwar kein Budget, aber sämtliche Freiheiten und jede Menge an Material, das aufgrund

UP In the former cinema hall you worked very scenographically: Here you brought an inconspicuous object of daily use into the foreground.
UG The film projector, which we found hidden on a shelf in the former control booth, was a central element. We positioned the found stage elements, which could also be used as stairs, in the hall and staged them with light and shadow. For example, the projector illuminated two stair elements that were placed close to each other in such a way that their oversized shadows were projected onto the former stage, for me, this is in a minimalistic way what cinema does. Associations are awakened in a very simple way.

UP The whole concept is called 'MINING'. In the conventional sense, this refers to invasive and exploitative processes in dealing with raw materials, whereas your practice contrasts with this. How did it develop, working with existing and used material?
UG In my diploma thesis period, conversion and demolition processes already played a role. The building of the University of Applied Arts at Oskar-Kokoschka-Platz was being rebuilt at that time and many people had to move out. Accordingly, I worked with what I found in terms of rooms and materials. I removed wooden walls from our former classrooms and reinstalled them elsewhere, thus working with the space in perspective. Working with the existing material and the spatial situation felt very meaningful to me. Why should I go shopping in the DIY store, make an exhibition and then everything goes in the trash?
FE The joint concept developed during and after 'MINING: Untertage'. The project came up during an artist residency in São Paulo and marked the beginning of our collaboration. The space we were given was a business centre at the FAAP University with the characteristics of a classroom. It was immediately clear to us that we wanted to change it a lot. We didn't have a budget, but we had all the freedom and a lot of material that had accumulated due to the heavy renovation. We started with: "What has to go?", so we shaped the space by taking it away and removing it, rendering in the classical sense.
UG So it gets very sculptural...
FE Exactly, and due to the spatial situation—an event room on the ground floor without windows.
UG We really went down there for four days...
FE Indeed, without daylight, hence the title 'MINING: Untertage' (German for underground, below-ground); and that's how the link to mining came about. We 'dug', layer by layer, for materials that we didn't even know existed. By uncovering underlying structures and materials, the process sometimes also takes on an archaeological component.
UG Right at the entrance, by cutting out the walls of small rooms one behind the other, the illusion of a corridor going into the depths was created, which

der starken Renovierung angefallen ist. Begonnen haben wir mit „Was muss raus?", somit formten wir also den Raum durch das Wegnehmen und Entfernen, also bildhauerisch ganz im klassischen Sinne.

UG So wird es sehr skulptural...

FE Genau, und durch die räumliche Situation – ein Veranstaltungsraum im Untergeschoß ohne Fenster.

UG Wir sind da wirklich vier Tage abgetaucht...

FE Tatsächlich ohne Tageslicht, daher der Titel *MINING: Untertage*; und so kam auch die Verknüpfung zur Minenarbeit. Wir 'schürften', Schicht für Schicht, nach Materialien, von denen wir noch gar nicht wussten, dass es sie gibt. Durch das Freilegen von darunter liegenden Strukturen und Materialien gewinnt der Prozess zuweilen auch eine archäologische Komponente.

UG Direkt am Eingang wurde durch das Herausschneiden der Wände von hintereinander liegenden kleinen Räumen die Illusion von einem in die Tiefe gehenden Gang erzeugt, der die Besucher*innen in die Dunkelheit geführt hat. Wie der Abgang in eine Mine.

FE In der großen Halle waren in den Deckenpaneelen Lautsprecher installiert, die überraschenderweise noch funktioniert haben. Wir haben sie abgehängt und mit einem Sound bespielt, der an Tropfsteinhöhlen erinnert. Zusätzlich haben wir die Klimaanlage auf Maximum hochgedreht.

UG Es war kalt und windig... In diesem Raum haben wir einen Boden aus quadratischen PVC-Fliesen vorgefunden, den wir skulptural bearbeitet und zu einer schuppenartigen Struktur geformt haben. Die große Ecke mitten im Raum, die sich aus vielen kleinen Fliesen zusammensetzte, hat fast bis zur Decke gereicht.

FE Der Boden schält sich ab, die Materie, der Raum selbst, ist im Begriff sich aufzulösen.

UG Hinter dem großen Raum gab es noch einen Korridor, den Lüftungskanal, in den man ein paar Treppen hinunter gehen musste. Hier gab es in den Wänden zwei konvexe Ausbuchtungen. Wir haben diese aufgegriffen und wieder mit dem Maßstab gespielt, indem wir die vorhandenen Leuchtstoffröhren kreisbogenförmig bis auf Hüfthöhe abgehängt und mit gelber Folie versehen haben, die wir dort gefunden hatten. Beim Durchschreiten dieses ‚Minenschachts' hatte man den Eindruck, zur Mitte hin größer und dann wieder kleiner zu werden...

UP Ihr habt euch mit dem abgebautem Material aus *MINING: Filmhaus* einen kleinen Fundus angelegt, welchen ihr für zukünftige Projekte weiterverwenden wollt. Habt ihr von *MINING: Untertage* auch etwas archivieren können?

FE Von der Arbeit in São Paulo besitzen wir nur Foto- und Videomaterial. Es stellt sich natürlich für uns die Frage, wie man mit so einer ephemeren Arbeit umgeht, von der am Ende nichts anderes übrig bleibt als die Dokumentation.

UG In *MINING: Filmhaus* entwickeln sich unsere Fragestellungen und Arbeitsweisen weiter. Ein Unterschied ist, dass wir von der Stöbergasse Schlüsselobjekte auf-

led the visitors into the darkness. Like the descent into a mine.

FE There were loudspeakers installed in the ceiling panels in the large hall, which surprisingly still worked. We took them down and played them with a sound reminiscent of stalactite caves. In addition, we turned up the air conditioning to maximum.

UG It was cold and windy... In this room we found a floor made of square PVC tiles, which we worked on sculpturally and formed into a shed-like structure. The large edge emerged in the middle of the room, which was made up of many small tiles, almost reached the ceiling.

FE The ground peeled away, matter, space itself, in the process of dissolving.

UG Behind the main room there was another corridor, the ventilation duct, into which one had to go down a few stairs. Here, the wall bowed out in two convexities. We picked these up and played with the scale again by hanging the existing fluorescent tubes in a circular arc down to waist-height and covering them with yellow foil that we had found there. When walking through this 'mine shaft', one had the impression of growing larger towards the middle and then shrinking again...

UP You have built up a small collection with the mined material from 'MINING: Filmhaus', which you want to use for future projects. Have you also been able to preserve something from 'MINING: Untertage'?

FE There is only photo and video material left of the project in São Paulo. Of course, the question for us is how to deal with such an ephemeral work, of which in the end nothing remains but the documentation.

UG In 'MINING: Filmhaus' our questions and ways of working developed further. One difference is that we were able to pick up key objects from Stöbergasse that we call artefacts and want to continue working with. For example, the façade lettering, a staircase or the master key to the building that no longer exists. The latter also represents the trust that was placed in us.

UP Between the polarities of the ephemeral and the artefact, there is the question of the preservation and mediation of your work.

FE The question: "How can you preserve an atmospheric spatial experience of temporary duration and also convey it afterwards?" plays an important role. 'MINING: Office' or 'MINING: Spaces in Transition' are possible answers to this. We are also thinking about taking it to another level, e.g. digital. We used photogrammetry to recreate the sculpture from the gym, which no longer exists. This virtual 3D object, fed by photos by different visitors, is a manifestation of collective memory.

UG The outcome was very surprising for us as some parts of the reconstruction look extremely real. From

heben konnten, die wir Artefakte nennen und mit denen wir weiterarbeiten möchten. Zum Beispiel der Fassadenschriftzug, eine Treppe oder der Generalschlüssel zum Gebäude, das es nicht mehr gibt. Dieser repräsentiert auch das Vertrauen, das uns entgegengebracht wurde.

UP Zwischen den Polen des Ephemeren und des Artefakts stellt sich die Frage nach der Bewahrung und Vermittlung eurer Arbeit.

FE Die Frage: „Wie kann man eine atmosphärische Raumerfahrung von temporärer Dauer konservieren und auch im Nachhinein vermitteln?" spielt eine wichtige Rolle. *MINING: Office* oder *MINING: Spaces in Transition* sind mögliche Antworten darauf. Wir denken auch darüber nach, die Arbeiten auf eine weitere Ebene zu bringen, z. B. die digitale. Die Skulptur aus dem Turnsaal, die nicht mehr existiert, haben wir mithilfe von Fotogrammetrie nachgebaut. Dieses virtuelle 3D-Objekt, gespeist aus Fotos verschiedener Besucher*innen, ist ein Manifest der kollektiven Erinnerung.

UG Es war für uns sehr überraschend, was da rausgekommen ist, denn manche Stellen der Rekonstruktion sehen extrem real aus. Aus anderen Blickwinkeln, von denen es sehr wenige oder keine Fotos gibt, löst sie sich in Undeutlichkeit auf. So wie auch Erinnerungen mit der Zeit diffuser werden. Für uns eine spannende Erweiterung unserer Arbeit.

UP Eure Interventionen öffnen sich auch für partizipative Situationen an unterschiedlichen Punkten.

FE Ein besonderer Aspekt von *MINING: Untertage* war die Interaktion der Besucher*innen mit dem Ort, allen voran den Studierenden der Universität. Wir haben einen Hammer an einer Rigipswand angebracht, der die Besucher*innen einladen sollte, diese damit im Kontext der Intervention zu demolieren. Wir wollten dadurch den Grat zwischen ‚Zerstören' und ‚Neues schaffen' nachvollziehbar machen.

UG Die Situation ist ziemlich eskaliert. Von überall kamen die Studierenden angeströmt und haben sich total ausgetobt. Das hat sich ziemlich schnell herumgesprochen. Es war sehr spannend zu sehen wie eine kleine Geste so ein überwältigendes Ausmaß annehmen kann.

FE Bei der Arbeit in Wien ging es uns darum, noch einmal die Möglichkeit zu geben das Gebäude zu entdecken und zu erkunden. Oder auch Abschied zu nehmen.

UG In der Nachbarschaft war definitiv eine gewisse Anspannung da. Sie sehen, da passiert was, und es gibt viele Fragezeichen. Was kommt danach? Die Angst vor dem Neuen war auch dabei, wenn man nicht weiß was kommt, kann man es schwer einordnen.

FE Ein Abriss ist auch immer ein Spektakel, für Vorbeigehende, für Anrainer*innen. Wir haben sie aufgefordert, uns Fotos vom Abriss zu senden und haben tolles Material erhalten. Eine Auswahl davon ist hier im Buch zu sehen. Es war sehr spannend zu sehen, wie sich die Bagger in das Gebäude reingefressen haben. Das

other angles, of which there are very few or no photos, it dissolves into indistinctness, just as memories become more diffuse over time. For us, this is an exciting extension of the project.

UP Your interventions also open up to participatory situations at different points.

FE A special aspect of 'MINING: Untertage' was the interaction of the visitors with the site, especially the students of the university. We attached a hammer to a sheetrock wall, inviting the visitors to demolish it in the context of the intervention. We wanted to make the line between 'destroying' and 'creating something new' comprehensible.

UG The situation escalated quite a bit. Students flocked in from all over the place and went totally wild. Word got around pretty quickly. It was very exciting to see how a small gesture can take on such overwhelming proportions.

FE In Vienna, our intention was to give people the opportunity to discover and explore the building once again. Or also to say goodbye.

UG There was definitely some tension in the neighbourhood. You see something is happening and there are many question marks. What will come afterwards? The fear of the new was also there, if you don't know what's coming, it's hard to place it.

FE Tearing down a building is always a spectacle, for passers-by, for those living in the neighbourhood. We asked them to send us photos of the demolition and received great material. A selection of them can be seen here in the book. It was very exciting to see how the excavators ate their way into the building. The hollowed-out stairwell–a real stage set. The tiled façade, emblematic of the Filmhaus, was left untouched until the end...

UP Like the most precious piece...

FE Yes, in a way.

UP Ursula, you got very involved with the building and spent the night there.

UG I travelled to Vienna with a tool kit in my luggage, including a sleeping bag. I had chosen a room on the 2nd floor, the former dance hall with a huge mirror and washing facilities. When I arrived, however, I hardly recognized the rooms. The parquet floor was already ripped out, everything was dirty and dusty. But I really wanted to stay there for a few days. The first night was a real horror, because every time I heard a noise I thought the workmen were going to come in and resume working. Well, and all alone in the house... I managed to stay there for three days. At least I could use the showers on the ground floor, but there was no electricity in parts. It was an important moment for me in coming to terms with the building. I felt very vulnerable.

ausgehöhlte Stiegenhaus – ein richtiges Bühnenbild. DieemblematischfürdasFilmhausstehendegeflieste Fassade blieb bis zum Schluss unangetastet...

UP Wie das schönste Stück...
FE Ja, irgendwie schon.

UP Ursula, du hast dich ja sehr intensiv mit dem Gebäude eingelassen und hast dort übernachtet.
UG Ich bin mit dem Werkzeug im Gepäck nach Wien angereist, inklusive Schlafsack. Im 2. Stock habe ich mir einen Raum ausgesucht, den ehemaligen Tanzsaal mit riesigem Spiegel und Waschgelegenheit. Als ich ankam, habe ich die Räume aber kaum wiedererkannt. Das Parkett war bereits rausgerissen, alles war dreckig und staubig. Ich wollte es aber unbedingt für ein paar Tage durchziehen. Die erste Nacht war schon ziemlich der Horror, weil ich bei jedem Geräusch dachte, jetzt kommen gleich die Arbeiter reinmarschiert und die Baustelle geht los. Naja und so ganz allein im Haus, ich habs dann drei Tage durchgehalten. Wenigstens konnte ich im Erdgeschoss die Duschen nutzen, aber teilweise gab es keinen Strom. Es war für mich ein wichtiger Moment in der Auseinandersetzung mit dem Gebäude. Ich habe mich sehr verletzlich gefühlt.
FE Wenn man die Tage und Nächte mit der Erkundung eines Ortes verbringt, und sich hauptsächlich dort aufhält, ist es so als würde man dort leben. Da kennt man dann das Gebäude wie seine eigene Westentasche und verinnerlicht den Ort und seine Architektur.

UP Wie würdet ihr eure Zusammenarbeit als MINING Kollektiv beschreiben?
UG In unserer Zusammenarbeit pushen wir uns sehr positiv gegenseitig. Jeder geht mit seinen Ideen rein, es gibt einen intensiven Austausch.
FE Unsere Persönlichkeiten sind eher unterschiedlich, würde ich sagen, aber dadurch ergänzen wir uns gut...
UG Und wir sind beide stur, manches will ich unbedingt haben, manches du..., aber wir geben uns gegenseitig genug Spielräume. Wir gehen aufeinander ein...
FE Wir fahren auf jeden Fall Achterbahn.

FE When you spend days and nights exploring a place, and you stay there most of the time, it's like living there. You know the building like the back of your hand and you internalise the place and its architecture.

UP How would you describe your collaboration as MINING Kollektiv?
UG Working together, we push each other in a very positive way. Everyone goes in with their ideas, there is an intensive exchange.
FE Our personalities are rather different, I would say, but that makes us complement each other well...
UG And we are both stubborn, some things I want so badly, some things you want so badly, but we give each other enough leeway. We respond to each other...
FE It's definitely a roller coaster ride.

Ulrike Payerhofer ist Initiatorin und Kuratorin der Plattform „Projektwerkstatt – creating collaborations for sustainability (2022–2024)" an der Universität für angewandte Kunst Wien, welche disziplinenübergreifende Projekte und Kollaborationen zum Thema Nachhaltigkeit aufbaut und konzipiert. Ihre kuratorische Praxis und Forschung konzentriert sich auf multidisziplinäre Kollaborationen und partizipative Methoden an der Schnittstelle von Kunst, Wissenschaft und Gesellschaft.

Ulrike Payerhofer is the initiator and curator of the platform "Projektwerkstatt–creating collaborations for sustainability (2022–2024)" at the University of Applied Arts Vienna, which fosters and conceptualises cross-disciplinary projects and collaborations on sustainability. Her curatorial practice and research focuses on multidisciplinary collaborations and participatory methods at the intersection of art, science and society.

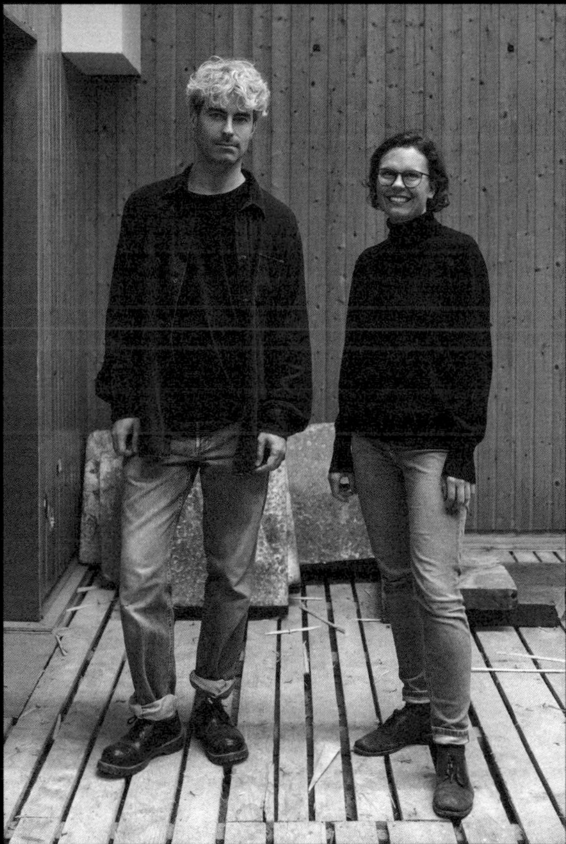

Notas sobre UNTERTAGE

[pausa]

É interessante pensar a ideia do próprio espaço e da construção, ou melhor, (des)construção-demolição, em contraste a essa estrutura elitista de universidade, [...] usando os termos atuais, poderíamos dizer que isso é uma espécie de ocupação ou manifesto. [pausa]. [...] Ocupação fala sobre resistência, privilégios e a falta de privilégios... espaços "que não devem mais ser habitados", morte e destruição. [pausa]. O som da instalação remete à caverna. Eu gostei dessas escamas-superfície, feitas por lâminas quadradas arrancadas do próprio chão, de modo orgânicos e/ou padronizado. [...] A crosta me remete, ora para uma representação do mar, com aquelas leves borbulhas brancas que só ele produz, mas também uma agressividade, uma coisa réptil, [...] pisar sobre eles me deu a impressão de estarmos sobre um animal, me sinto sobre o grande peixe que engoliu Jonas, ou sobre um Dragão-de-komodo... [...] Eu preciso assumir que tenho medo desses animais. [...] Afora o conjunto de pontas submersas, nos deparamos com uma maxi-estrutura. Aqui já não refere mais a uma onda ou a uma besta, seria, na verdade, um vagalhão que só vemos em lugares específicos do globo. Essa forma no espaço, devido ao seu peso e o pensamento sofisticado de sustentação, é uma construção autônoma [...] uma curva perfeita que se desloca do chão e se suspende até o meio do vazio, uma superfície-flutuante [...] eu sou suspeito para falar, uma arte pautada na ressignificação do espaço, na reinvenção do existente e das ruínas, me atraem [...] todos os materiais utilizados para a reconfiguração do espaço são pertencentes ao próprio espaço [...] o contraste da riqueza da FAAP (lado externo), com a demolição aqui dentro, me faz pensar um pouco na ação performativa que aconteceu durante o evento. Estudantes adentram e quebram uma parede. [...] Eu consigo sentir um desejo de destruição muito forte desses jovens participantes [...]. Então, em um mesmo espaço, você consegue ter essas relações de riqueza e devastação [...]. No espaço expositivo temos um "salão principal" com essas escamas de peixes e esses sons de caverna que se propagam no ar, temos essa parede-extinção, parede da performance da destruição, um terceiro espaço-sala, completamente iluminado, vazado-geométrico, com chapas de madeira [...] regular-simétrico [...] que me remete à costelas... esqueletos, estruturas de sustentação e que, ao mesmo tempo, possibilita atravessamentos... fantasmagórico quase... o que dantes limitava, paredes-limitantes, agora é passagem transgredida... atravessável... [...] De modo geral, o que nos é apresentado nesses espaços, são as partes que sobram... são essas carcaças... é como se você pegasse uma parede, ou melhor uma construção e fosse tirando sua vestimenta... e você consegue ver essas estruturas... [...] Volto mentalmente na performance dos meninos e meninas quebrando as paredes... eu acho que isso representa muito, fala muito dessa exposição, desse contraste que eu disse anteriormente, desse desejo, dessa sede de destruir, que poderia ser usada para outro fim, ou que fosse a própria destruição dessas instituições [...]. me fez pensar muito na relação desse prédio caro, elitista, e dessa ocupação aqui dentro sendo destruído pelas próprias mãos de seus alunos-habitantes... [...] por fim nós temos uma sala, descendo as escadas, por trás de tudo, um ambiente vazio, iluminado por luzes amarelas, onde predomina o silêncio.[...] [pausa longa].

Tulio Costa, uma bixa-trapeira colecionadora, artista, mestrando em artes visuais pela Unesp

Notes on UNTERTAGE

[pause]

It is interesting to think of the idea of this space and of this construction, or better yet, of the (de)construction-demolition, in contrast to the elitist structure of the university [...]. Using current terms, we could say that this is a type of occupation or manifesto. [pause]. [...] Occupation speaks of resistance, privileges, and the lack of privileges... spaces "that shouldn't be inhabited anymore", death and destruction. [pause]. The sound of the installation remits the cave. I like these scaly surfaces, done with square splinters ripped from the very ground, organic and/or patterned. This crust reminds me of the sea, with those fine white bubbles that only the sea produces, but also an aggression, something reptilian.[...] Stepping on it gave me the impression that I was on an animal, on top of the giant fish that swallowed Jona, or on top of a komodo dragon... [...] I must confess that I am afraid of these animals. [...] Aside from the set of submerged tips, we encounter a maxi-structure. This is no longer a wave or an animal, but a rogue wave, such that only occurs in certain places on the planet. This shape in space is a construction in itself due to its weight and the well thought-out supporting structure [...] a perfect curve that lifts off the ground and rises in the middle of the void, a floating surface [...] [...] I may sound biased here, but art based on the resignification of space, the reinvention of the existing and of ruins, attracts me [...] all the materials used to rearrange the space came from the place itself. [...] The contrast of the richness of FAAP, external side, with this demolition here inside, made me think a little of the performance that happens during the event. Students come inside and break a wall. [...] I can sense a very strong desire for destruction from these participants. [...] So in the same space, you can have a relationship between richness and devastation. In the exhibition we have a "main hall" with these fish scales and these cave sounds that propagate in the air, we have this wall-extinction, the wall of the performance of destruction, a third space, completely illuminated, geometrically hollow, with wooden planks, symmetrical-regular, that reminds me of ribs... skeletons, supportive structures and at the same time still allowing one to traverse... phantasmagoric almost...what was limiting, confining walls, now is a transgressable passage... crossable... [...] But in general, what we are presented with in these spaces are the parts that are left over... these carcasses... it's as if you have a wall, or rather a building and took off its clothes... and so you can see these structures... [...] I mentally go back to the performance of the boys and girls breaking the walls... I think this represents a lot, speaks volumes about this exhibition, about this contrast I mentioned before, about this desire, this thirst to destroy, that could be used for another purpose, such as the destruction of these institutions themselves [...]. It made me think a lot about the relationship of this expensive, elitist building and this occupation in here being destroyed by the very hands of its student-inhabitants... [...] In the end, there is a room, down the stairs, behind it all, an empty room, illuminated by yellow lights, where silence prevails. [...] [long pause].

Tulio Costa, fag-ragpicker-collector, artist, master's student in visual arts at Unesp

Notizen zu UNTERTAGE

[Pause]

Es ist interessant, über diesen Ort und diese Konstruktion – oder besser gesagt: diese (De)konstruktion-Zerstörung – nachzudenken, die in Kontrast zur elitären Struktur der Universität steht [...], man könnte sagen, dass es sich um eine Art Besetzung oder Manifest handelt. [Pause]. [...] Besetzung spricht von Widerstand, Privilegien und dem Fehlen von Privilegien... von Räumen, die „nicht mehr bewohnt werden sollten", von Tod und Zerstörung. [Pause] Der Klang der Installation erinnert an eine Höhle. Mir gefallen diese schuppigen Oberflächen, aus dem Boden herausgelöste quadratische Platten, organisch und/oder musterhaft. [...] Die Kruste erinnert mich an das Meer, mit diesen feinen weißen Schaumbläschen, die nur es hervorbringt, aber auch an etwas Aggressives, Reptilisches, [...] auf sie zu treten, gab mir den Eindruck, auf einem Tier zu stehen, auf dem riesigen Fisch, der Jonas verschluckt hat, oder auf einem Komodowaran... [...] Ich muss gestehen, dass ich Angst vor diesen Tieren habe. [...] Weg von den versunkenen Spitzen stoßen wir auf eine große Struktur. Hier handelt es sich nicht mehr um eine Welle oder ein Tier, sondern um eine Monsterwelle, wie sie nur an bestimmten Orten auf dem Planeten vorkommt. Diese Form im Raum ist durch ihr Gewicht und die durchdachte Tragstruktur eine eigenständige Konstruktion [...] eine vollkommene Kurve, die sich vom Boden abhebt und in der Mitte der Leere aufsteigt, eine schwebende Fläche [...] […] Ich bin vielleicht voreingenommen, aber ich mag Kunst, die sich mit der Resignifikation des Raumes, mit der Neuerfindung von Bestehendem und Ruinen beschäftigt [...] alle Materialien, die für die Neuanordnung des Raums verwendet wurden, stammen aus dem Ort selbst. [...] Der Kontrast zwischen dem Prunk der FAAP (im Außenbereich) und dem Abriss im Inneren lässt mich über die performative Aktion nachdenken, die während der Ausstellung stattfand. Die Studierenden kommen herein und durchbrechen eine Wand. [...] Ich kann einen sehr starken Wunsch nach Zerstörung bei diesen jungen Teilnehmer*innen spüren [...]. Im selben Raum kann es somit diese Beziehungen von Reichtum und Verwüstung geben [...]. In der Ausstellung haben wir also eine „Haupthalle" mit diesen Fischschuppen und den Höhlengeräuschen, die sich in der Luft ausbreiten, wir haben diese Wand-Vernichtung, die Wand der Zerstörungs-Performance, und einen dritten Bereich, komplett ausgeleuchtet, geometrisch hohl, mit Holzplanken [...] regelmäßig-symmetrisch, das erinnert mich an Rippen... Skelette, tragende Strukturen und gleichzeitig die Möglichkeit, sie zu durchqueren... nahezu phantasmagorisch... was vorher einschränkend war, begrenzende Wände, ist jetzt eine durchschreitbare Passage... begehbar… [...] Aber im Allgemeinen werden uns in diesen Räumen die Teile gezeigt, die übrig geblieben sind... diese Karkassen... es ist, als würde man eine Wand oder ein Gebäude nehmen und es ausziehen... und so werden diese Strukturen sichtbar... [...] Ich komme gedanklich zurück auf die Performance der Jungen und Mädchen, die die Wände einreißen... Ich denke, das sagt viel aus, spricht Bände über diese Ausstellung, über diesen Kontrast, den ich zuvor erwähnte, über dieses Verlangen, diesen Durst nach Zerstörung, der für einen anderen Zweck genutzt werden könnte, wie der Zerstörung dieser Institutionen selbst [...]. Es hat mich dazu gebracht, viel über die Beziehung zwischen diesem prunkvollen, elitären Gebäude und dieser Besetzung darin nachzudenken, wie es durch die Hände seiner studentischen Bewohner zerstört wird... [...] Am Ende gibt es einen Raum, die Treppe hinunter, hinter allem, ein leerer Raum, durchflutet von gelbem Licht, in dem Stille herrscht. [...] [Lange Pause].

Tulio Costa, Tunte-Lumpensammler-Sammler, Künstler,
Masterstudent der bildenden Künste an der Unesp

APPENDIX

APPENDIX

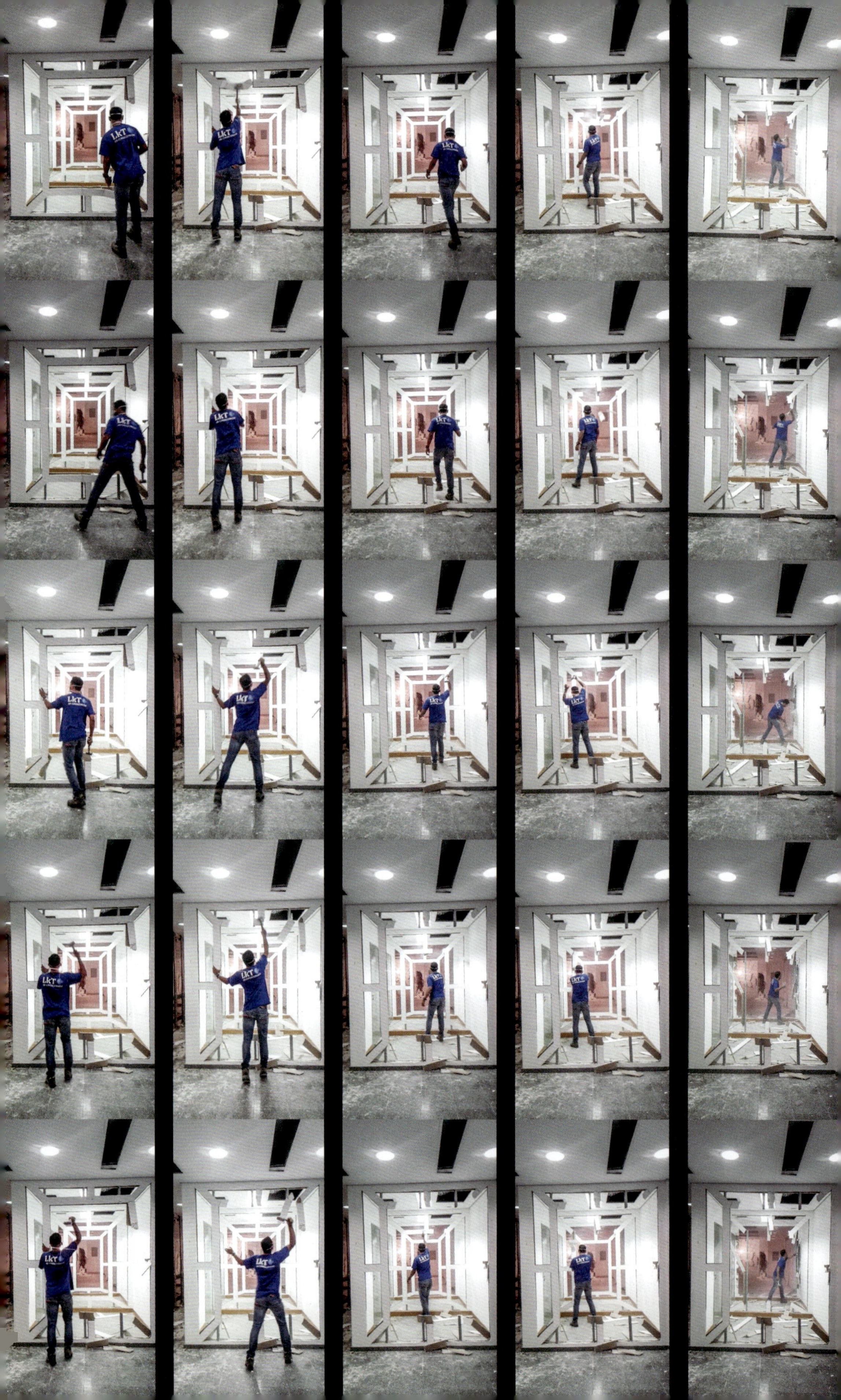

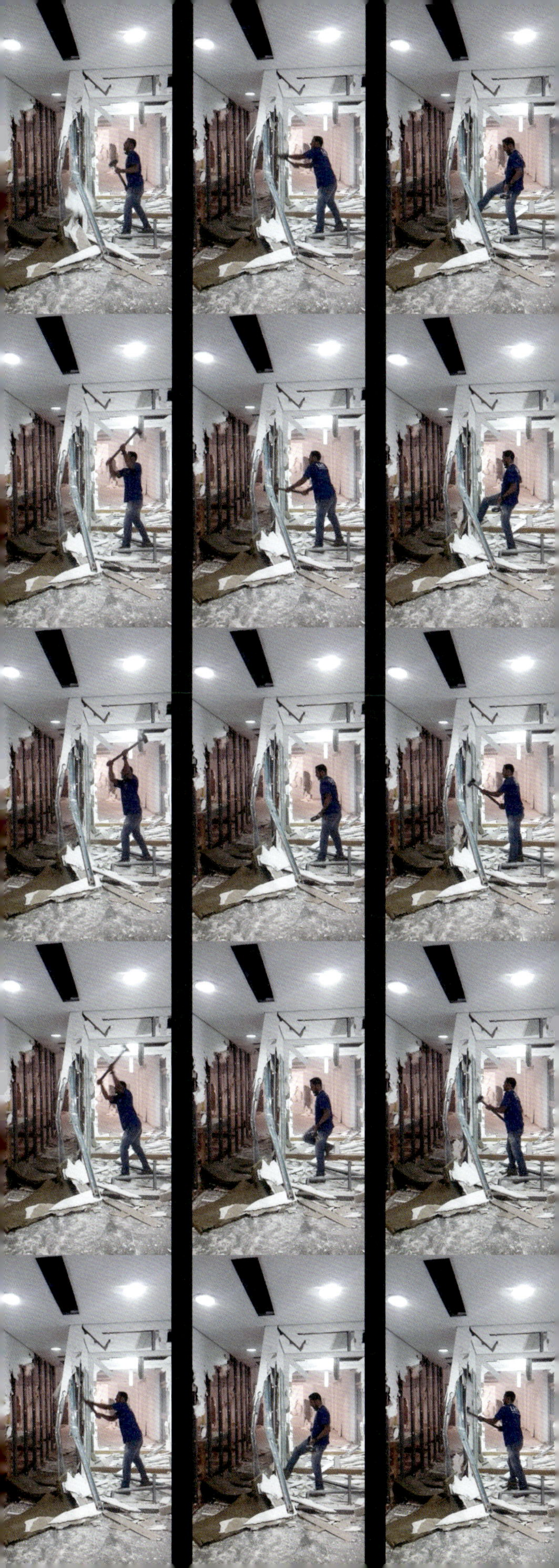

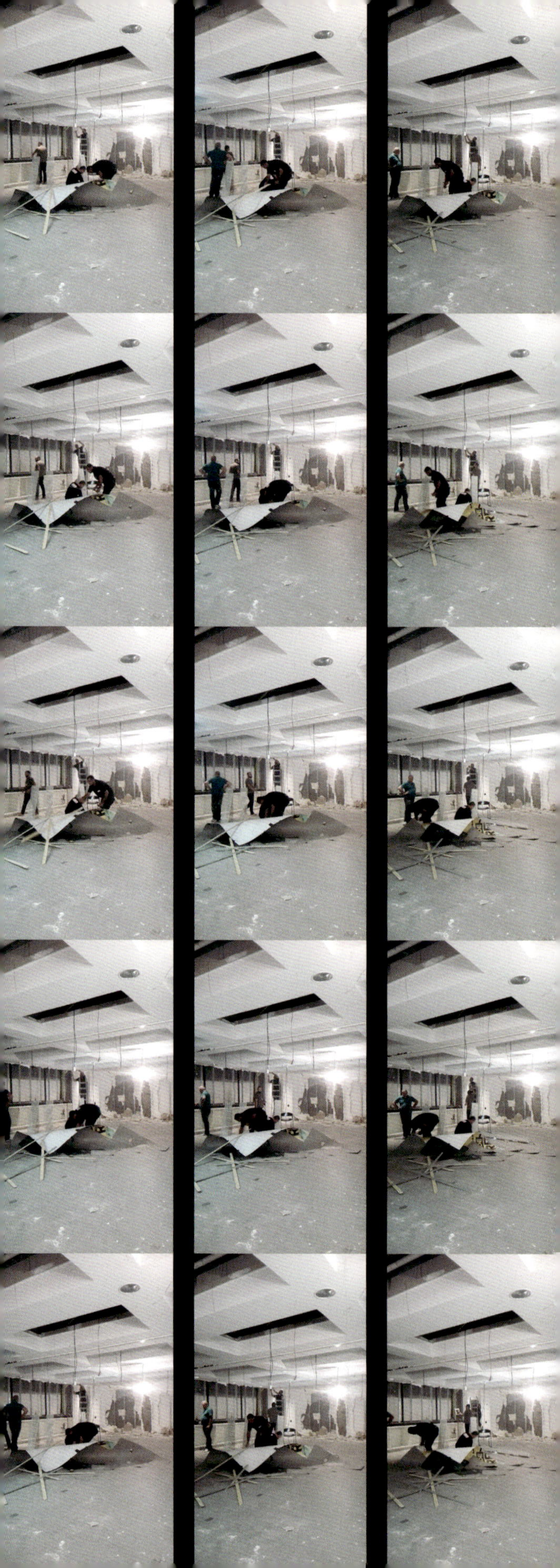

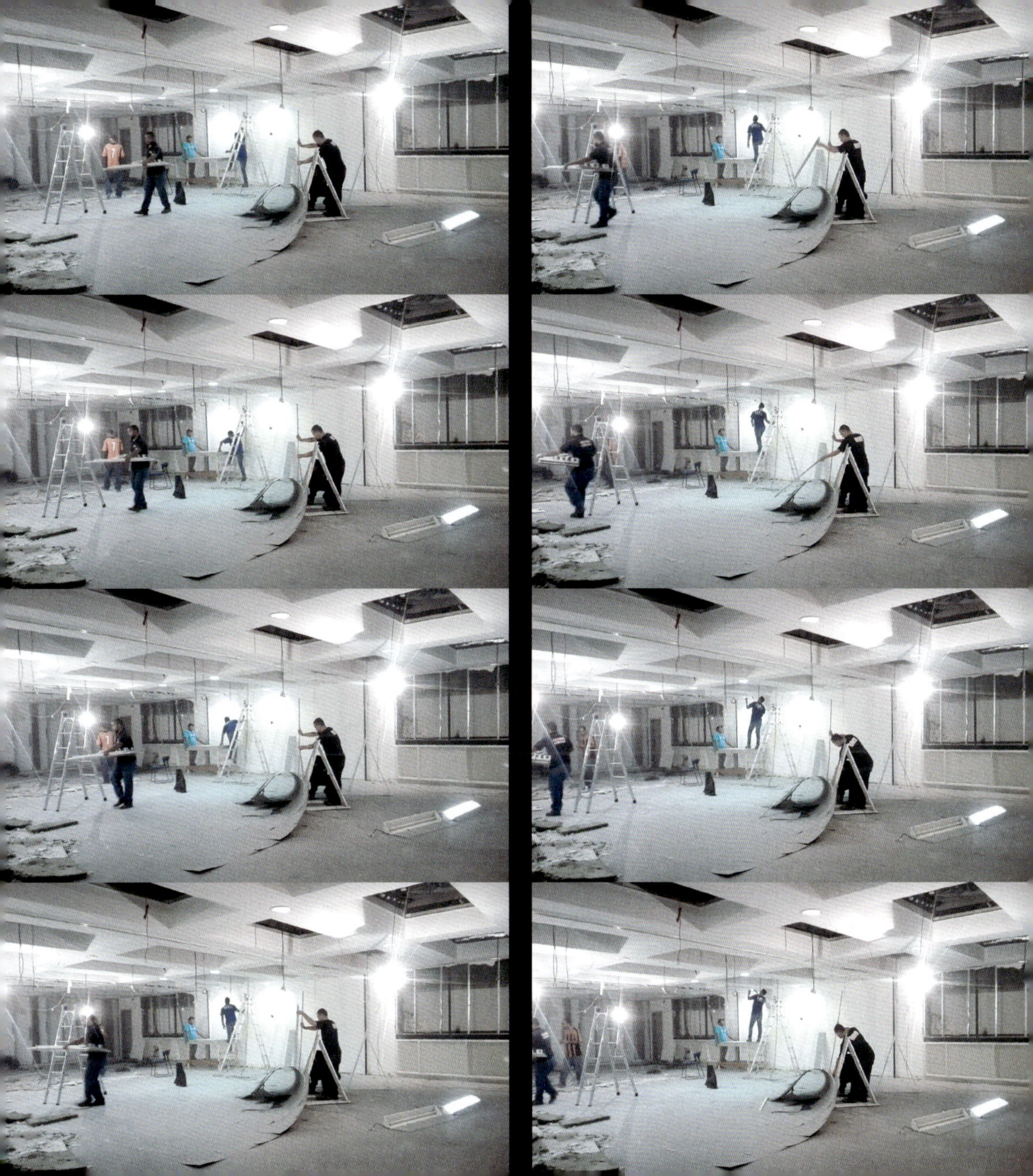

DEMOLIERUNG
(Auflösung)

DEMOLITION
(Resolution)

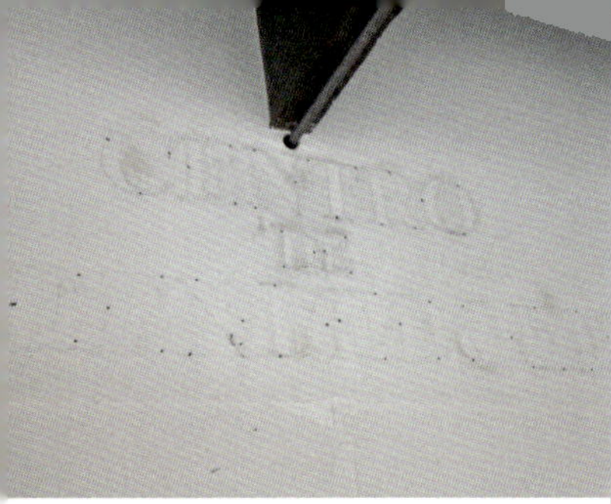
CENTRO
DE

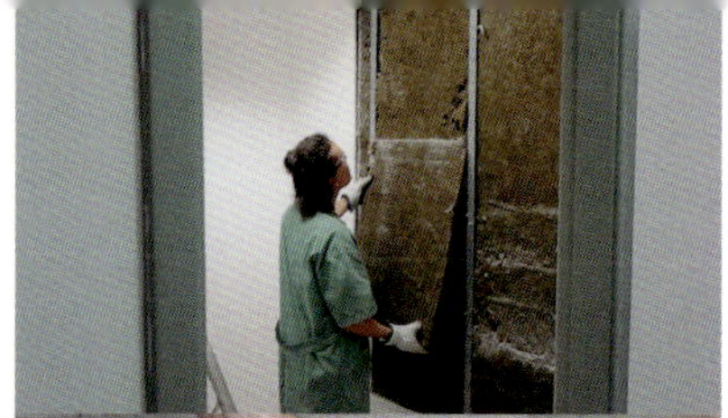

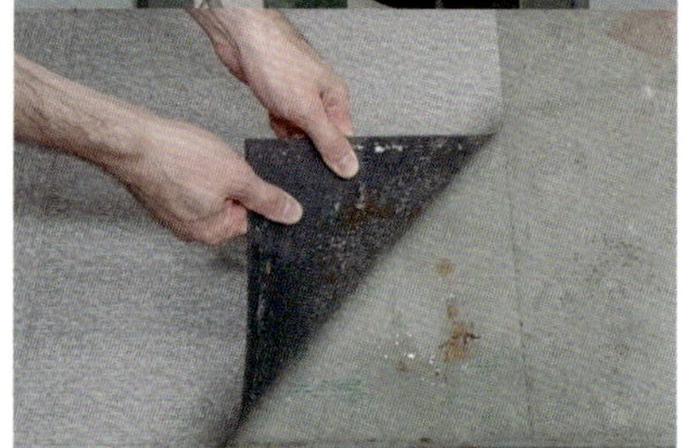

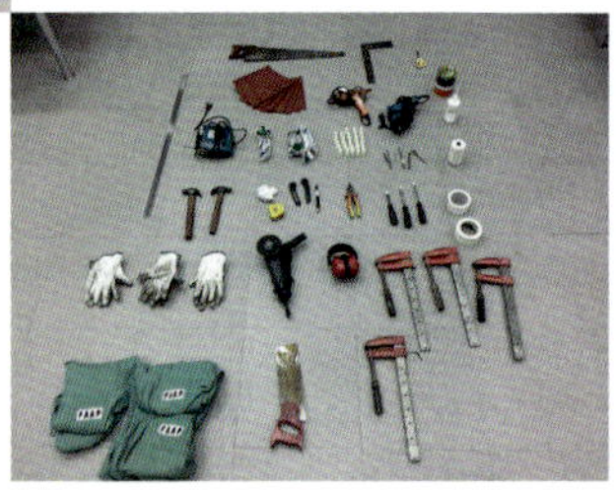

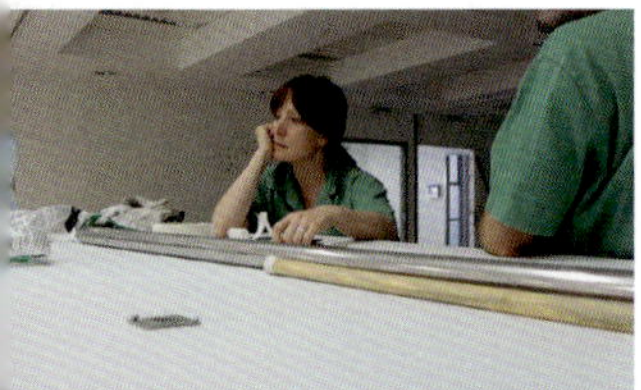

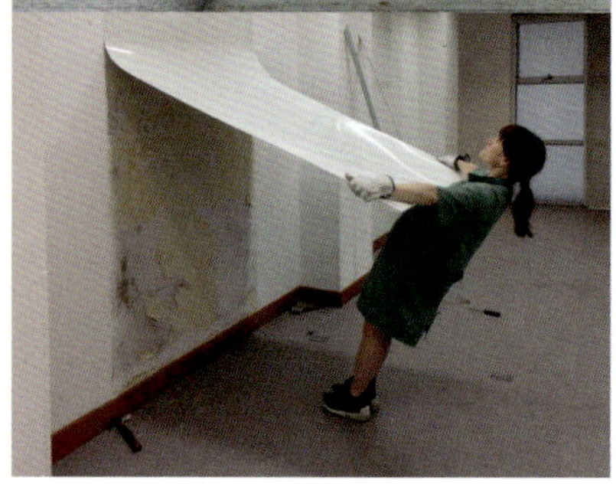

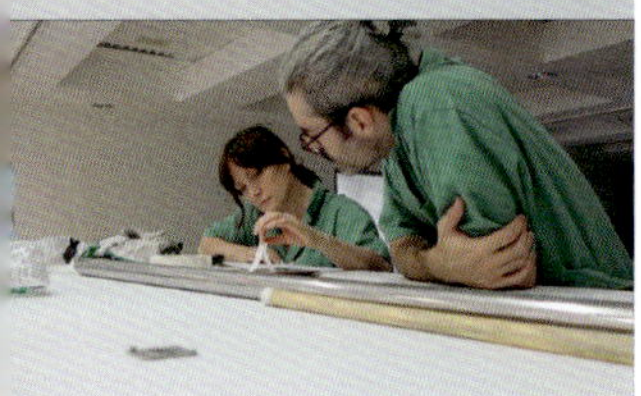

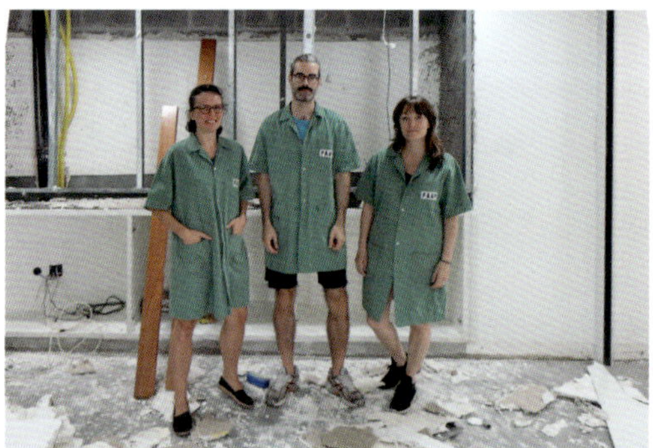

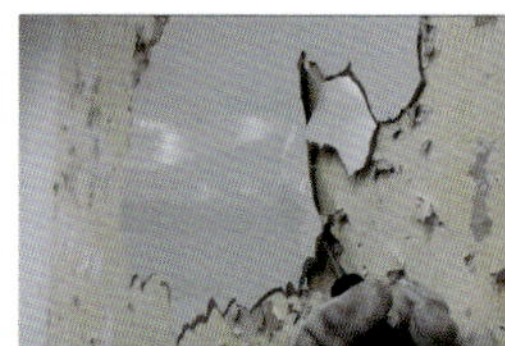

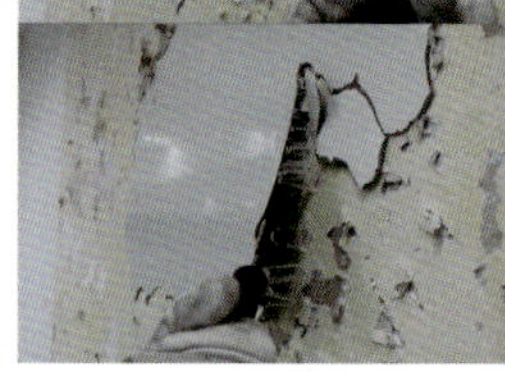

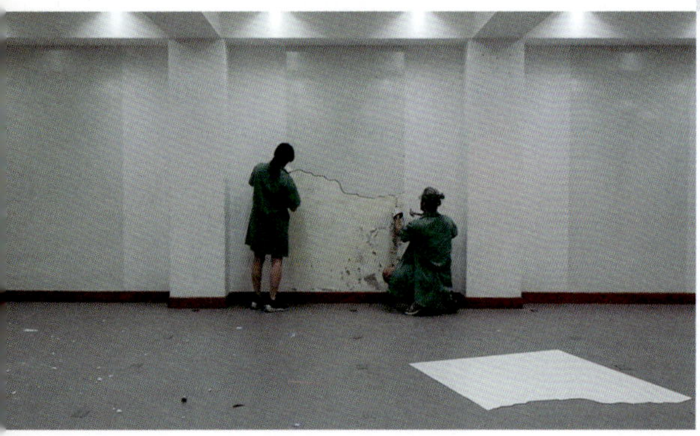

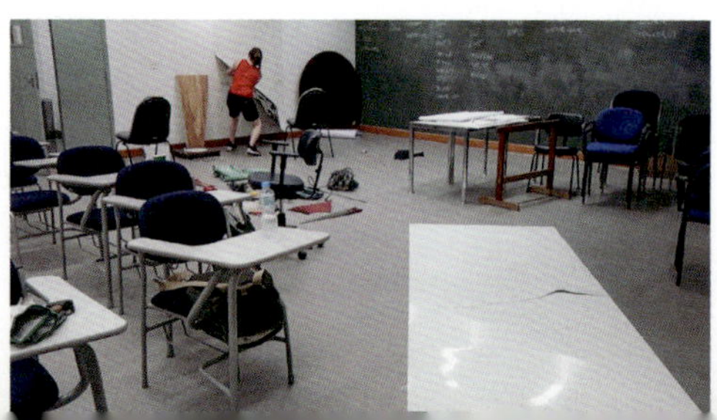

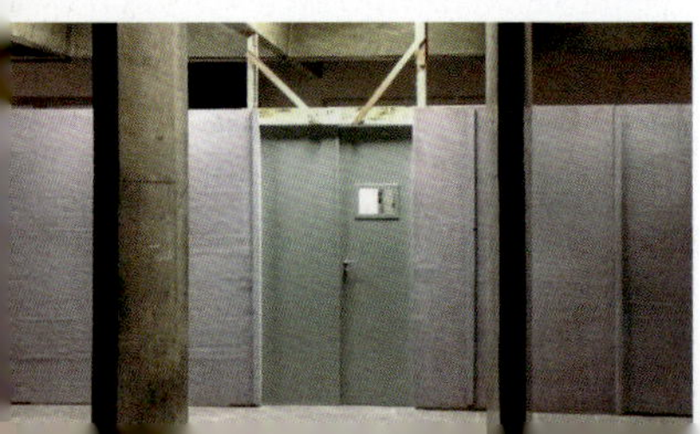

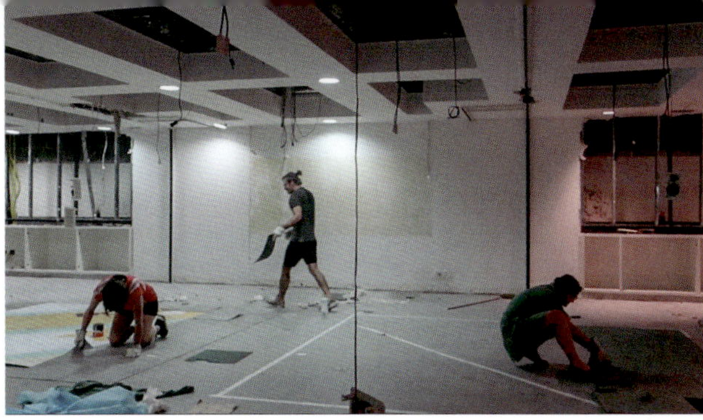

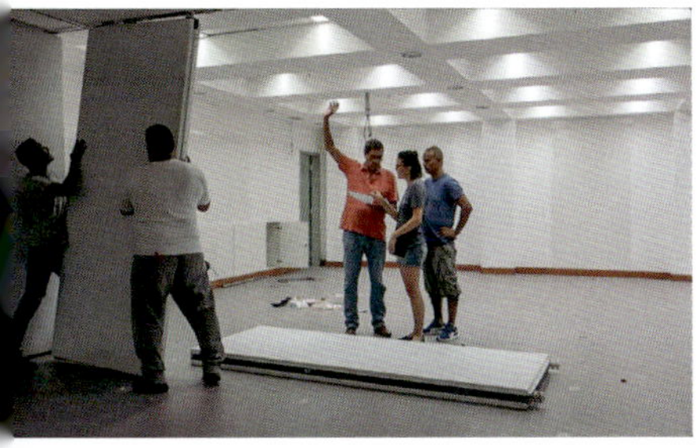

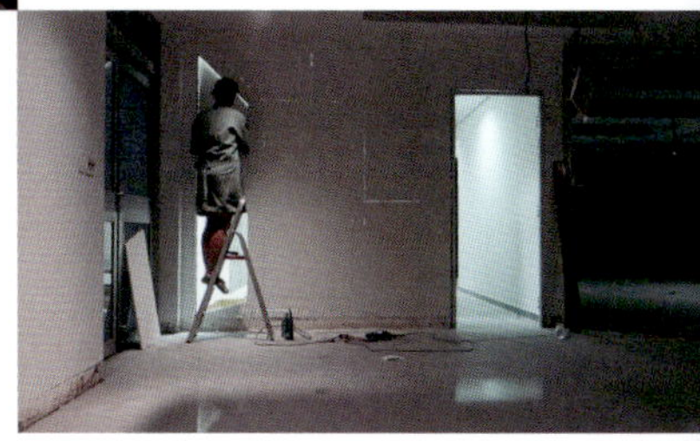

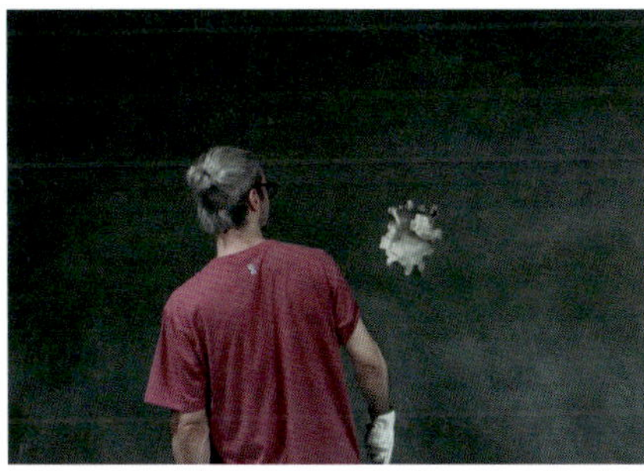

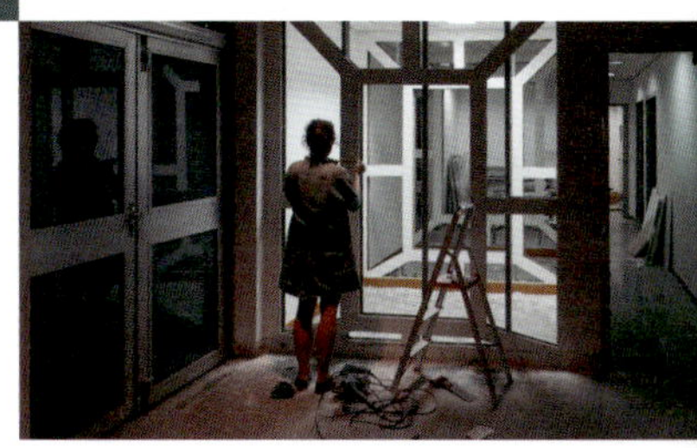

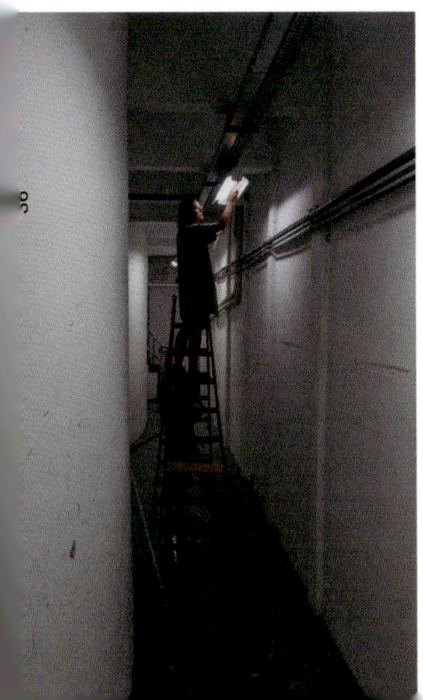

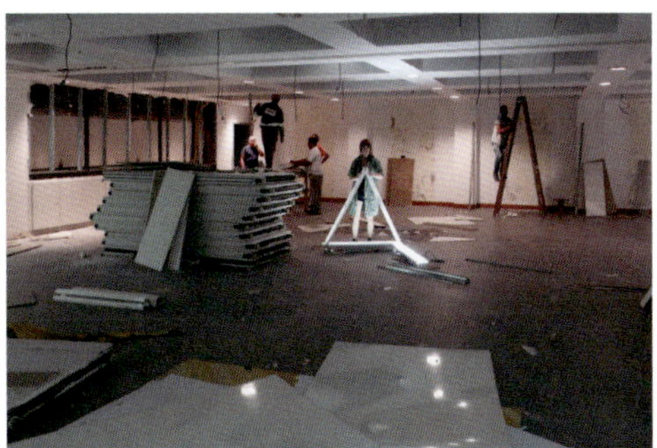

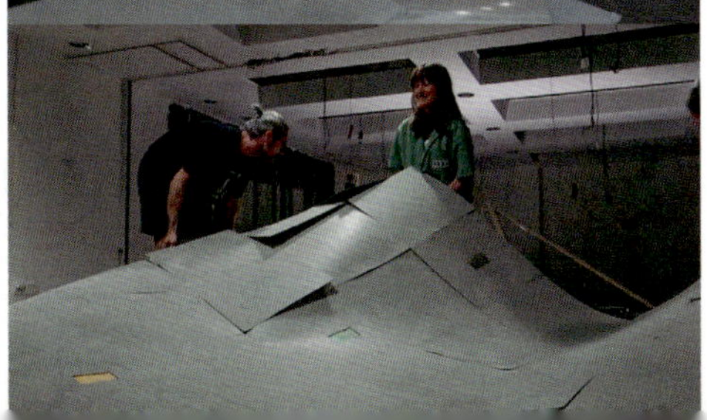

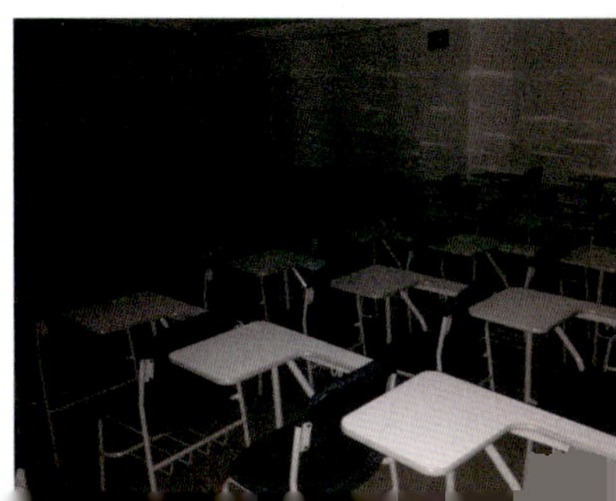

PROZESS
(Exposition)

PROCESS
(Exposition)

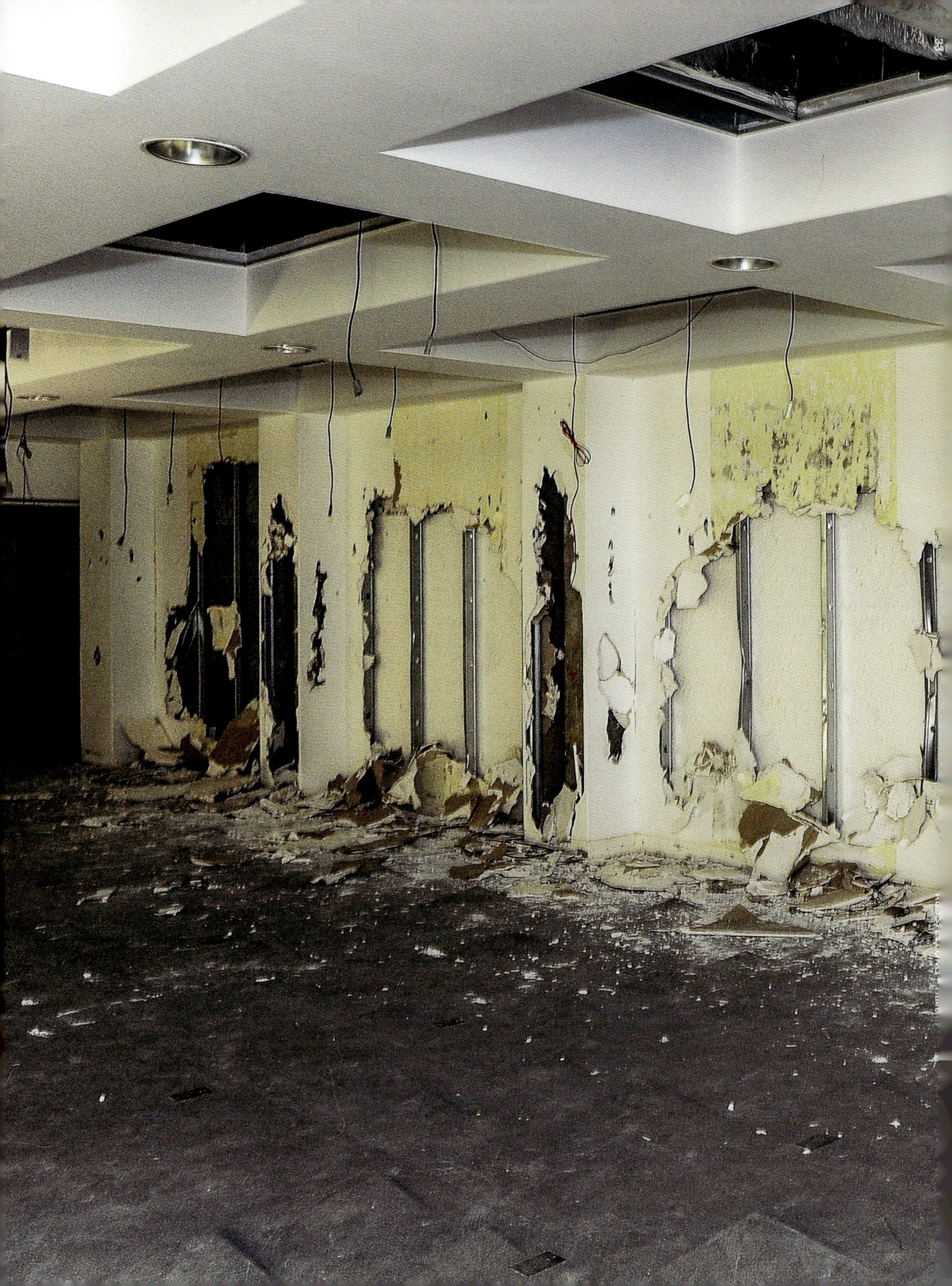

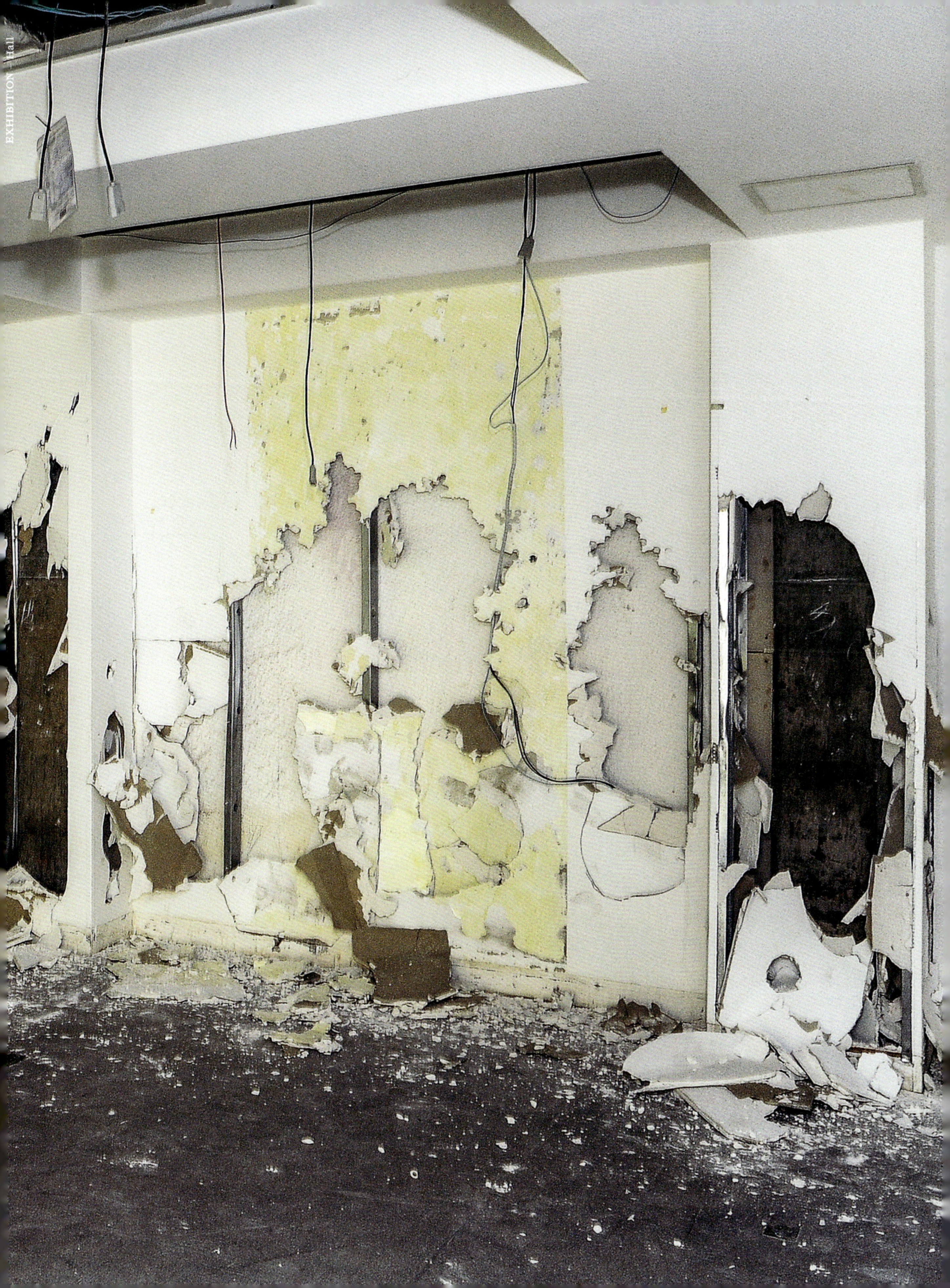

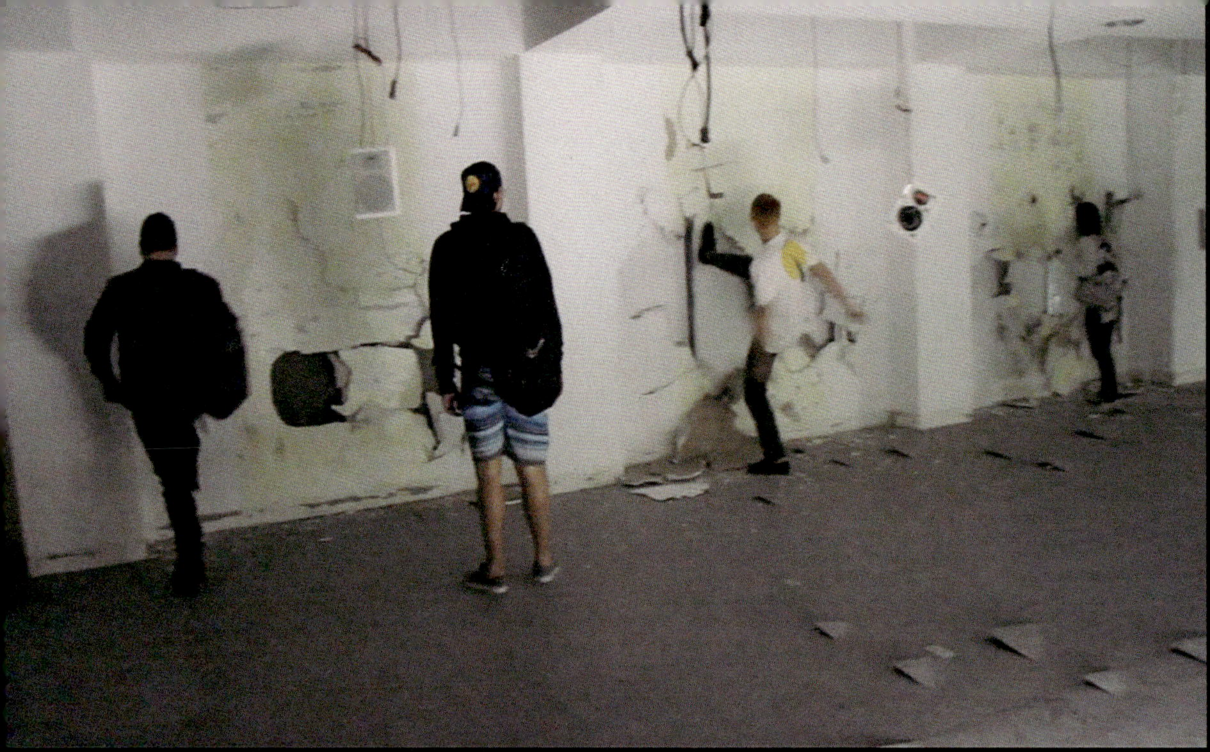

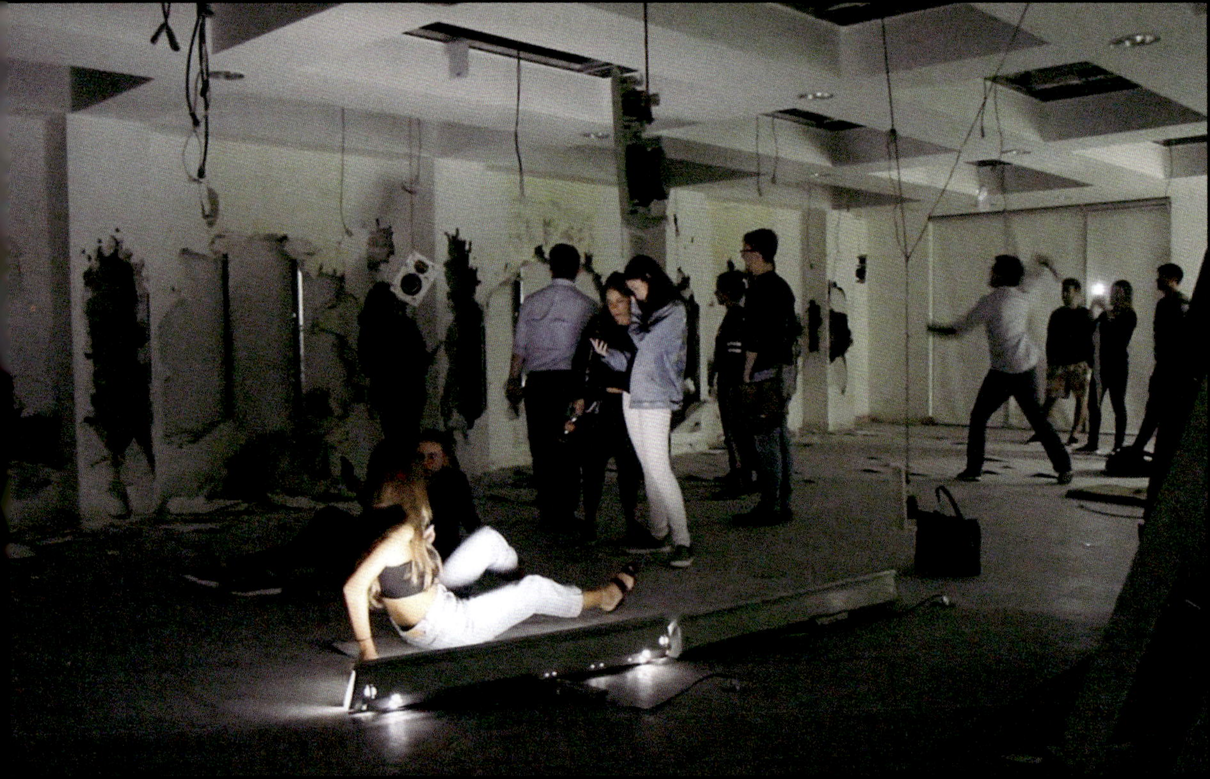

Video: *MINING: Untertage*, 2018
04:10 min

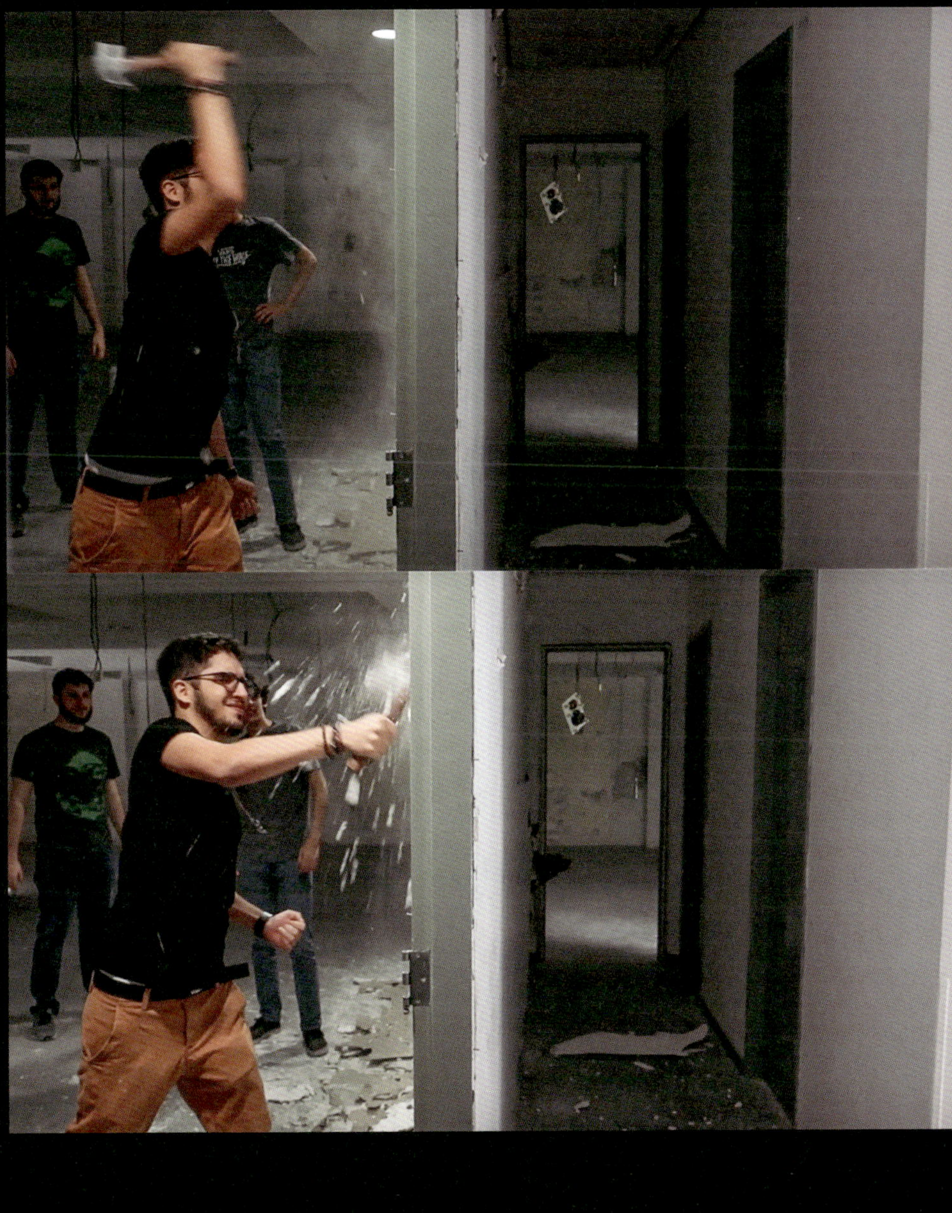

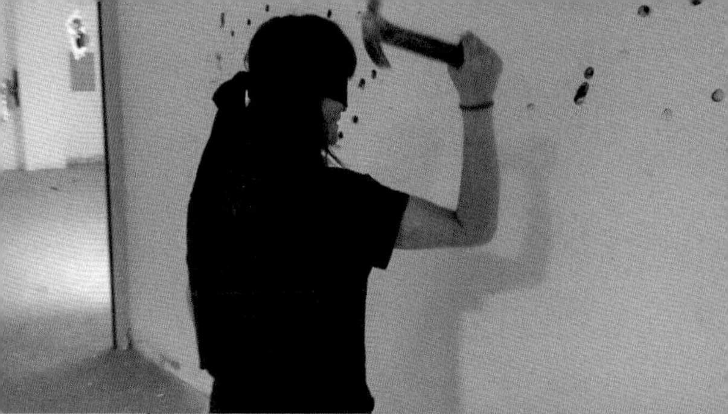

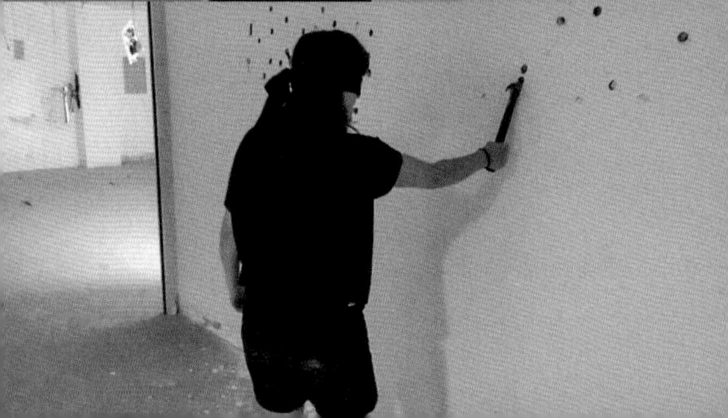

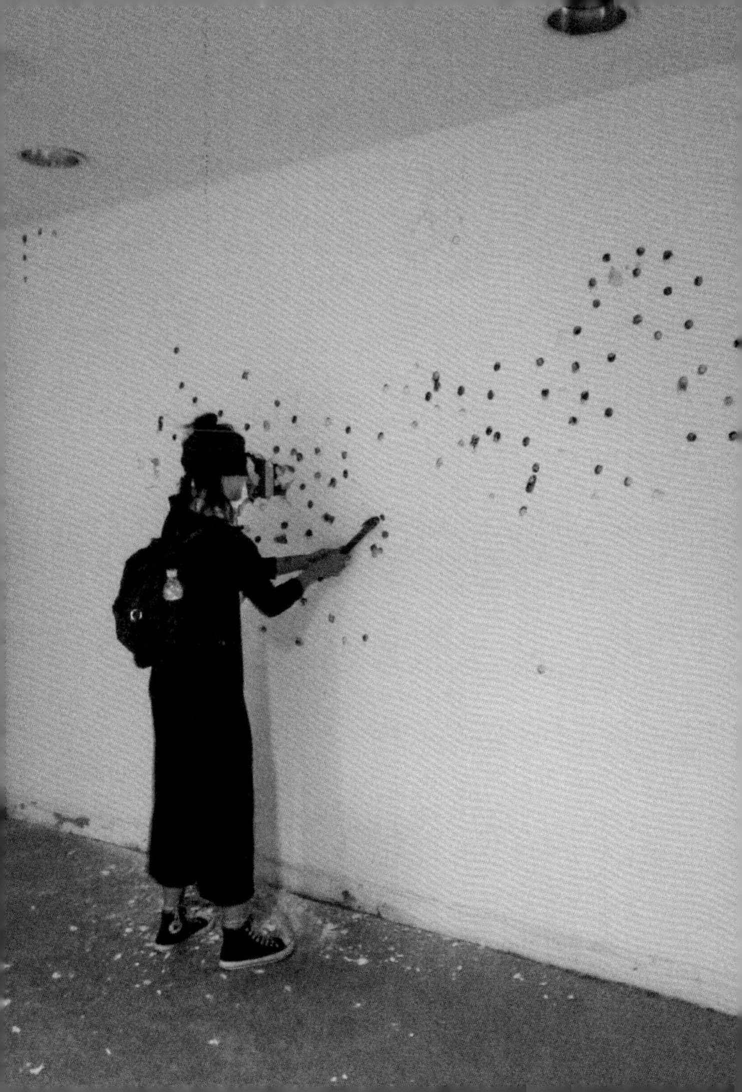

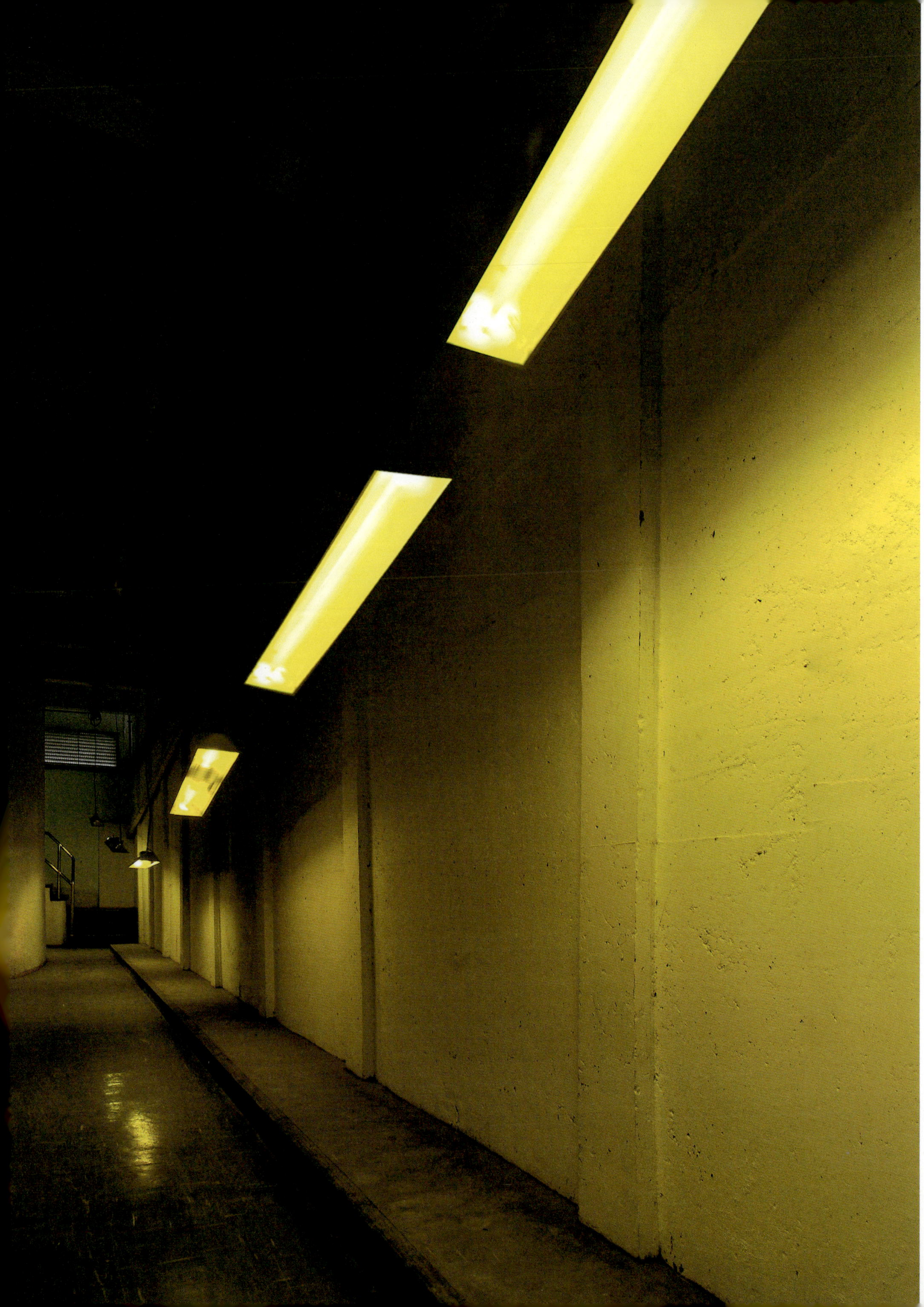

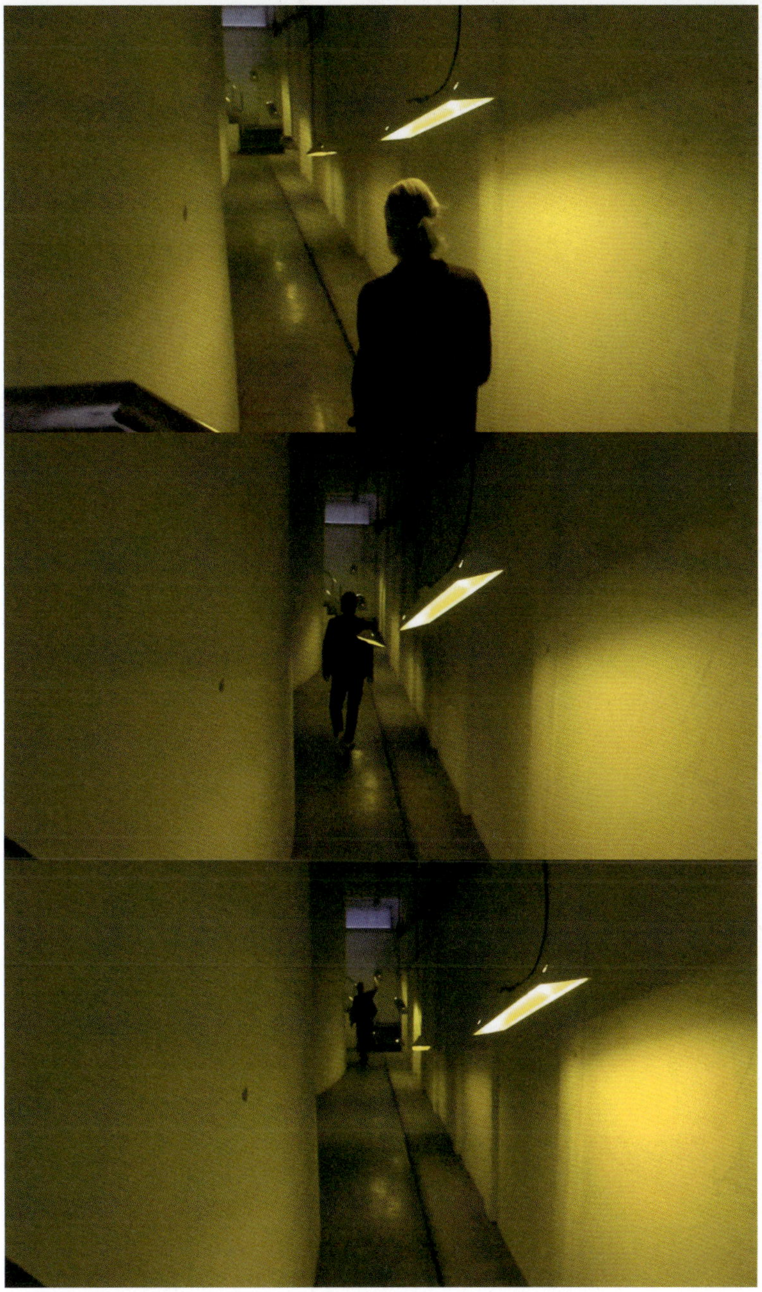

Video: *MINING: Untertage*, 2018
04:10 min

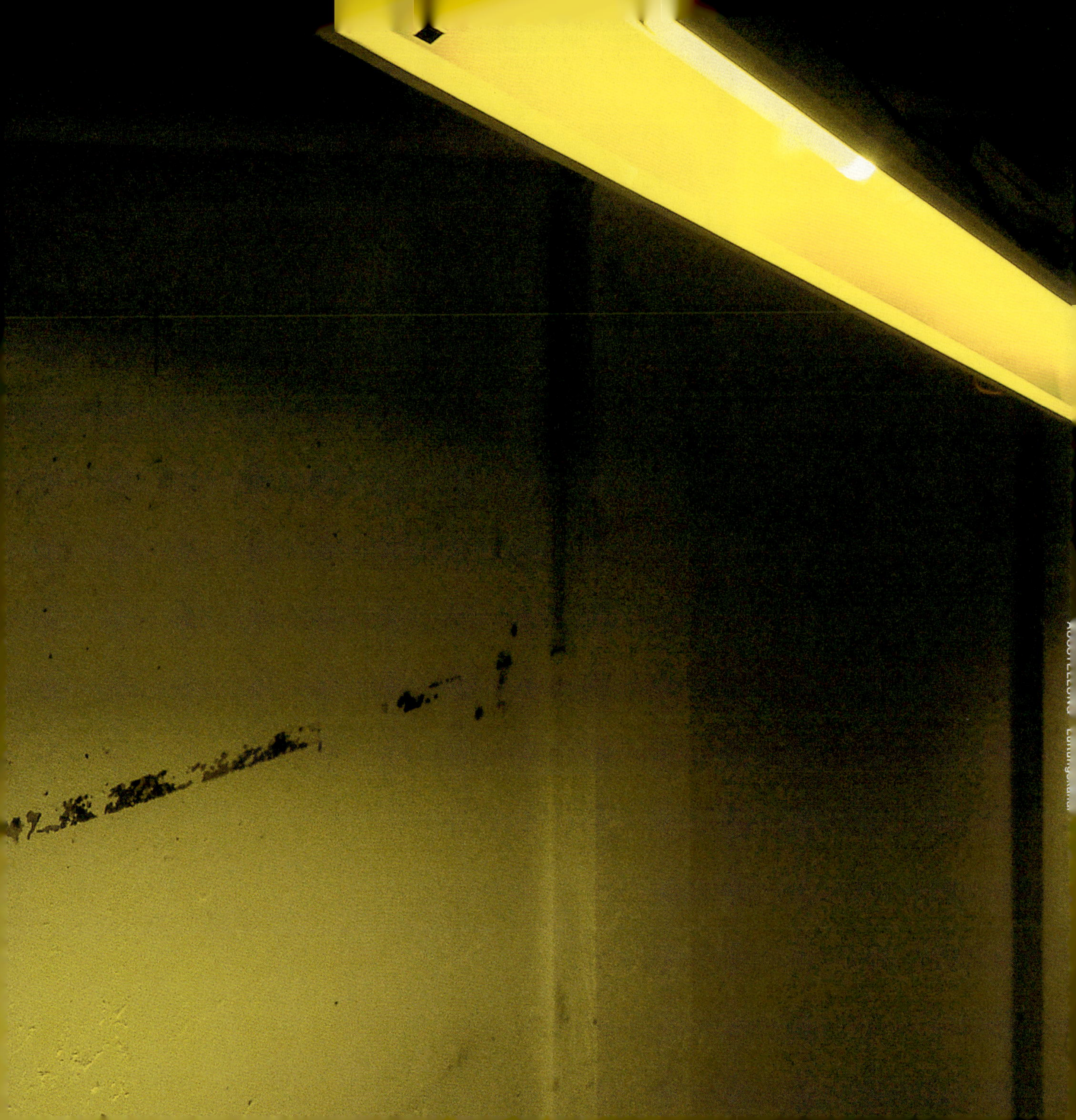

EXHIBITION – ventilation duct

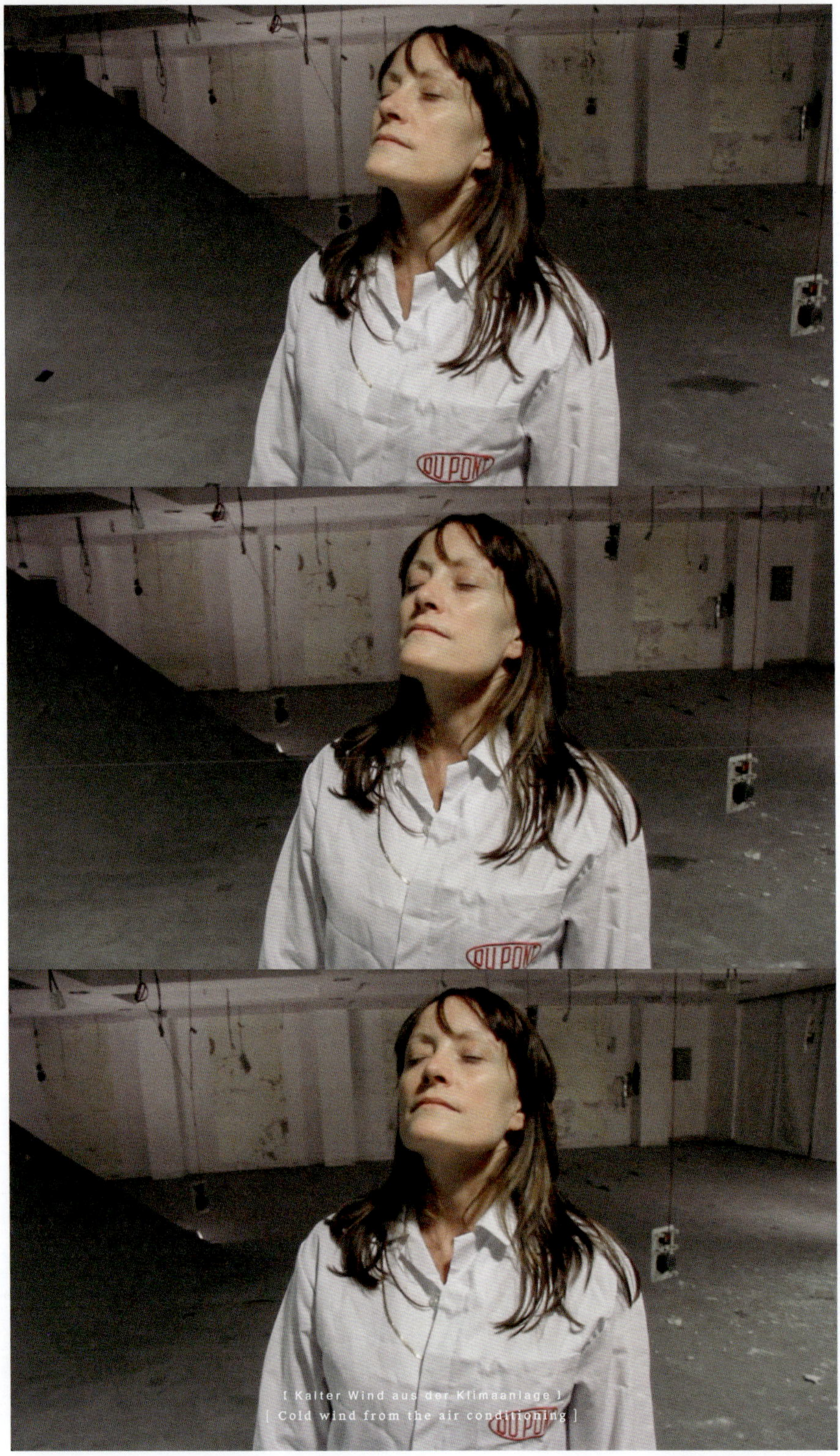

Video: ***MINING: Untertage***, 2018
04:10 min

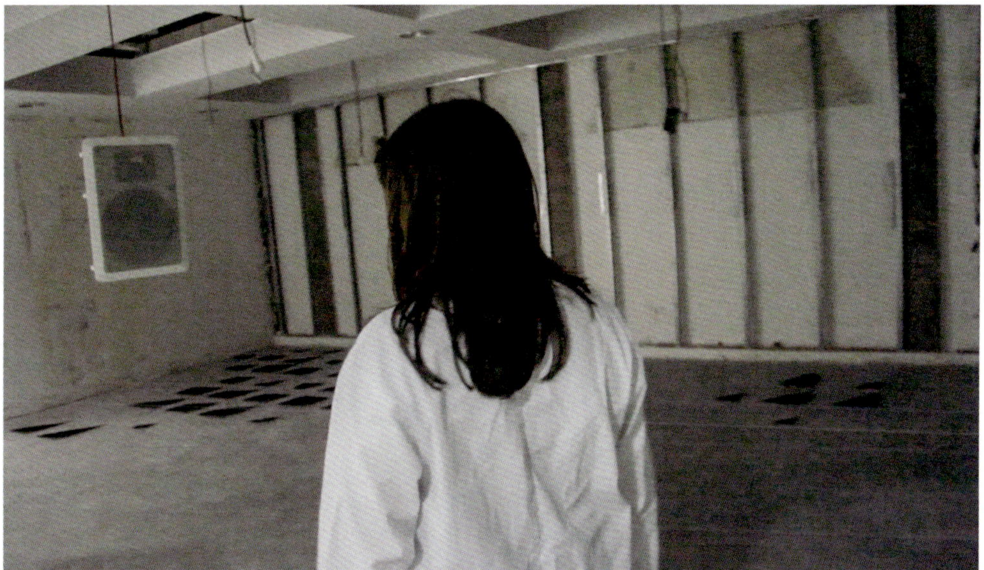

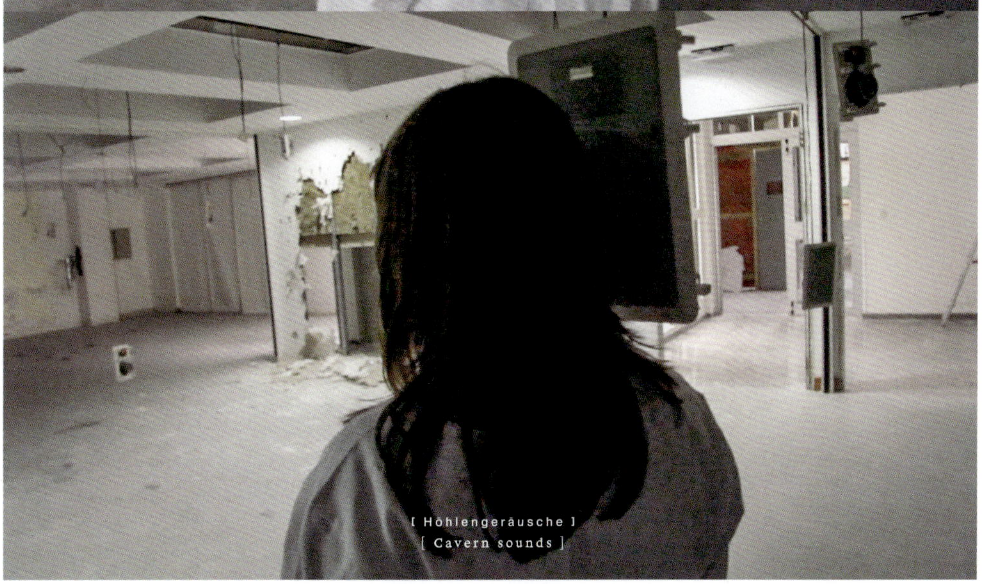
[Höhlengeräusche]
[Cavern sounds]

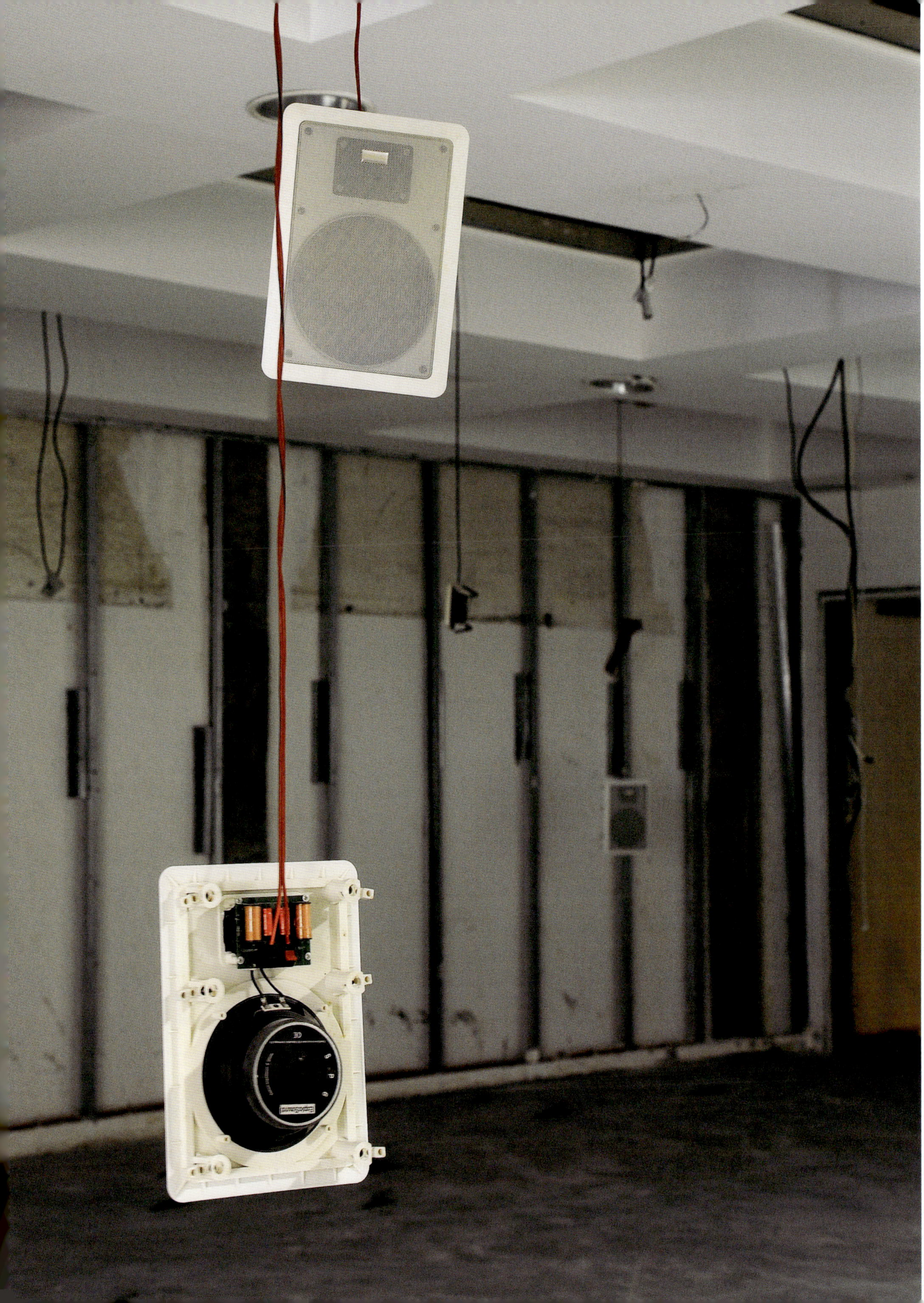

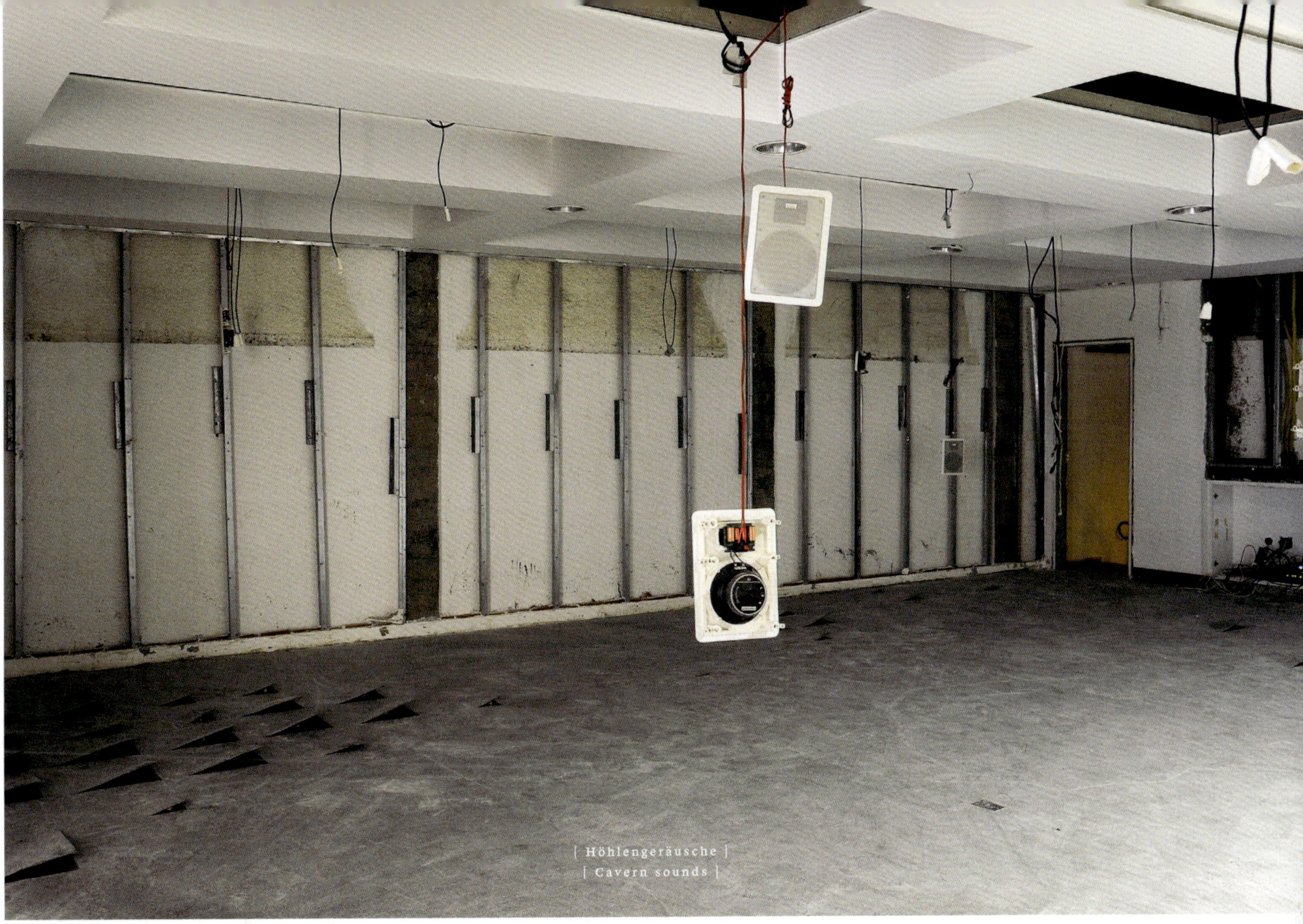
[Höhlengeräusche]
[Cavern sounds]

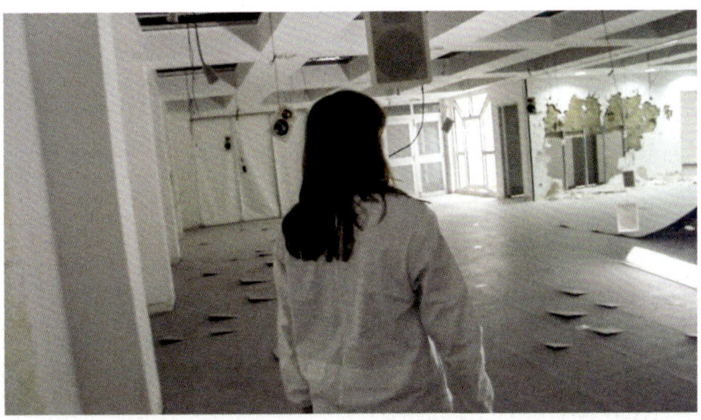

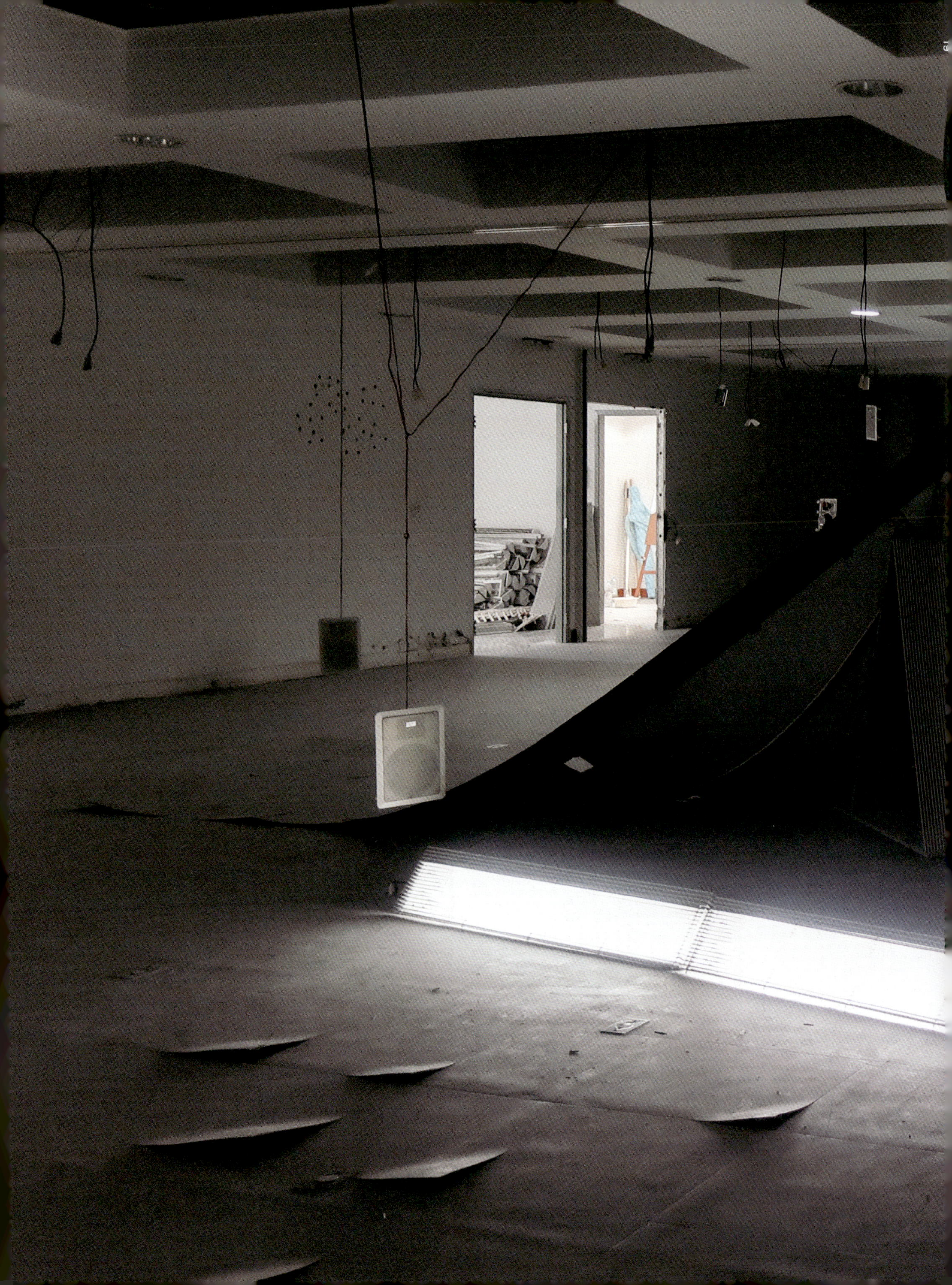

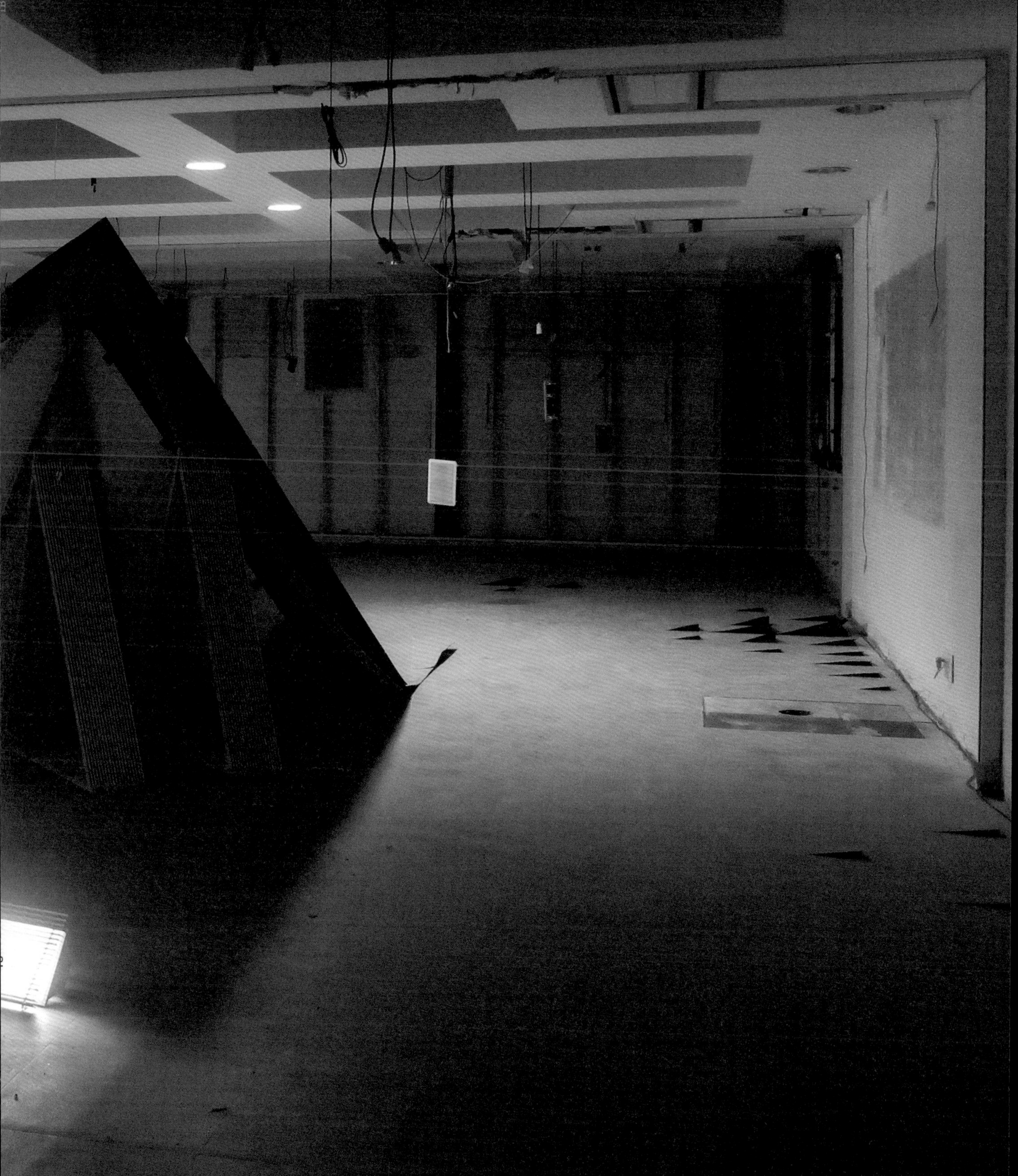

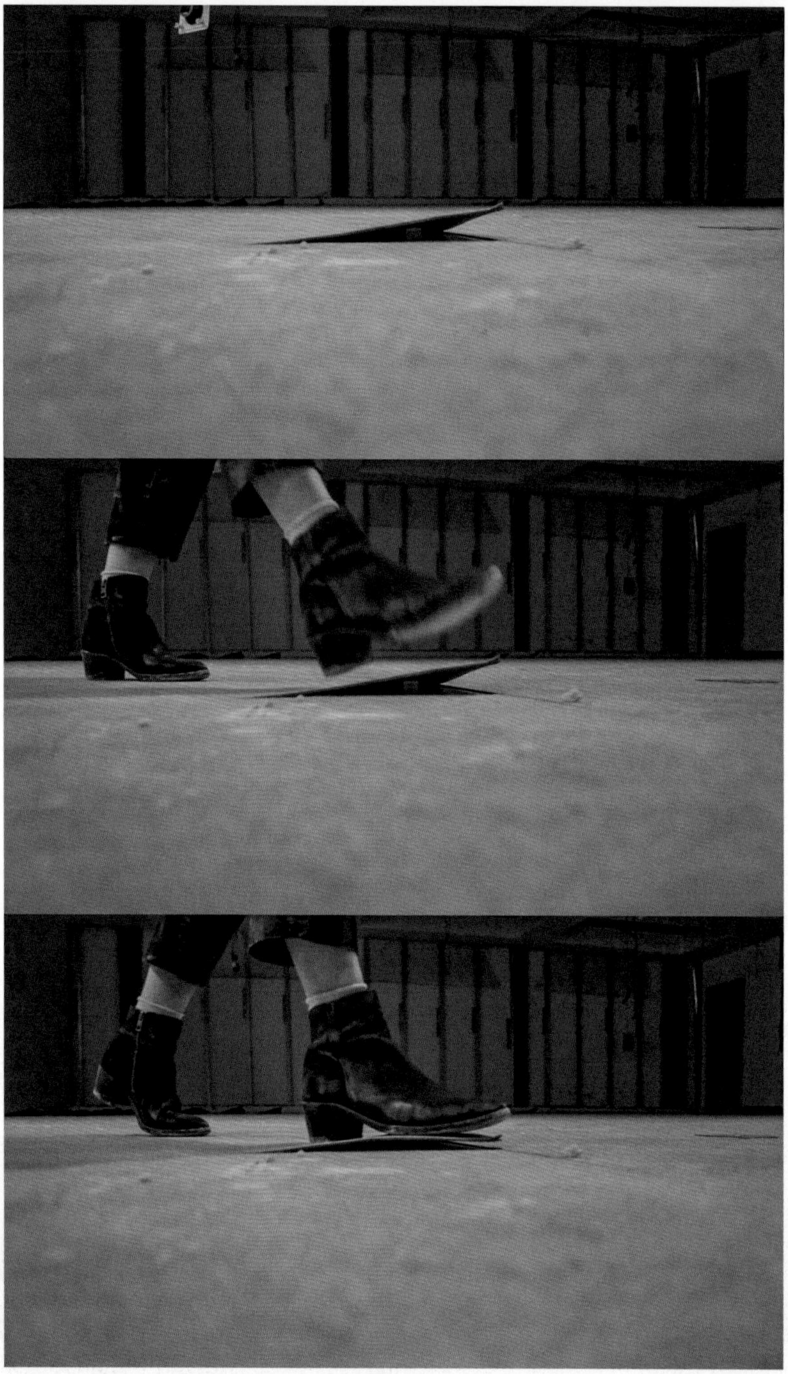

Video: *MINING: Untertage*, 2018
04:10 min

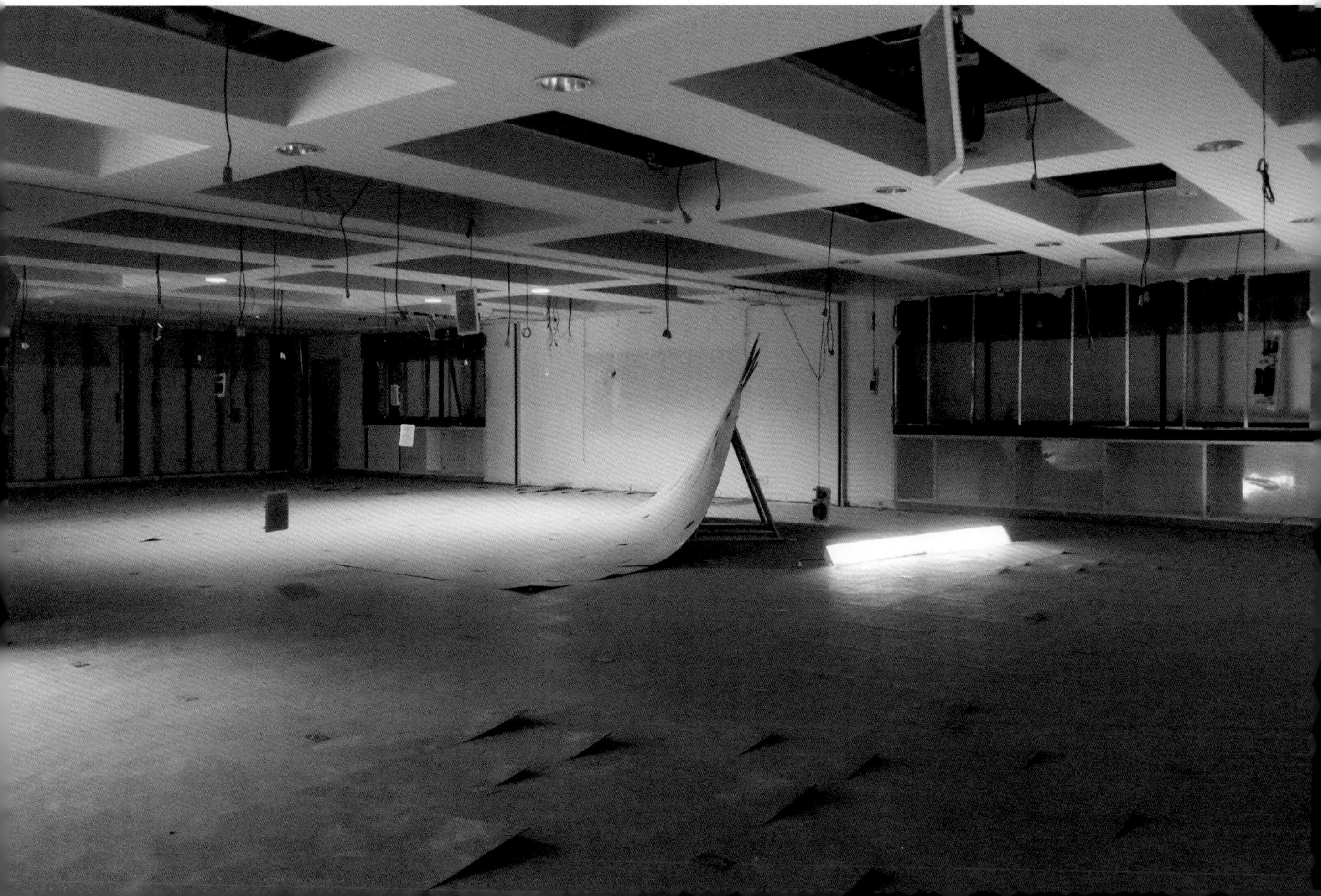

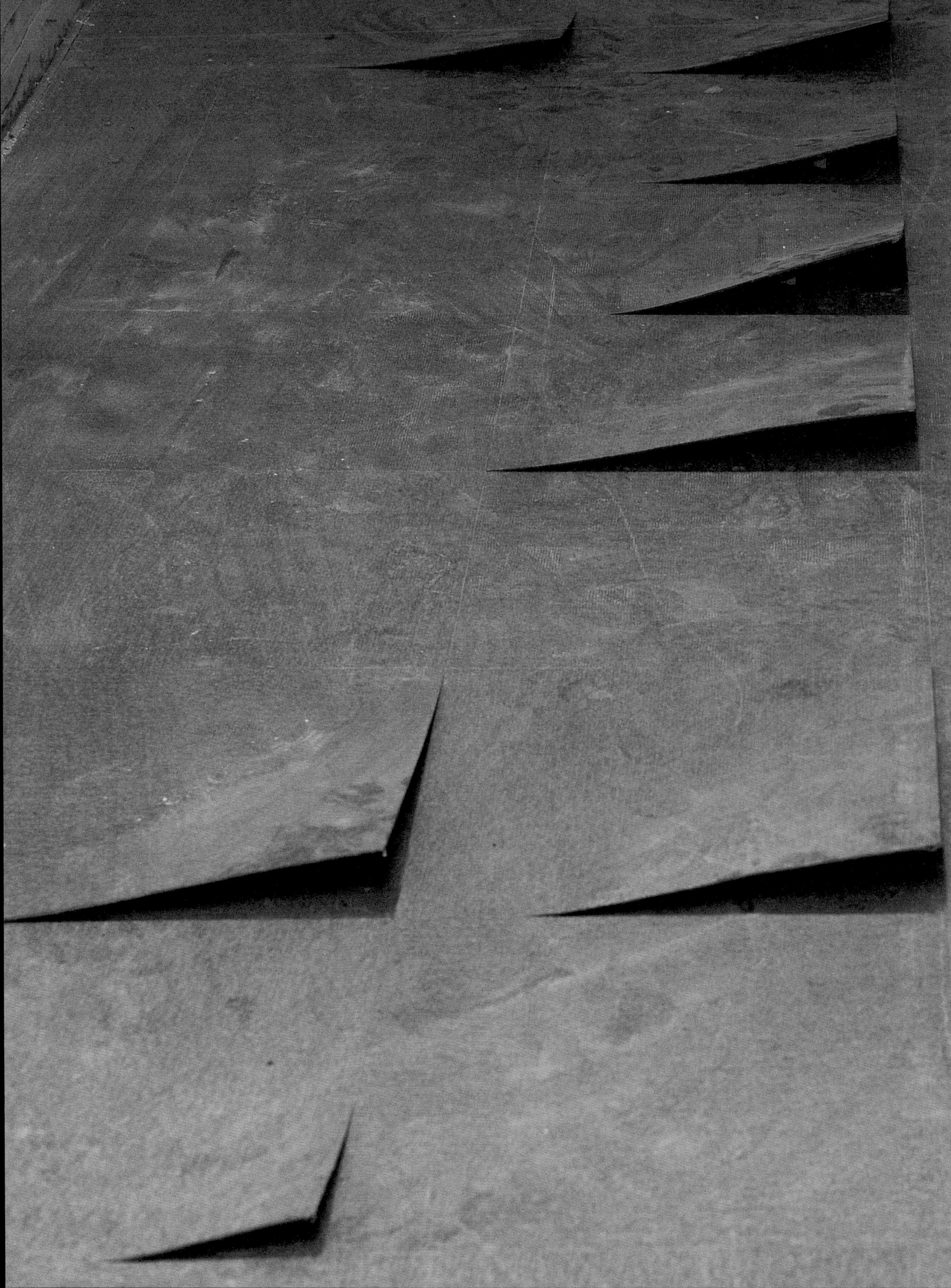

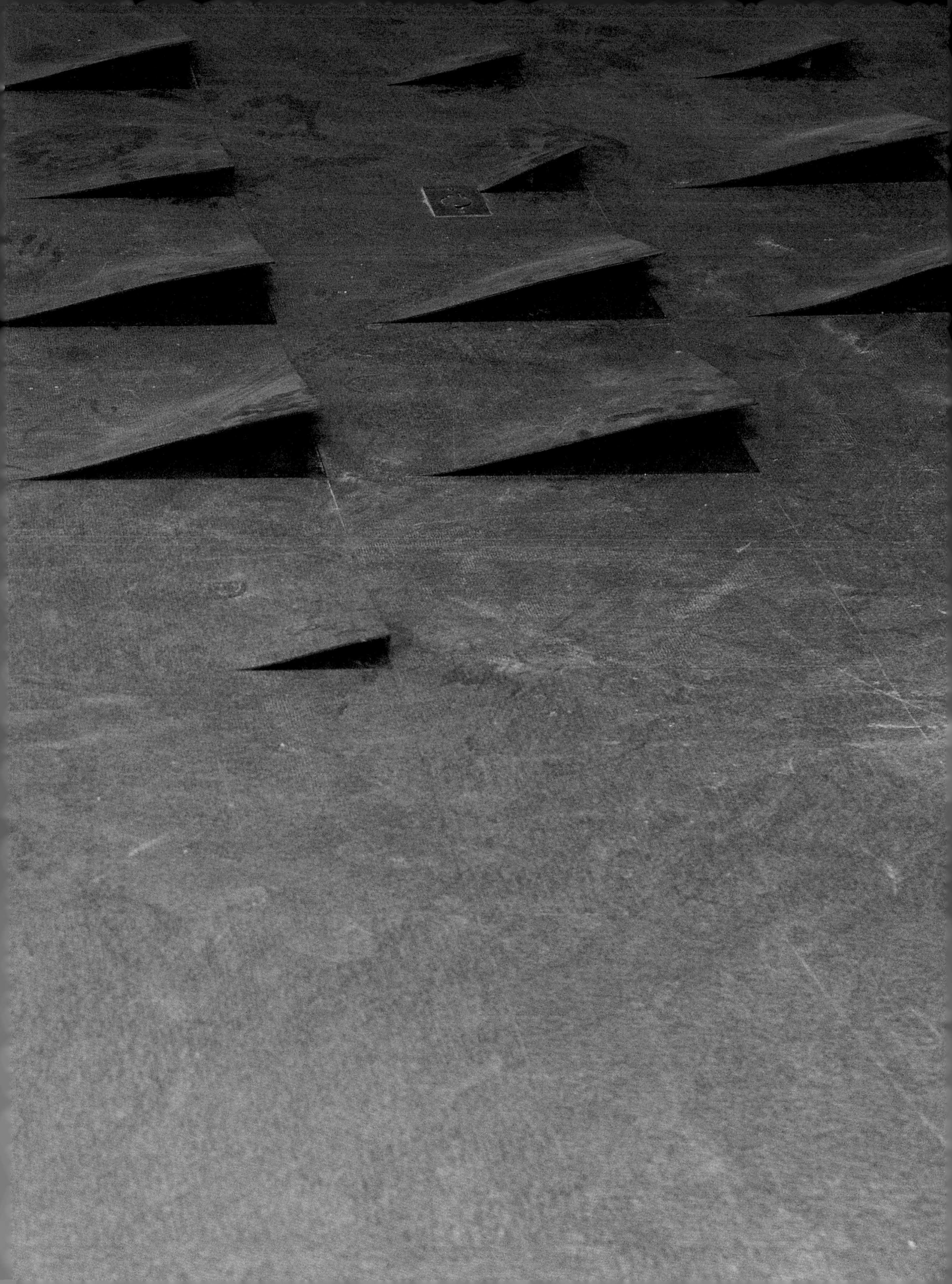

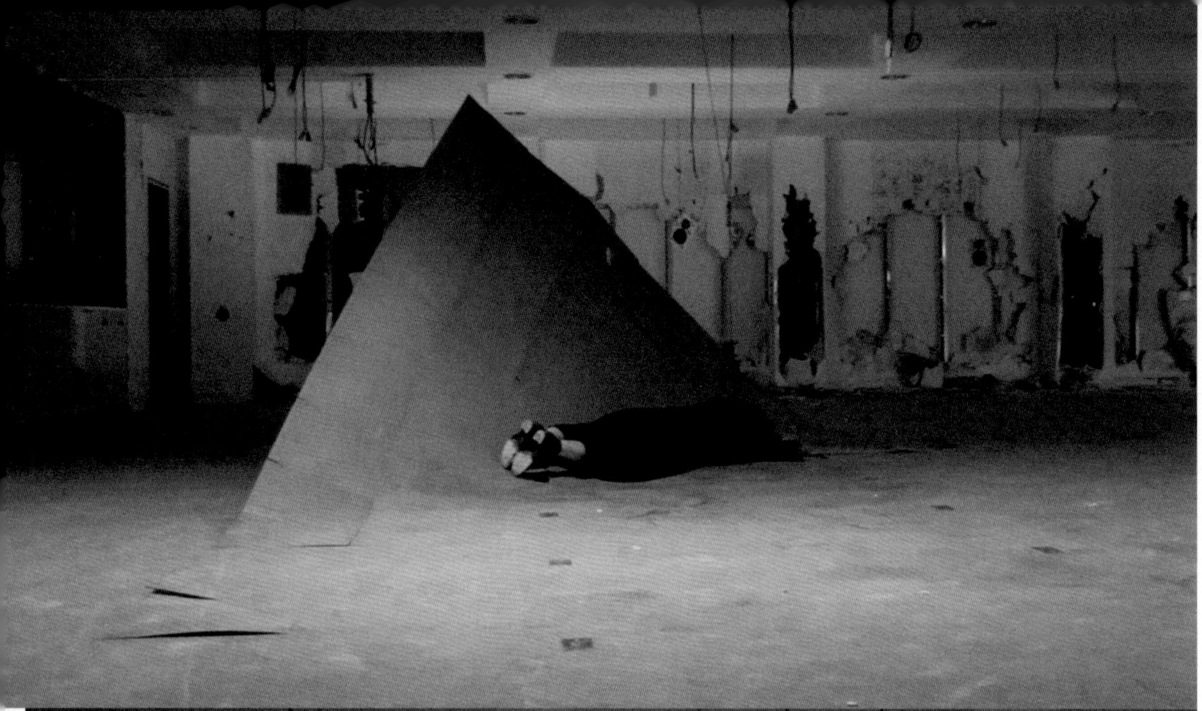

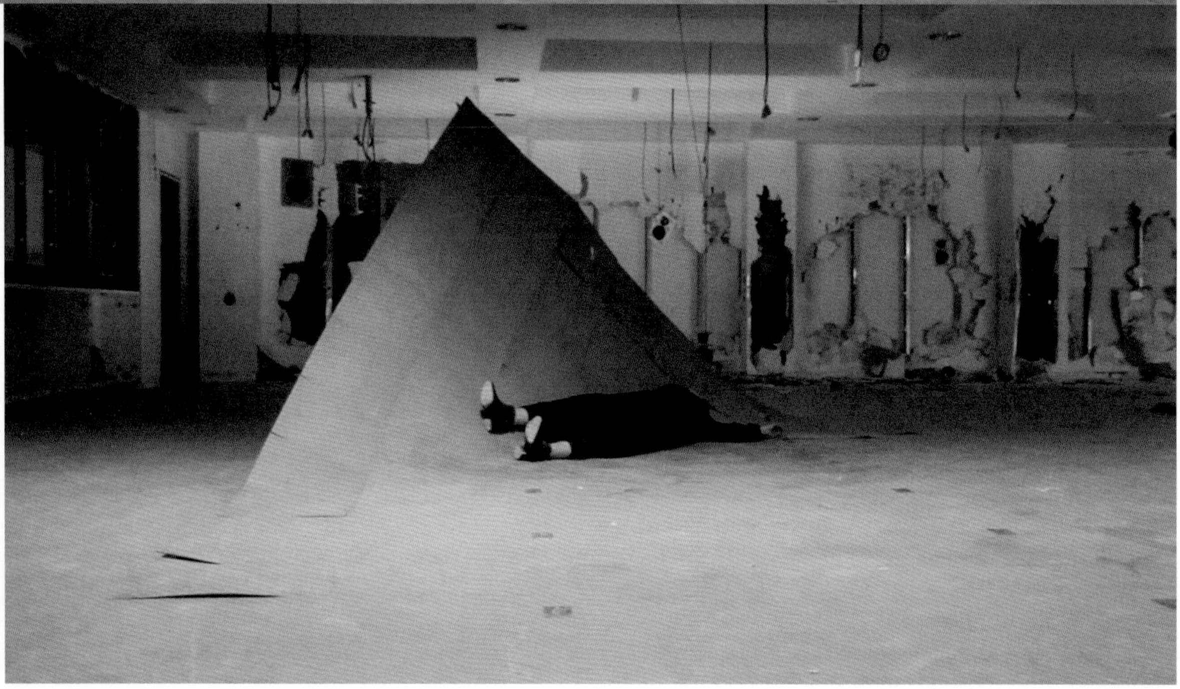

Video: *MINING: Untertage*, 2018
04:10 min

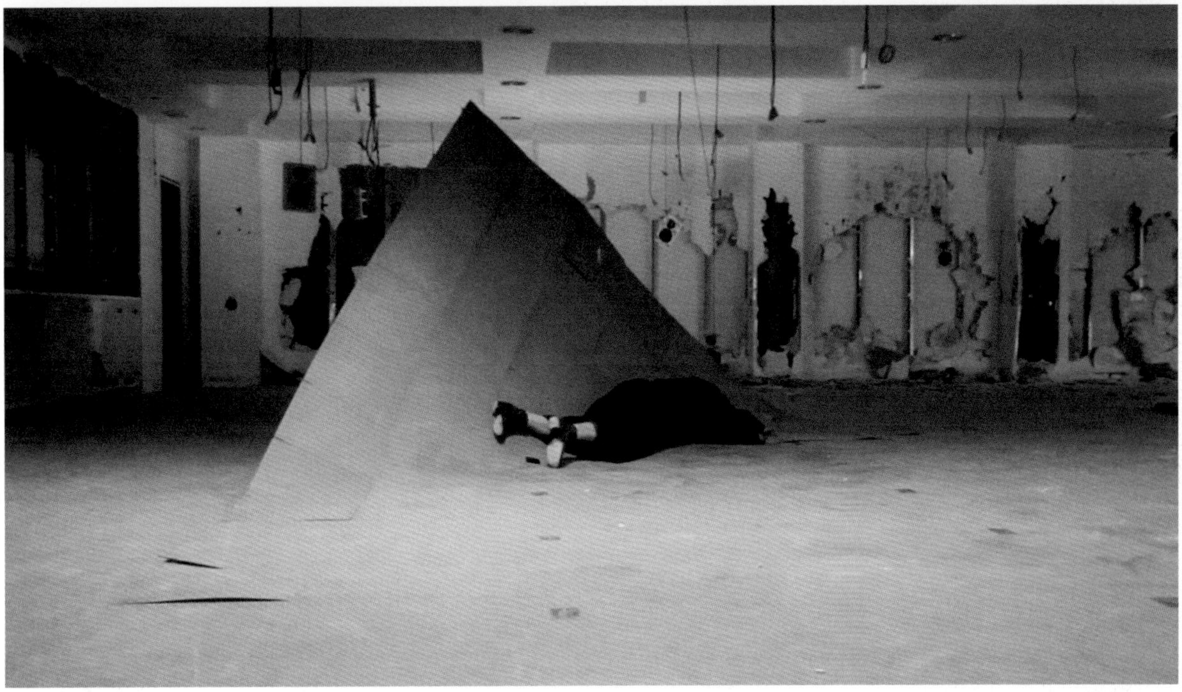

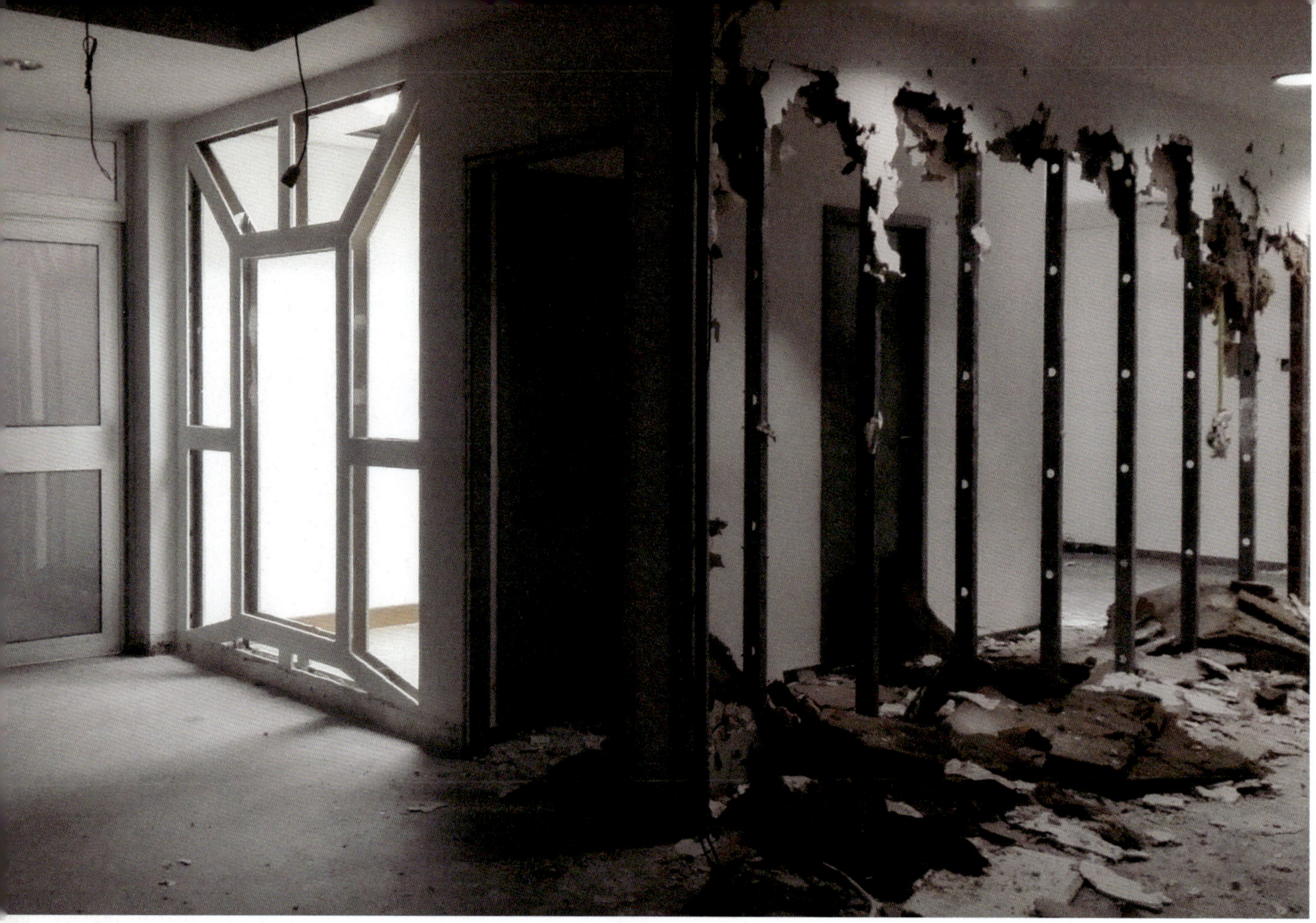

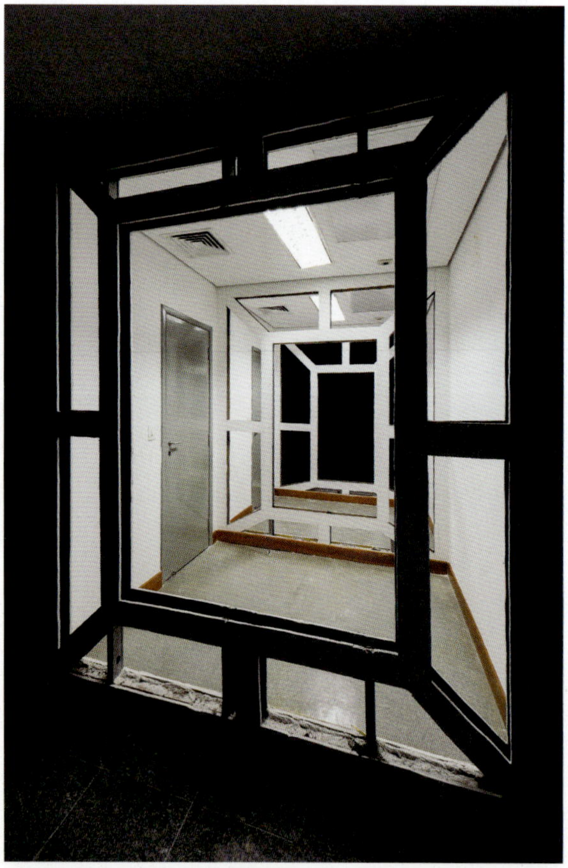

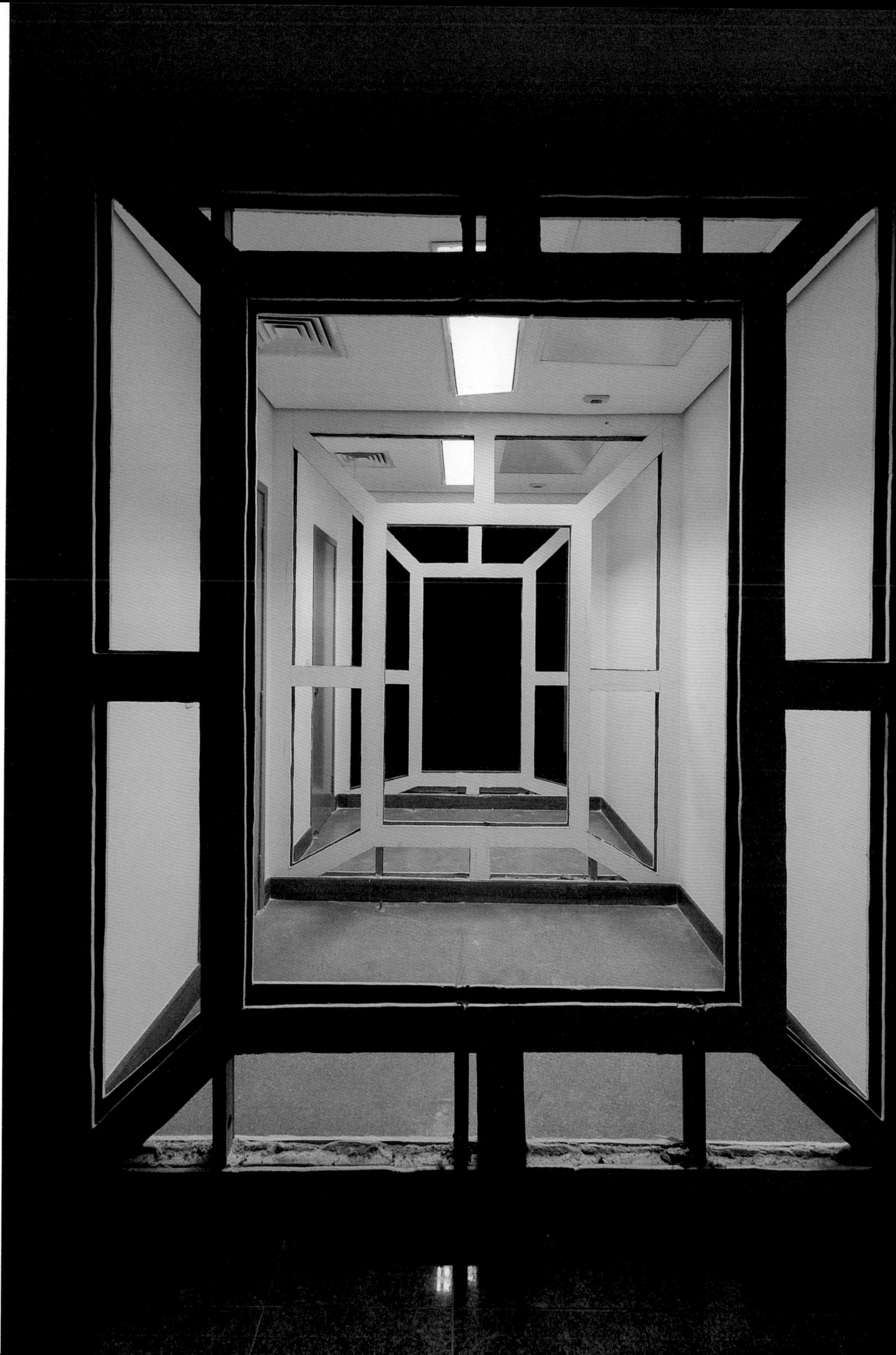

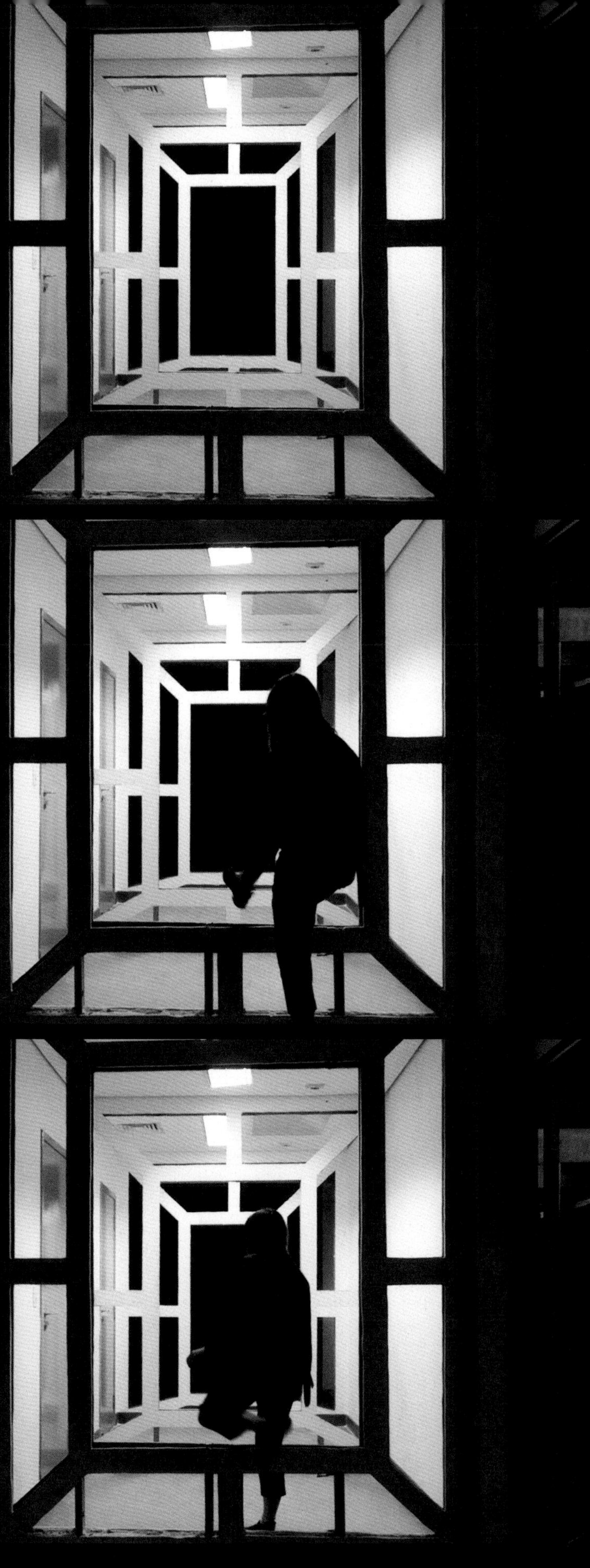

Video: *MINING: Untertage*, 2018
04:10 min

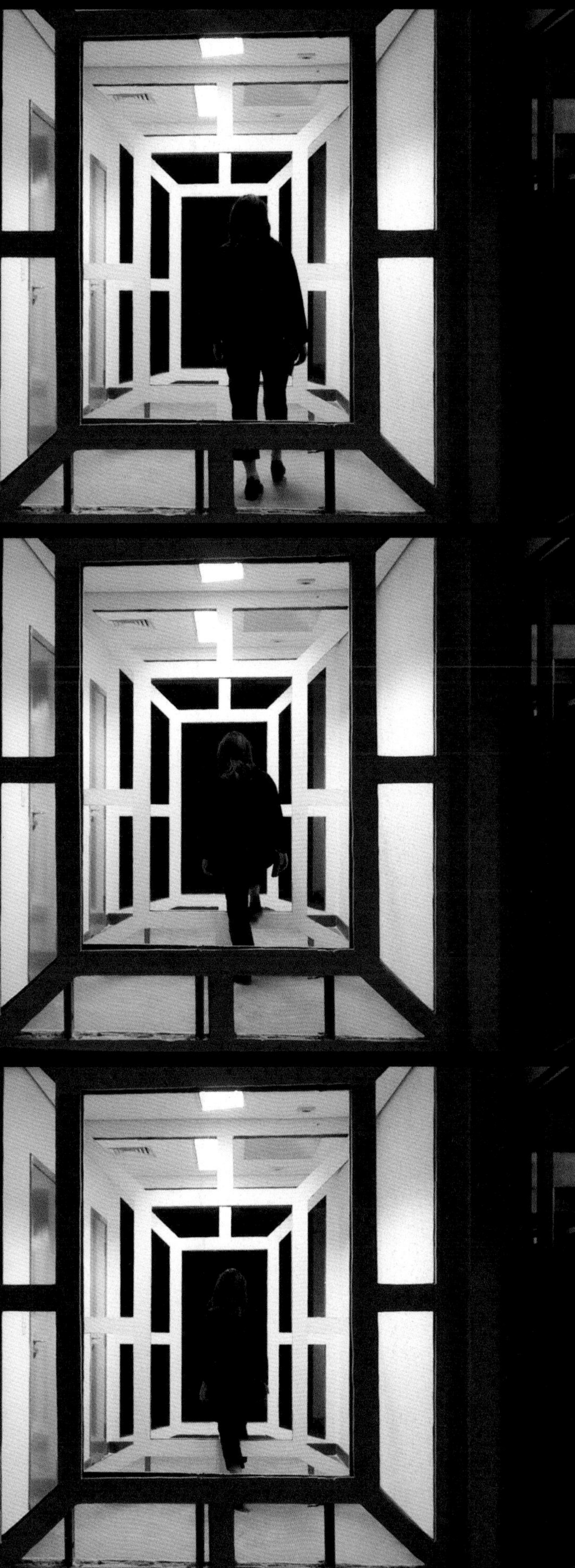

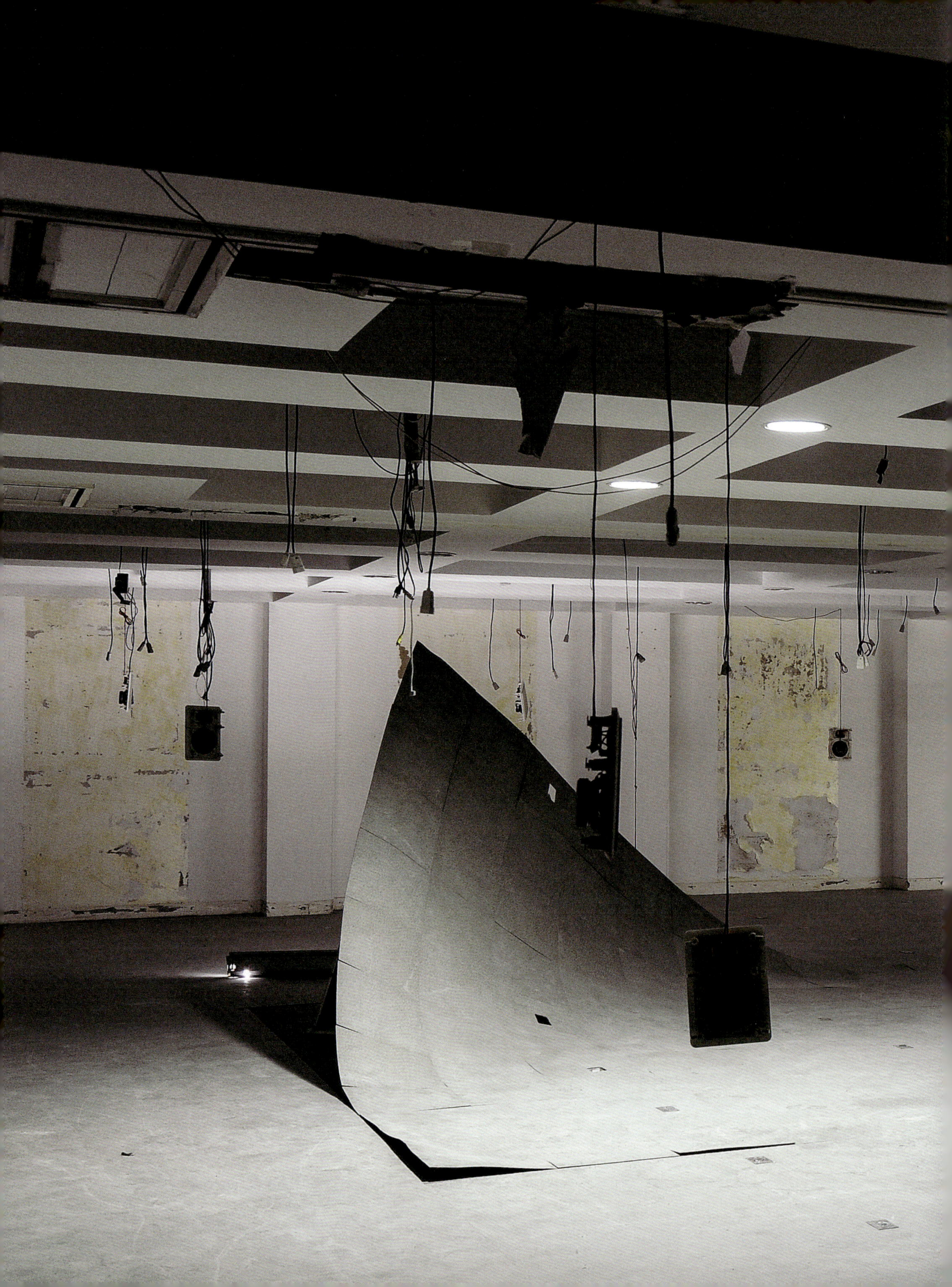

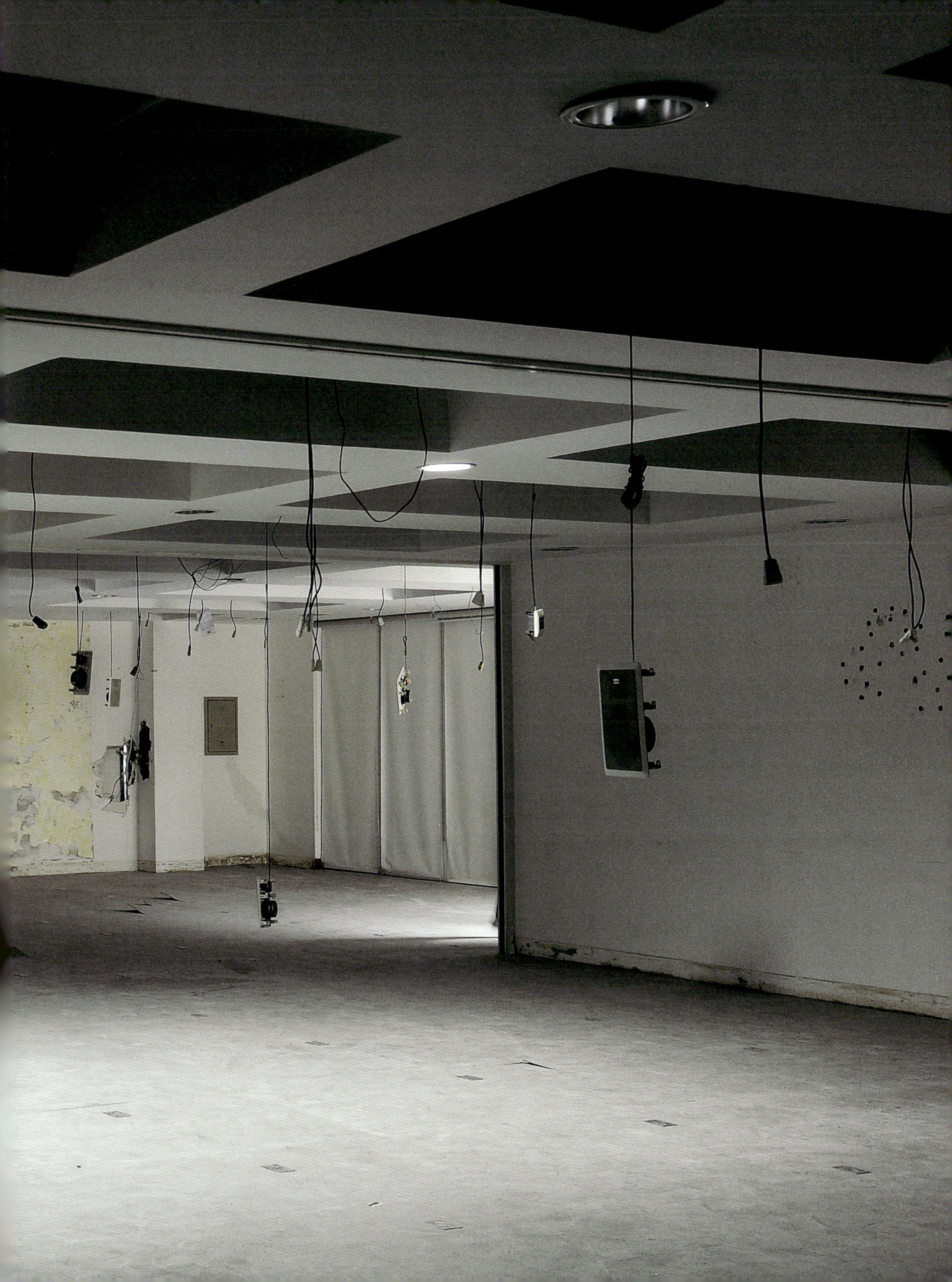

AUSSTELLUNG
(Höhepunkt)

EXHIBITION
(Climax)

MINING: Untertage

Eine räumliche Intervention des MINING Kollektivs (Ursula Gaisbauer & Friedrich Engl) und Rhona Byrne

mit 8 Akteur*innen, realisiert im Mai 2018

Skulptur, Sound, Performance, Partizipation, Video

Space in Transition:
Business-Center, Universität FAAP, Rua Alagoas, 903, São Paulo, Brasilien

Fläche:
Ca. 300 m²
Baujahr:
Unbekannt
Architektur:
Unbekannt
Bauherrin:
Universität FAAP

Intervention:
4 Tage / 4.–7. Mai 2018
Ausstellung:
2 Tage / 8.–9. Mai 2018

Im Zuge von Renovierungsarbeiten des Business-Centers der Universität FAAP begaben sich die Künstler*innen für die Dauer von drei Tagen in einen höhlenartigen Raum ohne natürliches Licht. Charakteristisch für *MINING: Untertage* ist die ausschließliche Wiederverwendung der Materialien on site sowie die Zusammenarbeit mit den Abbrucharbeitern vor Ort, deren Arbeitsprozesse auch durch Zerstörung und Umgestaltung des Raums geprägt sind. Mit bildhauerischen Interventionen sowie Licht, Klang und Temperatur, wurde der Ort zu einem archiskulpturalen, immersiven Environment inszeniert. Der an einer Wand angebrachte Hammer lud Besuchende dazu ein, Teil des Abrissprozesses zu werden. Ein performativer Rundgang der Intervention wurde filmisch dokumentiert.

MINING: Untertage

A spatial intervention by the MINING Kollektiv (Ursula Gaisbauer & Friedrich Engl) and Rhona Byrne

with 8 acteurs, realised in May 2018

Sculpture, sound, performance, participation, video

Space in transition:
Business-center, University FAAP, Rua Alagoas, 903, São Paulo, Brazil

Area:
Approx. 300 m²
Year of construction:
Unknown
Architecture:
Unknown
Builder:
University FAAP

Intervention:
4 days / 4–7 May 2018
Exhibition:
2 days / 8–9 May 2018

In the course of the renovation at the business centre of FAAP University, the artists entered a cavernous space without natural light for three days. Characteristic of 'MINING: Untertage' is the exclusive reuse of materials from the site and the collaboration with the demolition workers, whose work processes are also defined by the destruction and transformation of the space. With sculptural interventions as well as light, sound and temperature, the space was turned into an archisculptural, immersive environment. The hammer mounted on a wall invited visitors to become part of the demolition process. A performative walkthrough of the space was documented on camera.

Über das Projekt
Hard Facts

MINING: Untertage

Inhalt / Content